Saṁnyāsin
in the Hindu Tradition
Changing Perspectives

Saṁnyāsin
in the Hindu Tradition
– Changing Perspectives –

T.S. Rukmani

D.K. Printworld (P) Ltd.
Publishers of Indian Traditions

Cataloging in Publication Data — DK

[Courtesy: D.K. Agencies (P) Ltd. <docinfo@dkagencies.com>]

Rukmani, T. S. (Trichur Subramaniam), 1930-
Saṁnyāsin in the Hindu tradition : changing perspectives / T.S. Rukmani.
p. cm.
Includes bibliographical references (p.).
ISBN 13: 9788124605745
ISBN 10: 8124605742

1. Saṁnyāsī. 2. Saṁnyāsī – India – Interviews. 3. Ascetics – Hinduism. I. Title.

DDC 294.50922 22

First published in India in 2011

ISBN 13: 978-81-246-0574-5 ISBN 10: 81-246-0574-2

Published and printed by:
D.K. Printworld (P) Ltd.
Regd. Office: 'Srikunj', F-52, Bali Nagar
Ramesh Nagar Metro Station
New Delhi-110 015
Phones: (011) 2545 3975; 2546 6019; *Fax*: (011) 2546 5926
E-mail: indology@dkprintworld.com
Website: www.dkprintworld.com

Preface

THIS book has been a long time in the making. A grant for this research on the Hindu *saṁnyāsin* and the institution of *saṁnyāsa* was provided by the FRDP (Faculty Research Development Program) by my University, without which I could not have visited the countries I did and have a series of interviews with both scholars of Indology as well as of *saṁnyāsins/saṁnyāsinīs* with their consent, during the years 1998 to 2000. I thank the Concordia University for that support. My stay at the Indian Insitute of Advanced Study at Shimla for six months in 2007 as a fellow also enabled me to use its excellent library for this research and helped me in realizing how varied and diverse the tradition of *saṁnyāsa* was and the wide variety of *saṁnyāsins* who come under that designation. For a textual scholar as myself this was indeed a revelation.

The very many people who facilitated the interviews with both scholars of Indology and the *saṁnyāsins/saṁnyāsinīs* themselves are too numerous to be mentioned by name. I thank them all sincerely as this would not have been possible without their help. The interviews themselves were based on a questionnaire which is given as Appendix I at the end of the book.

I regret to say some of those who were interviewed have passed on and as a token of my gratitude to them I dedicate this book to their memory. It may also be noted that the information given in the book regarding the *saṁnyāsins* and the *saṁnyasāśramas* is from the time of the interviews and because of the very many people involved, it was not possible to update the information.

No book is written by the author alone. There are always a number of people who help in crafting a book and that is equally true in this case as well. Apart from the interviewees themselves a number of my friends and colleagues have helped me in many ways and it is not easy to thank them individually. I will just say a big thank you to everyone of them and leave it at that. My husband S. Rajamani has always been there as a pillar of support to see this project through. My thanks are also due to D.K. Printworld who by their gentle reminders and their great patience pushed me into finally completing this book.

Contents

Introduction

RELIGION has been part of human civilization from ages past and continues to consume the interest of both the layperson and scholar alike. And the Hindu *saṁnyāsin*/*saṁnyāsinī* whether in isolation or in an institution, who defines Hinduism in a very special way, is very much part of the Hindu landscape in the imagination of the world at large and has captured the minds of the common folk, scholars working in the Humanities and the Social Sciences as well as some scientists. The powerful image of a *saṁnyāsin* who renounces the much coveted worldly life which an ordinary person finds difficult to renounce is of perennial interest and there is a fascination to learn more and more about this *saṁnyāsin* phenomenon in the Hindu tradition.

The *saṁnyāsin* has not always been an object of admiration alone though; he/she has been the subject equally of praise as well as ridicule. But no one has been able to ignore the notable presence of the *saṁnyāsin* in the Hindu social structure from ancient times and the curiosity regarding their lives has never been diminished and consumes the average Hindu's life to this day. While some have looked upon the *saṁnyāsin* as a person in whom the highest value of *mokṣa* (liberation) has been achieved, there are others who have vilified the *saṁnyāsin* as a parasite in society living off the labour of other people. These are two extreme views and it is surely possible to have *saṁnyāsin*s who are representatives of both these viewpoints. However, this study does not concern itself with these issues but starts off with the assumption that the *saṁnyāsin* is a vital part of Hindu society and is also a much respected part of the tradition. It has sought to verify that assumption not solely by relying on textual sources dealing with *saṁnyāsin*s and the institution of *saṁnyāsa* but also through face to face interviews with both scholars of Indology and the different *saṁnyāsin*s belonging to a variety of traditions.

As the subject of this book is about *saṁnyāsins* and their institution, some may pose the question as to whether there is a need for such a book at all as there are already quite a few books which deal with this topic from many angles such as textual, anthropological, ethnic and sociological. I am aware of these studies and a number of them are listed in the bibliography at the end. However, the point of departure for this book is that the conclusions arrived at are based solely on personal interviews with *saṁnyāsins*, in most cases, in their *āśramas* themselves. I would, however, like to draw attention to three books which deal with this subject in more or less a similar manner as I am doing here. These are by Ghurye (1964), Tripathi (1978) and David Miller (1976). While Ghurye attempts a broad historical survey of the many *saṁnyāsins* in the land, Tripathi's book concerns itself mainly with the Uttar Pradesh area as does David Miller's book which concentrates on the State of Orissa alone. One should also realize that these books were written some time ago and there is a need to look at the changing perspectives that have come to govern both the individual *saṁnyāsin* as well as the *saṁnyāsāśrama* as well, since the time these books were written. Though these three books base their findings on interviews and participant observation, the results are communicated by the authors in their own words to the readers.

In this book however, I, as the author, am in the background and I let the interviewees speak for themselves without injecting my words into what they have to say about their *sampradāyas* and their own views. In other words, the author is practically absent in this book or sometimes minimally present when some views of the interviewees are summarized for clarity alone. In the presence of differing views amongst the different *sampradāyas* and individual *saṁnyāsins*/*saṁnyāsinīs*, even on basic topics like *mokṣa*, initiation rites, women *saṁnyāsinīs* and so on, the author has allowed the interviewees to speak for themselves and the result has been to reveal the rich variety within the broad framework of the *saṁnyāsa* tradition itself within Hinduism. As the study was based on a prepared questionnaire, the questions asked of the interviewees were the same and one limitation of this methodology was that very often the answers to the same questions tended to have the same ideas repeated. I could have glossed over them saying that the answer for a particular question did not differ from the previous person, etc., but I preferred to state what was narrated and let the reader make his/her own conclusions regarding the person being interviewed rather than intrude into the views of the person. This has resulted sometimes in repetitive ideas on some topics like *mokṣa*, concept of *saṁnyāsa* and so on, but that was unavoidable in this kind of a study.

Apart from the reasons stated above for the need of a book of this kind, one has to also take into consideration the constant influx of change that creeps into both individuals as members of a society they live in as well as into the institutions that are within the society. *Saṁnyāsin*s and the institution of *saṁnyāsa* are also subject to the phenomenon of change and this has been particularly pronounced in this age of globalization wherein *saṁnyāsin*s are no more confined to the Indian landscape but are visibly present in foreign lands as well. All classical material whether they are texts or institutions need to be studied afresh every few decades and that is what this endeavour is all about. There is also still a lot of ignorance regarding the lives of the Hindu *saṁnyāsin*s and one more book on the subject can contribute, in, however small a measure, to give a proper perspective on the subject. That in itself is a justification for another attempt to study and inform the public about the life of these *saṁnyāsin*s and the institution in which they live. In time this study will also be superseded by another, more representative of the age it will be dealing with.

In all some fifty-five *saṁnyāsin*s were interviewed for this book, but eventually only thirty-one interviews have been included here keeping the size of the book in view. By and large I have tried to include a variety of *āśram*s like the Advaita, Viśiṣṭādvaita, Dvaita, Śaiva-Siddhānta, Vīraśaiva, Ramakrishna Mission, Sivananda Ashram, Chinmaya Mission and many more. I have also looked at the different branches of the Ramakrishna Mission, Sivananda Ashram and others which have come to be established outside of India such as South Africa, the UK, and North America, which give a broader picture of how these organizations function in foreign lands and make adjustments to different cultures. Just as diaspora groups living outside their homelands adjust to changed circumstances, these *āśrama*s also exhibit similar strategies of changing some of the customs and introducing new ones to suit the places they live in, in order to better adjust to foreign lands. The names of the *āśram*s and Missions as well as the names of the persons interviewed have been given as they are published in their own respective publications even if sometimes they may differ from the Sanskrit spellings. Similarly, in view of the multiple spellings used for words like *peeṭha/pīṭha/peeṭham, maṭha/maṭham/mutt, āśram/āśrama/āshram* etc., no attempt has been made to change them. They have, by and large, been indicated in the glossary.

The book is planned in four chapters. The first one titled "Swāmīs/Saṁnyāsins/Monks/Ascetics in the Cultural World of the Hindus", tries to place the topic in a historical context using texts as well as traditional and cultural understanding. This chapter makes the point that though the institution of *saṁnyāsin*s came into being later, traditionally associated with Śaṅkarācārya, the concept itself can be traced to Vedic times and is very much part of Hindu culture. It also traces the many twists and turns that the concept itself underwent in its long journey from Vedic to modern times. The dramatic changes that have come in the wake of technological advances to this age-old institution is also a focus of this chapter.

The second chapter is based on interviews with some scholars of indology as to their understanding of the *saṁnyāsin* and the institution of *saṁnyāsa*. Amongst these scholars some talk about *saṁnyāsa* in general, while some others belonging to particular *sampradāya*s like Viśiṣṭādvaita and Dvaita dwell on the minute points of differences that *saṁnyāsin*s from their *sampradāya*s have and yet others look at individual *saṁnyāsin*s and highlight the many ways in which they reinterpret the very concept of *saṁnyāsa* itself in their institutions. The views of the scholars are sometimes given in their own words and at other times they are summarized to give the gist of what they meant. Even though these scholars are familiar with the textual *saṁnyāsa* material, what comes out loud and clear in these interviews is that there is no single way in which the scholar of Indology views both the *saṁnyāsin* and the institution they belong to. This chapter thus presents the tradition as is seen to be practised on the ground and brings to focus the truism that the reality is very often not always what is represented in the texts themselves.

The third chapter continues the same format as the second, of presenting the views of *saṁnyāsin*s based on interviews with individual *saṁnyāsin*s from many lineages. Here again we find what was highlighted by scholars in the second chapter, i.e. that there is no one way of understanding the concept of *saṁnyāsa* and the institution itself.

Here, as in Chapter 2, the views of *saṁnyāsins* are given in their own words and sometimes summarized but in no way has the author intruded into what the *saṁnyāsins* had to say about the different points raised. The *saṁnyāsins* affiliated to centres like the Ramakrishna Mission, the Sivananda Ashram, etc., working outside India have also been interviewed separately from *saṁnyāsins* of these same *āśrams* in India, in order to get some perspectives on the different approaches when one works in an alien atmosphere.

The fourth chapter is a concluding chapter where some observations based on the information gathered in the foregoing chapters are made. For instance, different *sampradāyas* and individual *saṁnyāsins* have brought in many changes in the initiation ritual for entering *saṁnyāsa*; there is also a wide variety of views regarding what *mokṣa* stands for; another area of concern which still engages the minds of some *saṁnyāsins* is whether women are eligible for *saṁnyāsa* or not; *saṁnyāsins* also have differing views on whether they should enter or take interest in politics or not; how much of contact should a *saṁnyāsin* have with her/his family after taking *saṁnyāsa* is another area where differences are visible.

Little details that are normally not well known also come as surprises like the participation of Viśiṣṭādvaita *saṁnyāsins* in the *śrāddha* ceremony which is normally considered taboo for a *saṁnyāsin*. Similarly the way the foreign *saṁnyāsin* imbibes the observances of the *sampradāya* sheds light on the way how little changes creep in due to a changed atmosphere. Moreover, there is interesting information not widely known and also which one would not normally associate with a *saṁnyāsāśrama* such as the consultation of horoscopes to select a new head of an *āśram*, for instance. Similarly, the way the *saṁnyāsins* themselves explain certain practices can differ from how people in the outside world as well as scholars of Indology understand them. The fourth chapter tries to highlight any new information learnt from the *saṁnyāsins* themselves which adds to our understanding of the lives the *saṁnyāsins* lead in their *āśrams*. What comes out clearly in the fourth chapter is the theme that there are some interesting facts about the *saṁnyāsins* and their institutions which we as scholars are normally not familiar with.

I do not talk about the Daśanāmī *saṁnyāsins* specifically in this book as the origins of the Daśanāmī order are not very clear. There are some *saṁnyāsin*s who were interviewed who belonged to Daśanāmī *akhāḍā*s and I have discussed some points of the *akhāḍā*s in that context. There could have been many free roaming *saṁnyāsin*s like the *keśin* mentioned in *ṚV* (X.136) and their names such as *Giri*, *Vana*, *Araṇya* and so on do suggest their various locations. As there is a strong tradition mentioning their association with Śaṅkara's name it is also possible that these names were given to them by Śaṅkara based on their own traditions and Śaṅkara might have also got them affiliated to his different *maṭha*s as well (Ghurye, 1964; Giri, 1976; Tripathi, 1978; Wade, 1990). A number of them from these various lineages might have come together in later times, when the need arose, to form a militant group called the Nāgās, even while retaining their original affiliations. The considered opinion of scholars is that the Nāgā *saṁnyāsin*s came into being to fulfil a specific purpose during times when the Hindu *saṁnyāsin* was under threat after the time of Śaṅkara.

The mode of recruitment of the Daśanāmī *saṁnyāsin*s at the time of Kuṁbha Melās, as well as the way in which the chiefs of the *akhāḍā*s are selected, all suggest that the *āśram*s and the *akhāḍā*s had independent origins. Though in practice the Daśanāmīs seem to be staunch Śiva followers, they profess to follow Advaita philosophy. This minor point might very well give credence to the legendary association to the Nāgās of Madhusudana Saraswati at whose behest the Nāgā *saṁnyāsin*s got sanction to organize themselves as a militant group to protect the Hindu *saṁnyāsin*s at the time of the Mogul king Akbar. As Madhusudana was a staunch Advaitin, this could explain the loyalty to Advaita amongst the *akhāḍā sampradāya*s even though in practice, as mentioned earlier, they are Śaivites.

Scholars also talk about 52/53 principal *maṭha*s divided into eight *dava*s and how the Daśanāmī *akhāḍā*s grew out of these original *dava*s. It is probable that initially there was only one *akhāḍā* and from that grew the six *akhāḍā*s known today, whose origins are given between CE 856 and 1749 by Dr Sarkar (cited in Giri, 1976: 22). What is relevant for our purpose is that a number of *saṁnyāsin*s interviewed for this book, specially in the north, are both *saṁnyāsin*s of traditional *āśram*s and are also Mahāmaṇḍaleśvaras/Maṇḍaleśvaras belonging to an *akhāḍā*. It is also worth noting that I did not come into contact with any Mahāmaṇḍaleśvaras or Maṇḍaleśvaras of *akhāḍā*s in the south of India. Books by Ghurye (1964), Tripathi (1978), Giri (1976); Wade (1990) and others can be consulted for more information regarding the Daśanāmī *saṁnyāsins*.

Though I have not included independent *sādhus* in this study, I did interview a few evolved independent *sādhus* in order to substantiate the claim that even today the practice of adopting *saṁnyāsa* for spiritual and other reasons is still very much alive in the Hindu tradition. There have always been such *sādhus* in the land not only amongst the Hindus but within Buddhism and Jainism as well. The Hindu *sādhus* are by and large free roaming ascetics on their own. They also wear, by and large, the ochre robes and generally follow the lifestyle of a *saṁnyāsin*.

One may notice, in the course of reading this book that there are a disproportionate number of *saṁnyāsins* who profess to follow the Advaita Sampradāya. While the first four or five *āśrams* started by Śaṅkarācārya cannot be duplicated, and in my interviews I did not come across any other *saṁnyāsin* calling himself Śaṅkarācārya which was solely reserved for the heads of the *maṭhas* established by Śaṅkarācārya himself, most independent *saṁnyāsins* profess to follow Advaita philosophy and I did not come across independent Viśiṣṭādvaita or Dvaita *saṁnyāsins*. The rigid rule of association with a temple which governs the Vaiṣṇava Sampradāyas as well as the Śaiva Sampradāyas does not easily lend itself to the formation of independent Vaiṣṇava or Śaiva Sampradāyas. The lack of any rituals and temple worship associated with the theoretical understanding of Advaita possibly made it easier for persons spiritually inclined to start *āśrams* based on Advaita philosophy. Sivananda, Chinmayananda, Dayananda Saraswati and others have all started their own *āśrams* and interestingly enough Chinmayananda was a disciple of Sivananda, and Dayananda Saraswati in turn was a disciple of Chinmayananda. Today the *āśrams* started by all three have their own branches all over the world.

This phenomenon of going to an established *guru* in a reputed *āśram* like Sivananda's, for instance, and then branching off to start one's own *āśram*, is very much part of the tradition which came into being specially after Swami Vivekananda. In time these subsidiary branches acquire their own reputation and sprout other *āśrams* much like a banyan tree with its hanging roots. We have many such examples like that of Swami Dayananda's Arsha Gurukulam, for instance. This is a phenomenon which continues to the present day.

1

Swamis/Saṁnyāsins/Monks/Ascetics in the Cultural World of the Hindus

An Overview

THERE has been a marked presence of the Hindu Swami, also called a *saṁnyāsin* or ascetic, in the Western world, increasingly since the 1960s. Swami Vivekananda who addressed the World Parliament of Religions at Chicago in 1893 can be considered the first Swami who kindled the curiosity of the Westerners regarding the way of life of a *saṁnyāsin* which has continued to the present day. The Vedānta centres started by Swami Vivekananda by providing some information regarding the institution and lifestyle of the Hindu *saṁnyāsin* and others after him like Maharshi Mahesh Yogi, Shrila Prabhupada, Swami Muktananda, Swami Sivananda, etc., have all helped in keeping the institution alive over the years. While this book deals with how *saṁnyāsa* is viewed by scholars and spiritual leaders themselves, this first chapter attempts a historical overview of the concept of *saṁnyāsa*/renunciation from Vedic times, in contrast to that of conventional ritual or religious action.

History and historical periods are difficult to be delineated within precise boundaries in any culture but is more so in Hindu thought which has a paucity of historical records. Moreover, the boundaries in Hinduism cannot neatly be divided into ancient, medieval or modern as is possible in some other religions. Therefore, when one talks about a historical overview, it is important to bear in mind that all the so-called historical periods which I talk about below have porous boundaries so that, what was perhaps pronounced in one period, was still present in both the antecedent and subsequent periods but perhaps with different emphases.

It is well known that the word *saṁnyāsin* itself came into use rather late in Hinduism. The word *saṁnyāsin* today stands for one who practises *saṁnyāsa* (detachment/dispassion) from conventional worldly behaviour as a cardinal principle of spiritual advancement. Though initially this detachment was emphasized more towards ritual activity, gradually, by the time of the Bhagavad-Gītā, it came to denote detachment from the expectation of results from any action, religious or secular as well. In Hinduism since all action was subsumed under the broad umbrella of *dharma*, the lines drawn between religious and secular action was also not always clear. Thus I use *dharma* and religious action as interchangeable terms when needed.

Dispassion/*saṁnyāsa* is a cultural concept whose origins can be traced to Vedic times. The act of abandonment of whatever is sacrificed in the fire was expressed by the sacrificer in the Ṛgveda (ṚV) (*c.* 2000 BCE) as *agnaye idam na mama*: "This is for Fire; it is not mine." The Bṛhadāraṇyaka (Bṛ.) and Chāndogya (Chā.) Upaniṣads (Up.) also talk about *saṁnyāsa* and a *saṁnyāsin*'s way of life for spiritual attainment. So even if the word *saṁnyāsa* may not be used in the early texts one can argue that ideas of detachment can be traced in them. Thus, the chances are that the later *saṁnyāsin* evolved from within the tradition but got a life of its own when it came in contact with other religions like Buddhism, for instance, where there is a polarization of the life of one who renounces the world called a *bhikṣu*, with the one who is still of the world.

By the time of the Mahābhārata (*c.* 400 BCE – CE 400) both the concepts of *saṁnyāsa* and the *saṁnyāsin* were well entrenched in the tradition and the famous dialogue between a father and his son, one arguing for a conventional religious life while the other rejecting it in favour of a withdrawal from it, illustrates this clearly (Hiriyanna, 1993: 21). While the ṚV supports generally a conventional ritual life, by the time we come to the early Upaniṣads (*c.* 800–600 BCE), the tendencies towards *saṁnyāsa* as an alternate way of life, not in a negative sense of just withdrawal but in a positive sense of adopting knowledge as opposed to rituals for achieving one's goal in life called *mokṣa*, is accepted. In the Bṛ. Up. and the Chā. Up. complete withdrawal coupled with a life of reflection and meditation is advocated, as the best spiritual path. This could be viewed as the first specific evidence of the *saṁnyāsa* concept in the Upaniṣads, which is a combination of withdrawal from ritual action accompanied with intellectual inquiry on the nature of reality, also known as the path of knowledge.

However, it must be said that this combination between *saṁnyāsa* and knowledge was not always expressly maintained. There were many different kinds of renouncers following the *saṁnyāsa* path as time went by, and in subsequent periods of its history, we do find all kinds of people both genuine seekers and others adopting this mode of life. However, at least theoretically, even in its later interpretations such as being engaged ritualistically or otherwise in any action with a sense of detachment known as *niṣkāma-karma* in the Bhagavad-Gītā, there was a sense of its being chosen as a path because of the aspirant having knowledge of its greater efficacy as compared to the ritual path.

Thus by the Upaniṣadic times, a new model for spiritual upliftment has come into being, i.e. that of following a path of knowledge informed by detachment in the ephemeral worldly life. But what one notices in the Upaniṣads is that, though some passages advocate a path of renunciation as opposed to that of ritual action, there was always a coming around, and a polarization between these two paths was not allowed to happen. Many Upaniṣads like the Īśāvāsya Upaniṣad (verses 1 and 2), Praśna (I.9-10), Muṇḍaka (I.2.1, 11-12) and others talk approvingly of both the paths of ritual and withdrawal from them. And by the time we come to the Bhagavad-Gītā (*c.* second century BCE) there has been a happy reconciliation of both ritual and withdrawal and that state, one can say, continues to the present day.

This reconciliation was partly effected in Hindu culture by making provision for both paths by a division of the life of an individual into four stages. After an initial stage of studentship (*brahmacarya*) one could go through the householder stage (*gṛhastha*) and then come to the last two stages of gradual withdrawal from engagement in a conventional sense both ritually and socially called *vānaprastha* (living in the forest) and then *saṁnyāsa* or total renunciation from all conventional engagement with society. While one could renounce the world at any time after going through the student's life, the ideal would be to go through the different stages gradually and reach the highest goal or value of liberation (*mokṣa*) through total renunciation in the *saṁnyāsa* stage.

The Hindu *saṁnyāsin* is also called variously as a *swāmi, yati, sādhu, parivrajya* or *parivrājaka* (meaning a wanderer), *tapasvī*, and so on. A *saṁnyāsin* would normally denote one who has been formally initiated into the stage of a renouncer and stays in institutionalized places of residence of renouncers. The Hindu *saṁnyāsin* is really not outside of society. The *saṁnyāsin* and the *saṁnyāsa* institution called the *saṁnyāsāśrama* are built within the structure of society and the *saṁnyāsins* are very much part of society, fulfilling the role of consultants and even acting as counsellors to their disciples. The *saṁnyāsin* is only outside the conventions ordinarily followed by people in society, having chosen to renounce conventional life in society in order to achieve the highest value the Hindu believed in, through the act of withdrawal from the world.

For the purposes of this chapter I divide the periods heuristically as (1) the Vedic which includes the Vedas, the Brāhmaṇas, the Āraṇyakas and the Upaniṣads (*c.* 2000–500 BCE), (2) the post-Vedic or Classical which, following Hiriyanna, can itself be viewed in two stages, i.e when there is an intervening period (*c.* 500 BCE – CE 100), and the age of the philosophical systems (*c.* CE 200–500). This is also the time of the Dharmasūtras and the period when Upaniṣads devoted to special topics like yoga, *saṁnyāsa* (renunciation), etc., were composed. The Mahābhārata epic, which exhibits elements of both Vedic as well as non-Vedic ideas, also belongs to this period. By this time religious ritual action also expanded its meanings. The opposition was no more between pure withdrawal and religious ritual practices but between selfless non-egocentric action that characterized a *saṁnyāsin*'s way of life and selfish engagement in both rituals and in the world for one's own benefit.

(3) We then pass on to the age of the Purāṇas (*c.* CE 300-1000) which overlaps with the second classical age and which is the age of *bhakti* (devotion) and its efflorescence. Śaṅkarācārya of Advaita fame belongs to this period and his life and message was a watershed in the history of the growth of the *saṁnyāsa* ideal. Śaṅkarācārya himself was a *saṁnyāsin* and in his personal life promoted the ideal of *saṁnyāsa* while allowing rituals for those not ready for liberation. His Advaita philosophy promoted this ideology and his was a major religious influence in all subsequent periods of Indian history. (4) Phase four (about CE 1000–1900) can be associated with reformers like Raja Rammohun Roy and others who worked within the householder's stage combining both religious behaviour and *saṁnyāsa* in a judicious blend while others like Swami Vivekananda donned the robes of a *saṁnyāsin* and enriched the ideas of *saṁnyāsa* by expanding it to include welfare activities called *lokasaṁgraha*. (5) Phase five is the pre-Independence period (1885–1947)

which follows closely phase four as Swami Vivekananda and other *saṁnyāsin*s were also active in this period. It was also witness to a number of individuals like Mahatma Gandhi and Vinoba Bhave who, though not *saṁnyāsin*s in the true sense of the term, gave a new meaning to the word *saṁnyāsa*. (6) And the last sixth phase is the post-Independence period, which itself can be viewed in two ways: one as an initial stage of euphoria between 1947-1970s when there was a proliferation of *saṁnyāsin*s, followed by a scenario, which continues to the present, where both selfish action and *saṁnyāsa* have porous boundaries.

VEDIC AGE (*C.* 2000–500 BCE)

The concept of liberation (*mokṣa*) characterized by complete withdrawal from the world of action, is not generally mentioned in the R̥V; this is yet to come at the time of the Upaniṣads. But the future *saṁnyāsin* as a wanderer is already foreshadowed.

R̥gvedic society is a robust one where the members live comfortable lives within a harmonious concept of a principle of Unity amongst all that exists. Its commitment to the sacred was expressed through its *yajña*s (sacrifices). While the notion of *dharma* as strict adherence to rituals as understood in the Dharmaśāstras is still far away, the metaphysical concept of *r̥ta* as a cosmic force which sustains the universe within a physical and moral order has come to stay. It was also believed that humans sustained this physical and moral order by the correct performance of sacrifices. In the early Vedic period, we also have *mantras* (sacred words) that state that this cosmic force, which is also called *satya* (truth) and which underlies the universe, the *r̥ṣi*s (sages) directly perceived as "unfolding through successive layers of reality" (Rajendra Pandeya in *Hindu Spirituality*, 1989: 6). And furthermore, any person performing sacrifices with faith can envision this Truth.

There was built into the sacrifice-performance the cultivation of a sense of selflessness, i.e. a forgetting of one's ego. The notion of giving up the ego *(saṁnyāsa)* will assume great importance in a *saṁnyāsin*'s life later. Even in the R̥V, sacrifices and *saṁnyāsa* were not opposed to each other but could be achieved in the very act of living in harmony with nature and did not demand an abdication of worldly life. One could visualize that at this time, someone abandoning the path of sacrifice would not be looked upon with favour.

It may appear from the above, that the life of a wanderer and a renouncer cannot fit this early society. But there we are mistaken. Even in the ṚV we discover individuals who are wanderers and who are described as living in the world of *apsaras*, *gandharvas* and wild beasts, "Treading the path of *apsaras*, of *gandharvas* and wild beasts, the long-haired man who knows the heart comes, a sweet friend, most gladdening" (ṚV, X.136.2). It is significant that the wanderer is long-haired, a reference perhaps to his unconventional lifestyle. He is credited with upholding the earth and heaven (*rodasī*), [capable of seeing] all lustrous visions and is designated as light (*jyoti*). They are called *munis* wearing soiled yellow clothes, and [they] travel with the wind to where the *devas* (deities) are (X.136.2 & 4).

Verses like the above make it clear that there were individuals who did not conform to the Vedic sacrificial path for attainment of a good life, here on earth, as well as ensuring for themselves an auspicious future existence, post mortem. If one pays attention to the *munis* travelling to where the *devas* are and also upholding the earth and heaven, the wanderers were perhaps those who were concerned with "reality" as such, and not just leading a virtuous life in the world as prescribed in the Vedic code.

One question that crops up, however, is: what is the meaning understood by "reality" here? We have statements in the ṚV such as "Reality is One; but it can be viewed in many different ways" (ṚV, I.164.45) and "Four grades of speech that have been measured, men of divine knowledge, who are wise know them. Three of these kept in secret make no motion, people speak only the fourth grade of speech." (ṚV, I.164.46). These statements appear to be linked to intuiting the highest Ṛgvedic principle called *ṛta* which appears to stand for "reality." *Ṛta* is the basic principle of physical and moral order and humans have a large role to maintain that order, as mentioned earlier, by the correct performance of rituals. But the *muni* strikes a discordant note here. Was he just walking out of ritual conduct out of scepticism or is he also trying to find an alternate path for intuiting the same *ṛta*? His action smacks of *saṁnyāsa* as we have come to understand it. But is it coupled with knowledge that will come to characterize *saṁnyāsa* in the Upaniṣads or was he just discarding his obligations and walking out?

In the early Vedic period, we also find many other words used along with *ṛta* to signify "reality." Thus the word *sat* is very often used in the sense of "reality/essence." For instance, in the Nāsadīya-Sūkta (R̥V X.129), *sat* (truth) and *asat* (untruth) refer to the reflections of the seer as to the nature of the primal entity. *Sat* and *asat* are here visualized as positive and potential existence of the primal entity, respectively. In the Yajurveda, Vena is described as having seen that *sat*, which is hidden in mystery and which is the single home of the entire world. There are three words used prominently in this period which are closely linked with each other. They are *r̥ta, satya* and *tapas*. If *r̥ta* stands for moral and physical order, *satya* will indicate truth or a rootedness in that being. And both *satya* and *r̥ta* are described as born of *tapas* (sacrifice/restraint) in R̥V (X.190.1), AV (X.7.1, XII.1), etc., (Bose, 1966: 7-8). Thus one can understand *tapas* or sacrifice to be at the root of intuiting the cosmic force, and the essence of being. A path of *saṁnyāsa* can now be identified with the religious path of performing sacrifice/*yajña*, because, in one sense, it was an externalization of an eternal truth and, in another sense, the *r̥ṣi*s were convinced that in that state of purity, *r̥ta* can be intuited (Bose, 1966: 30, 33, 127, 355), (R̥V VI.9.4-6, X.154.1-5, X.85.1).

If, then, we concede that the intuitive understanding of one's "true essence," as shown above, can come through a conventional ritual life, we can ask ourselves whether the *muni*s walking out of this way of life, were also seeking to intuit the same "true essence." There is no doubt that the *muni* has stepped out of this conventional life of sacrifice, either out of disillusionment or through scepticism. But it is not difficult to imagine that both disillusion and scepticism can feed on each other and lead in the end to abandoning the path of sacrifice. We have many *mantra*s in the R̥V which express doubts in the minds of some *r̥ṣi*s about the meaning of all that exists. One *mantra* significantly questions the very existence of Indra, who by all accounts is one of the important Vedic *devatā*s (deities). "There is no Indra" it says, "who has ever seen him? Whom shall we praise?" (R̥V, VIII.100.3). It is therefore, not unreasonable to assume that these *mantra*s indeed refer to groups of individuals who questioned the accepted sanctity and efficacy of the ritualistic mode of life, to accomplish its avowed objectives.

We now have a clue to unravel the mystery of the path of the *muni*s. The twofold divergence of paths as the path of religious action and the path of knowledge (*jñāna/saṁnyāsa*) have their seeds sown in the conventional performance of sacrifices by the *r̥ṣi*s and the free path of the *muni*s respectively. These two paths continue to doggedly follow the trajectory of Hinduism throughout its history up to the present day. While the performance model came to be identified with the path of *dharma* or religious action, which assured *abhyudaya* or worldly welfare for its performers along with the promise of intuiting the ultimate *ṛta* gradually, the knowledge model advocated a withdrawal from the performance aspect but assured the attainment of *ṛta* which in itself was a complete value. We can thus assume that the *muni*, because of the description of his being close to the *deva*s and moving with the winds, withdraws from the conventional mode of action and chooses the path of *saṁnyāsa*, as it were, and seeks the ultimate reality, *ṛta*, within the mystery of his heart.

The Upaniṣadic period, probably, is the time when a number of new ideas got associated with Hinduism. There is enough evidence to indicate that the fourfold *varṇa* (class) division of society had hardened and we also know that the four *puruṣārtha*s or values of human existence (*dharma, artha, kāma, mokṣa*), as well as the *karma* theory connecting the self with transmigration, were all well entrenched in the tradition. Bṛ. Up. (4.4.22) and Chā. Up. (5.10.1-2), indicate that the fourfold *āśrama*s (stages of life) were also open as choices for individuals without being as yet a sequential hierarchy. The *puruṣārtha*s came to be related to the *varṇa*s as well as the four *āśrama*s (student, householder, forest-dweller and *saṁnyāsin*: the four stages of life). In this fourfold scheme of both the *puruṣārtha*s and the *āśrama*s, the ultimate value was defined as *mokṣa* or liberation, and the *āśrama* in which to achieve it was the *saṁnyāsāśrama* (stage of life as a monk). This was withdrawal *par excellence*. The other values were dubbed together as religious action (*dharma*) and they dealt with life in the world while leading the life of a student or householder. The third *āśrama* (*vānaprastha,* literally meaning starting for the forest) was only a preparation for the ultimate goal *mokṣa,* and was neither religious action nor *saṁnyāsa in toto*.

As the formative period of these different ideas, one also notices an accommodation and flexibility in pursuing the twin paths of religious action and *saṁnyāsa* in this second phase. While ideally only those who withdrew from the world and embraced the *saṁnyāsāśrama* (monastic order) qualified for the ultimate goal of *mokṣa*, the *jīvanmukta* ideal (liberated while still embodied), which was again introduced in the Upaniṣads, also accommodated persons like Janaka and Ajātaśatru, who could fulfil their obligation to society and gain *mokṣa* by engaging in action in a detached manner. There was thus a combining of an active life with a mental attitude of detachment. We thus see the *muni*s withdrawing from a conventional lifestyle during the early Vedic period, undergoing some modifications in this phase. While there was a hardening of attitudes by allowing *mokṣa* to be realized only by a *saṁnyāsin* (monk), examples like that of Janaka and Ajātaśatru also tell us that the values of religious action or fulfilling one's *dharma* and *saṁnyāsa* were possible as public and private goals, respectively.

Liberation while still embodied called *jīvanmukta*, was perhaps another attempt not to divorce action from being a value in society. After all, the presence of Buddhism and Jainism must have been a strong pull towards adopting the renunciate's life for the common folk. Hinduism had to reject the polarization of the two models and find a balance within its own interpretation of action which can also satisfy spiritual aspirants. At a time when non-Vedic schools like Jainism and Buddhism asserted their presence with their questioning of the authority of the Vedas and valorizing the life of a monk in a *saṁgha* (community), Hindu culture had to reassert itself and find new ways of preserving its way of life. It did so immediately after in the post-Vedic period, by composing different kinds of texts which are mentioned under the classical or Post-Vedic Phase.

Reality came to be understood in the Upaniṣads as an identity between the individual self (*ātman*) and the absolute supreme self (*paramātman)* and *mokṣa* was the state in which to realize this truth. The earlier *ṛta* concept of unity has taken on a new garb as an identity between *ātman* and *paramātman* in the Upaniṣads. Whereas in the early Vedic period, even those who led a householder's life dedicated to sacrifices were assured a realization of *ṛta,* in this period the experience of *paramātman* was restricted only to those who abandoned selfish interests. Ideally those were the ones that chose the last stage of life of a *saṁnyāsin*. Even in exceptions like Janaka, there was an emphasis on the mental attitude of detachment. Thus, for the ordinary human, life led in accordance with *dharma* prepared him for the final withdrawal by adopting the last *saṁnyāsāśrama*. In this period then, conventional religious action and *saṁnyāsa* coexisted in a friendly way; thus *dharma* (ritual action) continued to hold sway in some circles, even while *saṁnyāsa* was acknowledged as the ideal path for attainment of the highest value of *mokṣa*.

CLASSICAL OR POST-VEDIC PHASE (*C.* 500 BCE – CE 500)

The classical phase (*c.* 500 BCE – CE 500), ushered in the composition of *sūtras* for the six schools of Vedic thought and the compilation of the Rāmāyaṇa and Mahābhārata (epics) and the early Dharmasūtras like that of Āpastamba, Gautama and Bodhāyana as well as the Smṛtis like that of Manu, Yājñavalkya, etc.; it is also a definitive phase when both religious action (*dharma*) and *saṁnyāsa* got defined both in a religious and philosophical sense as well as in the lived world. One can view this cluster of literature as setting down the values to be followed in an individual's life.

One can say that *saṁnyāsa* was gaining ground and that it assumed a dominant role in the cultural history of Hinduism at this stage. *Mokṣa* as the highest value and *saṁnyāsāśrama* as its expression were also gaining importance at the time. This could be due to the influence of *nāstikas* (non-believers in the Vedas) like the Buddhists, Jains and Ajīvikas on the one hand, and, on the other, due to the reformulation of the ritualistic mode of life in the rise of *bhakti* or devotion which was gaining an upper hand over the Vedic sacrificial mode. The Bhagavad-Gītā and the Mahābhārata as well as the Rāmāyaṇa talk about the importance of *bhakti* (devotion to a personal deity). But whatever the religious expression, *mokṣa* was the highest value sought after, whether through withdrawal from the world or by practising devotion. And *mokṣa* could only be achieved by subordination of the ego; thus there was an emphasis on *saṁnyāsa*, more by pointing to its psychical aspect of selflessness than by withdrawing from the world, in this phase. By now *saṁnyāsa* (monk's life) was already incorporated into the social fabric as an individual choice (as mentioned earlier) and allowed individuals to assume the *saṁnyāsa* or monastic mode of life anytime they chose. The elaborate Āgama texts dealing with temple rituals were still in the making and so we can assume that the concept of *saṁnyāsa* was paramount in this classical period. Since the institution of *saṁnyāsa* was also not institutionalized like the Buddhist *saṁgha* as yet, there must have been a proliferation of *saṁnyāsins* wandering about and recalling to mind the wandering *muni* of Vedic times.

The Bhagavad-Gītā which belongs to this period presents the concept of *saṁnyāsa* in a number of ways including that of *niṣkāma-karma* (action done with detachment to the outcome), a reformulation of the very concept of action in a *saṁnyāsa* mode. One could generally state that *saṁnyāsa* is being redefined in this phase. Even though there were examples of liberated individuals like Janaka and Ajātaśatru continuing in the world and engaging in selfless action, those were exceptions and had not become the norm. But desireless action (*niṣkāma-karma*) was eloquently argued for by the Bhagavad-Gītā in this phase. That was *saṁnyāsa par excellence;* not a running away from the world of action but action done in a certain spirit. Since devotion to a preferred deity (*iṣṭadevatā*) as a religious practice had also come to the fore, religious action also got defined in that context as dedication of all acts to Īśvara, again conveying the sense of non-attachment. This reformulation was reiterated in many different ways in the Bhagavad-Gītā. *Saṁnyāsa* is no longer restricted to the recluse's domain but has been brought within the householder's realm, a subtle transformation of the ideal into the lived world.

PURĀṆA PHASE (*c.* CE 300-1000)

This is the heyday of *bhakti* when a number of Purāṇas were composed on the religious front and commentaries on philosophical *sūtra*s held sway. There was also a revival of Vedic sacrifice and we hear of emperors like Pallava Śivaskandavarman and Candragupta I performing the horse sacrifice. The Vedic Dharma was revived by the kings and existed side by side with worship of Śiva and Viṣṇu. Buddhism as well as Jainism were also in existence along with other sectarian movements. It was a time when there was an outburst of devotional religious poetry in the south and a number of the eighteen great Purāṇas were composed which glorified devotion (*bhakti*) as the way to *mokṣa*. The Gupta kings, in this period, attempted to reconcile the new *bhakti* cults with the old Vedic rituals and social theories, (Classical Age, 1988: 297-98) and they succeeded in great measure due to their spirit of toleration of all religious expression. One can even say that this was the period that defined Hinduism's many phases like worship of icons in temples, pilgrimage, fasts, festivals, etc., all part of popular Hinduism even today.

Along with the developments of Vedic Dharma and popular devotional movements, rigorous philosophical debates based on original philosophical texts (*sūtra*s) and commentaries on them, made sure that the value of *mokṣa* as the highest value to be aspired for, was not forgotten. The importance of *bhakti* and temple worship, as also the reaffirmation of Vedic sacrifice, catapulted religious ritual action back to centre stage during this period. Religion was more oriented towards the lived world and had a slight edge over *saṁnyāsa* now.

Śaṅkarācārya, the Advaita Vedānta philosopher, looms as a towering personality in this period, and in him we get a reaffirmation of total renunciation only to be achieved in the last stage of *saṁnyāsa* by abandoning worldly conventions. Śaṅkarācārya strengthened that belief by also establishing four institutions (*maṭhas*) where *saṁnyāsins* could reside, in Dwārakā, Purī, Jyotirmaṭha and Śṛṅgerī (Kāñcī is also mentioned as the fifth *maṭha* by some scholars) to continue the propagation of Advaita Vedānta. Thus, with Śaṅkarācārya, the lines were drawn between the domain of a *saṁnyāsin* and the non-*saṁnyāsins*. To a certain extent that perception is still present in the Hindu psyche. Till now the Hindu *saṁnyāsin* led a wandering life which resembled the lifestyle of the Ṛgvedic wandering *muni*. The Buddhist institution for the *bhikṣus* (*saṁgha*) was already in existence and it is likely that the success of the Buddhist *saṁgha* could have inspired Śaṅkara to do the same for *saṁnyāsins* of the Advaita persuasion. So, even though the importance of *saṁnyāsa* was devalued in an atmosphere of *bhakti* and revival of a householder's life based on domestic rituals at this time, *mokṣa* as the highest value to be pursued by practice of *saṁnyāsa*, which was already established on a firm footing during the classical period, was reinforced during this age through the commentaries and debates conducted amongst rival philosophical schools at Varanasi and other places and also by the establishment of the Advaita Vedānta *āśrams* by Śaṅkarācārya.

Śaṅkara also established the tradition of writing commentaries on important Vedānta works that kept the *saṁnyāsa* ideal alive in the minds of people. While so far, the *saṁnyāsin* worked for his own *mokṣa*, living very often a secluded life, Śaṅkara also expanded the functions of a *saṁnyāsin* to include what is known as *lokasaṁgraha,* i.e. action done selflessly for the welfare of the world. Śaṅkara himself travelled the length and breadth of the country working for the spiritual upliftment of the people at large. It is reasonable to argue that Śaṅkara must have preached Vedic Dharma (ritual) as well as the ideal of *mokṣa* as contrasting modes of living, with different ends in view.

One can say that though *saṁnyāsa* lost its hold on the minds of the people due to the upsurge of the devotional movements and a return to Vedic Dharma practices in this age, Śaṅkara's one-pointed effort of promoting *mokṣa* as an ideal and advocating a life of a *saṁnyāsin* in order to achieve it, and also his strengthening the institution of *saṁnyāsa* by establishing *maṭha*s for them to stay and promote this ideal, and also amalgamating it with *lokasaṁgraha*, helped in making, once and for all, *mokṣa* part and parcel of Hindu thought and praxis. His combining the *mokṣa* ideal with the *lokasaṁgraha* praxis also opened the way for new interpretations and innovations both in the ideal of *mokṣa* as well as in the *saṁnyāsa* institutions. An accommodation and mutual respect for religious action and *saṁnyāsa* was achieved by this time. Thus a religious minded Hindu was guided both by some idea of religious action (*dharma*) which helped in regulating one's life in the world and *saṁnyāsa* which assured *mokṣa* after death. The option to renounce was also always open for one so inclined. This was the message that was conveyed to an average Hindu through the stories related in the Mahābhārata and Rāmāyaṇa, the Purāṇas, Dharmasūtras/ Dharmaśāstras and popular tales. The concept of *lokasaṁgraha* in the world would also continue to engage religious developments in subsequent periods of Indian history.

The tradition of maintaining the culture through an oral recitation of the stories of the Rāmāyaṇa and the Mahābhārata and in particular the Bhagavad-Gītā, called *kathāprasaṅga*, was responsible, one could say, for disseminating these various ideas amongst the general population. After all, it was these gatherings which would be attended by large numbers particularly during festivities like Rāma's and Kṛṣṇa's birthday celebrations wherein the message of *niṣkāma-karma* (selfless action) for the attainment of *mokṣa* would make a big impact. Thus, one can surmise that, while in academic circles the philosophical schools and the commentarial literature kept the theoretical aspect of the *saṁnyāsa* ideal alive and healthy, the accessibility of popular epic and Purāṇic literature to the general public helped in emphasizing detachment and dispassion, and action performed as a dedication to Īśvara gained popularity. Thus a healthy accommodation between religious action or *dharma* and *saṁnyāsa* was maintained in this phase.

PHASE FOUR (CE 1000–1900)

This age can be associated with *saṁnyāsin*s like Swami Vivekananda. He belonged to a group of reformers like Rammohun Roy, Dayananda

Saraswati, Swami Ramtirtha and others who kept alive both the concepts of *dharma* and *saṁnyāsa* in the minds of the people (Rukmani in *Brahmavidyā* 1998: 30-50).

With Swami Vivekananda we come to the age of the Hindu idea of *saṁnyāsa* and yoga spreading to the West in a big way. Many Westerners adopted the Hindu saṁnyāsin's ideology of *mokṣa* and the saṁnyāsin's way of life as well, inspired by Swami Vivekananda. Swami Vivekananda did not just lecture in the west about India's spiritual heritage, but he also set up Vedānta centres in the places he travelled; thus there was established a permanent visible presence of the Hindu *saṁnyāsin* in the West. These gradually became important centres to spread the Ramakrishna Mission *saṁnyāsa* message. His contact with independent women in the West also allowed him to encourage women also in their spiritual quest, on par with men. This would later lead to the establishment of the Sarada Math in India which today has some branches outside India as well.

In Vivekananda we also have a person who believed, like Śaṅkara, that only a *saṁnyāsin* can pursue the goal of *mokṣa* single-mindedly without any distractions. It is mentioned that it was Ramakrishna Paramahamsa, his *guru*, who was responsible to turn his mind away from adopting the life of a *saṁnyāsin* and engage himself in worldly *dharma* activities. He did that applying the *saṁnyāsa* concept of *lokasaṁgraha* as a tool of social welfare. Others like Swami Dayananda also used the *lokasaṁgraha* concept to bring in reforms in Hindu society. Thus what distinguishes *saṁnyāsin*s like Vivekananda and Dayananda Saraswati from Śaṅkarācārya, is their strenuous effort to uplift society both materially and spiritually. While Śaṅkara had lived the life of a *saṁnyāsin* working for *lokasaṁgraha* as described in the Bhagavad-Gītā, the concept of *lokasaṁgraha* by *saṁnyāsin*s got enriched at the hands of reformers like Swami Vivekananda, Dayananda Saraswati et al.

Vivekananda used Upaniṣadic philosophy to strengthen the belief that humans have the potential to be their own masters. He called it "the philosophy of man-making" for which confidence in oneself, pride in one's heritage, commitment to the pursuit of a value that is perfect and a belief in the oneness of humanity are essential. The Upaniṣads and Śaṅkara's Advaita provided him with the necessary tools for this purpose.

The concept of *saṁnyāsa* had now come to stay in the Hindu psyche and was constantly present to the vision of a Hindu and, as pointed out above, it sometimes gained special recognition due to some powerful individuals but at other times it would lie dormant. But not once did the ideal ever disappear from the scene.

THE FIFTH PRE-INDEPENDENCE PHASE (1885–1947)

The fifth phase can be called the prelude to the post-Independence period, where the boundaries of engagement in ritual action or *dharma* and *saṁnyāsa* were getting increasingly blurred. We find individuals like Mahatma Gandhi and Vinoba Bhave who never donned the robes of a *saṁnyāsin* but led lives more akin to the life of a *saṁnyāsin* than a householder.

Even though Gandhi was married, he vowed to follow a celibate life like the *saṁnyāsin*s and considered the whole world as his family. The same was true of Vinoba Bhave who never married and both of them, though never initiated into the *dharma* of a *saṁnyāsin*, would fit the description of a *saṁnyāsin*. Gandhi talked about liberation and *mokṣa* at times and in his personal life always yearned one day to achieve liberation. His language of non-violence and truth, his pursuit of non-violence as a means to the realization of Truth which he equated to God, his willingness to suffer, his constant effort to "adapt the older notions of *mokṣa* and *tapas* [austerity] . . . to the practical needs of [Indian] society" (Raghavan 1973: 235), his willingness to reduce the individual ego to a zero and many more such ideas make him more a *saṁnyāsin* than one engaged within the conventional norms in society.

Gandhi's energies were, however, solely concentrated on achieving Independence for the country and his priority was for winning freedom or *mokṣa* (*svarājya*) for his people from colonial rule. And even his definition of *svarājya* (self-rule) was in spiritual terms as being in control and achieving "reform from within" and he defined the movement for *svarājya* as "a movement for self-purification" (Dalton 1993: 7). Thus Gandhi was reinterpreting both *dharma* and *saṁnyāsa* in his personal life. Like a *saṁnyāsin* he had no home called his own and his *āśrams* were modelled like the *saṁnyāsa* dwellings where the *saṁnyāsins* lived and carried on their activities. In Gandhi's *āśrams*, however, there was a judicious combination of spiritual and worldly concerns. Both his *āśrams* (Sabarmati and Wardha) were meant for *lokasaṁgraha* or working for the welfare of the world. A contemporary of Vivekananda but without much communication with him, Gandhi yet evolved a *saṁnyāsa* model similar to Vivekananda's Ramakrishna Math itself. The Ramakrishna Math characterizes a *saṁnyāsin* as one who, while pursuing his own *mokṣa,* is also engaged in working for the welfare of all people. This can easily fit into the kind of life that Gandhi led and he can thus be called a *saṁnyāsin.*

Vinoba Bhave, one of the most trusted of Gandhi's followers and a staunch follower of Gandhi's principle of Truth (*satyāgraha*), whom Gandhi called "one of the few pearls of the [Sabarmati] *āśram*" was even more of an exemplar of the *saṁnyāsa* path. Having given up his home and family at a young age, Vinoba never looked back and his detachment was genuine. It is said that he did not attend even his only sister's wedding. He himself never married and his *āśram* at Wardha continued to work for the welfare of the poorest of the poor. He is well known for his *bhūdāna* (donation of land) movement in which he was able to motivate the rich to give up their lands voluntarily in favour of the poor.

Both Gandhi and Vinoba living as they did between "pre" and "post" independent India and living practically the lives of ascetics, though never initiated into the monastic order, did have a lasting influence in shaping the *saṁnyāsa* ideology after them. Since Gandhi did not live too long after India's Independence, Vinoba probably was more of a model of *lokasaṁgraha* for those Swamis, who became prominent in the post-Independent phase of India. In general, then, this was an age of mixed messages for the *saṁnyāsa* model.

The earlier ideal of individual *mokṣa* had already been shortchanged as early as Śaṅkarācārya, and others like Vivekananda only added more and more dimensions to the concept of *lokasaṁgraha* introduced by the Bhagavad-Gītā. Gandhi and Vinoba Bhave are also in the same category. Thus the total *saṁnyāsa* concept advocated by the Bṛ. Up. of abdication of wealth, family and the world for personal *mokṣa,* seems to have been lost by the wayside. A new model of engagement in the world along with working for various projects for the welfare of all people, sometimes combined with one's own individual freedom, is the dominant model we see emerging in the post-Independent phase. So, *saṁnyāsa* has been reduced to a minimum value of "performing action without any desire for personal gain." The question that can then arise is whether it can be distinguished from working for social welfare. Maybe one can draw a distinction from social work by stating that the *saṁnyāsin*s abandoned any selfish interest and worked with a sense of detachment and with no desire of personal gain.

In post-Independent India the legacy of Vivekananda, Gandhi and others would lead to a free rendering of the word *mokṣa* in many ways as an engagement within society, not for one's personal gain but for the liberation or *mokṣa* of all people from different forms of injustice. *Mokṣa* was no more understood as just the ultimate eschatological liberation and we come across examples of *saṁnyāsin*s taking the vow of *saṁnyāsa* and going through initiation into the monastic order, staying in society immersed in the world and engaged in many different kinds of activities in the world including political activity which, after all, is what the great Mahatma Gandhi had done. To the common perception Gandhi's "spiritual approach" was indistinguishable from an ordinary pursuit of political activity and many Swamis in the post-independent phase will use Gandhi to justify their actions.

POST-INDEPENDENCE PERIOD

The sixth period comes with India winning its Independence from foreign rule in 1947. It can itself be viewed as having two phases; one (1947-1970s) in which euphoria in the new-found Independence triggered some renewed activities amongst *saṁnyāsin*s and a growing acceptance of women *saṁnyāsinī*s in the *saṁnyāsa* mode of life. In the subsequent phase after the 1970s, information technology also brought in new ways of living in the *saṁnyāsa* mode. At this time a number of Swamis started their own *āśram*s and gave *saṁnyāsa* to anyone they thought was spiritual enough. One name that comes to mind is that of Swami Sivananda who was one of the most well known of this group at the time. He himself was a medical practitioner in Malaysia before taking up *saṁnyāsa* in India at the age of 36 in the year 1923.

Though the Sivananda Ashram was started in 1932, its official birth as "The Divine Life Society" was in 1936. With the dawn of Independence, in 1948 the Yoga Vedanta Forest Academy was set up in Rishikesh at the foothills of the Himalayas, where classes on Vedānta and Yoga became a regular feature. One could call this a new innovation, catering to the educated middle classes in India as well as to those foreigners who started flocking to these *āśram*s from the 1960s, in large numbers. The instruction initially at the Academy was in English in order to attract this crowd. In the wake of Independence, Swami Sivananda also sent many *saṁnyāsin*s of the Divine Life Society to propagate the Vedānta ideal outside India. After all, Swami Vivekananda had already set the trend. The Sivananda Ashram at Val Morin in Montreal, for instance, was started by Swami Vishnudevananda, a disciple of Swami Sivananda in this period. Swami Sivananda was, perhaps, also the first spiritual head to include medical treatment as part of his *lokasaṁgraha*. Like Swami Vivekananda, Swami Sivananda also encouraged women into *saṁnyāsa*.

In this period of expansion *saṁnyāsin*s of all persuasions and schools of belief representing the *saṁnyāsa* way of life of a Hindu monk fanned out into the world. Sometimes they started independent movements or kept their affiliation to their parent body in India. Names such as Bhakti Vedanta Prabhupada (ISKCON), Maharshi Mahesh Yogi (Transcendental Meditation), Bhagwan Rajneesh (Osho), Swami Muktananda and many more come to mind. Hinduism was gaining more visibility in the West and the perception of the holy man clad in saffron robes in pursuit of enlightenment, as a repository of the spirituality of the East, got fixed.

This presence of Hinduism in a visible sense did kindle a desire to know more about Hinduism at the popular level and it also led to an attempt to understand its theology and spirituality in the Western world. There were even movies made based on books like the *Razor's Edge* of Somerset Maugham which glorified the eastern spiritual heritage. So, while in India, most of the *saṁnyāsāśrama*s were getting popular because of their social activities, outside India, the Swamis and *saṁnyāsin*s were drawing people into their fold out of a curiosity to understand more about its spirituality. Thus, *saṁnyāsa* in the garb of a *saṁnyāsin*, was gaining a global presence. However, in their own lives, the monks were combining both worldly action and *saṁnyāsa* by engaging in *lokasaṁgraha* activities.

The distinguishing feature of this period then, as opposed to all the earlier periods, is the hard work that these *saṁnyāsin*s put in, so as to make available the spiritual heritage of Hinduism to those interested, particularly outside the country. Swamis like Chinmayananda were in great demand for this very purpose. There were others like Swami Rama who were, again, able to authenticate the claims of Yoga and thus gain a number of followers. These Swamis, in turn, could consolidate their *āśram*s in India and use the funds earned abroad for *lokasaṁgraha* in India. Thus the *saṁnyāsin* combined the twin concepts of *dharma* and *saṁnyāsa* in his/her life, even though the original meanings underwent some significant changes.

The explosion of information technology beginning in the 1980s also had its impact on the saṁnyāsin's way of life and changed the very meaning of *saṁnyāsa*. While so far *dharma* and *saṁnyāsa,* by and large, coexisted in their own spaces and it was still possible to distinguish the borders that subtly divided them, in this new phase of technological development the borders became very porous and even the monastic institutions (*āśram*s) where *saṁnyāsa* conceptually reigned supreme succumbed to the allurement of modern technology. We, thus, find that the *saṁnyāsāśrama* also started being just one more institution in society without much emphasis on spirituality. While there were genuine seekers of *mokṣa* on the one hand, there were also pseudo-*saṁnyāsin*s aplenty. Today *mokṣa* is the buzzword and is still spoken of as the ultimate goal in the *āśram*s and by *saṁnyāsin*s and is perhaps still so, for the genuine seeker. But the stress now is more on "material well-being" and the *saṁnyāsa-dharma* is recruited to serve, in general, a material end, both in the *āśram*s and in the individual lifestyle of the *saṁnyāsin*s as well. In this last phase of the fifth period, we find examples of *saṁnyāsin*s even participating in elections and holding cabinet posts in a worldly sense. The boundaries between *dharma,* secular action and *saṁnyāsa* are totally blurred now. Furthermore, what distinguishes this phase is:

1. *Saṁnyāsin*s are more interested in the consolidation of their position in countries outside India particularly in North America and the U.K. This trend continues to the present day.
2. Many free lance *saṁnyāsin*s, without proper training and initiation into the *saṁnyāsa* mode of life, making their way to countries outside India and bringing a bad name to the institution.
3. The presentation of Vedānta and an interpretation of Hinduism in a neo-Vedānta way as the dominant form of Hinduism, because it fits better into the *saṁnyāsa* ideal.
4. A positive side now is a more open attitude to women recruits into the *saṁnyāsa* fold. Even though most of the women *saṁnyāsinī*s were not formally initiated they were given equal

respect and recognition within the tradition. There are today women *saṁnyāsinīs* like Uma Bharati who is also an active politician. Most of these women *saṁnyāsinīs*, called *swāminīs* and *brahmacāriṇīs* have their own institutions (*āśrams*) with a large following of both men and women. Names like that of Anandamayi Maa, Nirmala Devi, Amritanandamayi Maa (the hugging *swāminī*), and many others come to mind who have a large following throughout the world.

5. Adopting a so-called rationalist approach to spiritual teachings. This has led to a number of *saṁnyāsins* going to universities and being educated in the English medium. I know of PhDs amongst *saṁnyāsins* who also participate in conferences like any other academic. This tends to blur the boundaries between the two realms of the secular and the sacred.
6. A non-self-conscious appeal for funds in Western countries for *lokasaṁgraha* work in India.
7. A proliferation of community-oriented *saṁnyāsa* institutions. Today there are such *āśrams* amongst the Vālmīkis, Kurubas (shepherds), Yādavas (hunters), Uppukāras (saltmakers) and others. These *saṁnyāsāśramas* are just organizations for the furtherance of the welfare of their own community members.
8. There are now lay seekers who come to the *āśrams* for relaxation and for relief from modern-day stress in the workplace or elsewhere. The *āśrams* and the *saṁnyāsins* also have adjusted to this new clientele. Moreover, *saṁnyāsins/saṁnyāsinīs* are now catering to the commercial world where they give lectures not only on management techniques but also on stress-management based on Vedāntic precepts. They also have web-sites and can be accessed by people round the globe.
9. *Saṁnyāsins/saṁnyāsinīs* accept posts as ministers in the cabinet like Uma Bharati, and Swami Satchidananda and *saṁnyāsins* outside the political circle also jump in sometimes, acting as arbiters to political disputes. Just two such instances that come to mind are the efforts of Kāñcī Śaṅkarācārya Jayendra Saraswati and Sri Sri Ravi Shankar, founder of The Art of Living fame, trying to negotiate an agreement between contenders in the Ayodhyā dispute.

Thus, there are no clear boundaries between action — both religious and secular — and *saṁnyāsa* in this age.

CONCLUSION

We can conclude by stating that the concept of *saṁnyāsa* as exemplified in the life of a *saṁnyāsin* has now taken on many new garbs, sometimes totally different from the Ṛgvedic *muni*, with whom we started this analysis. There are at present, in general, two groups of *saṁnyāsin*s. The first kind is the one that wants to prove his rationalist approach to spirituality and the other is the one who is more of a traditional spiritual teacher. Both are not against "material well-being." The rational one tries to conduct classes very often in the English language and generally attracts a fair number of Western students and followers; they are also popular with the educated and monied sections of Indian society. These *saṁnyāsin*s also have *āśram*s both in India and in countries outside India and they are also quite prosperous. They usually give lectures on Vedānta and Yoga and also give Sanskrit lessons and practical Yoga classes. They are the ones who earn a lot of funds from their foreign disciples and their affluent Indian clients and use those funds for charitable work in India. They or their representatives travel regularly outside the country and succeed in attracting disciples who sometimes go and start living in India in their *āśram*s and are sometimes inducted into the *saṁnyāsāśrama* as well. The pursuit of *mokṣa* though acclaimed as the final goal, has fallen by the wayside due to preoccupation with goals that fit in more with the action ideal.

The other is the traditional *saṁnyāsin*s who advise their followers about how to lead a life in accordance with *dharma*. They would, by and large, lecture in the regional language and are easily accessible to their followers, unlike the first, who are not so easily accessible. The traditional *saṁnyāsin* mingles informally with his followers and also advises in their day-to-day lives. Their lifestyle is also more or less traditional and they have a rapport with all sections of society, particularly the middle classes and the not so affluent classes. They try to keep the spiritual tradition alive, though they also are not against advising their clients in "material well-being" but perhaps do it more subtly. In keeping with the general mood, they also engage in running charitable institutions but their clientele is mainly within the country. They also act as counsellors when called upon to do so. They are also not averse to dabbling in politics with the avowed purpose of bringing harmony amongst all sections of the population.

Both these kinds of *saṁnyāsin*s maintain the theoretical understanding of what it is to be a *saṁnyāsin* following the *saṁnyāsa* style of life. Most of them seem to be busy conducting classes on Vedānta and one wonders where they get the time for spiritual activity at all. I have also been told that *mokṣa* must be understood not in the age-old manner but as Swami Vivekananda said "as service to society." Swami Agnivesh, for instance, would define *lokasaṁgraha* as "fighting for justice." Thus, there are many definitions of *mokṣa* in today's vocabulary of the *saṁnyāsin*s.

We can say that this period is one where there is a tremendous upsurge of worldly activity even in the lives of these *saṁnyāsin*s, in the way they have prioritized their *lokasaṁgraha* activities.

Even though the *saṁnyāsāśrama* itself, as seen above, has not lived up to the initial ideals it was supposed to uphold, that is not the whole history of Hinduism. One cannot forget that the average Hindu (Hinduism) has never viewed the ultimate truth called variously as Brahman, Īśvara, Puruṣottama, Śiva, Viṣṇu, etc., as apart from oneself. Īśvara or Brahman is within oneself in the form of the *antaryāmin* (inner self) or as identified with oneself. Therefore, *mokṣa* at one level is the continuous search for this divinity within, and even an average Hindu will speak of the attainment of *mokṣa* as the value he/she most cherishes. In many ways, the average Hindu also tries *saṁnyāsa* or renouncing sense pleasures and cultivating a degree of detachment towards material goods. Thus a modicum of *saṁnyāsa* is part of a Hindu's worldly life. Even though renunciation defined by the Bṛ. Up. belongs to the complete renouncer/*saṁnyāsin*, it is good to remember that even for an average practising Hindu, the pendulum keeps swinging between worldly activity and *saṁnyāsa* and the desire to renounce is an ideal that s/he greatly admires. One must also add that even today one hears of genuine *saṁnyāsin*s who do not come into the limelight and who stay in faraway places hidden from common gaze genuinely pursuing the goal of *mokṣa*.

2

Saṁnyāsins and the Saṁnyāsāśrama as Seen by Scholars

SCHOLARS both Western and Indian have tried to understand the Hindu *saṁnyāsins* in all their various aspects. This chapter is based on interviews with well-known scholars of Indology regarding their views on *saṁnyāsins* and the institution of *saṁnyāsa* and is thus a first hand account of their understanding of the concept of *saṁnyāsa* and the institution. This first hand, objective analysis of scholars of Indology about *saṁnyāsa* and the institution, brings into focus how a textual tradition gets transformed and takes on new meanings in the lived world and does not always conform to what the texts represent both with regard to the concept and the institution as well. The views of the scholars have been presented faithfully as they responded to some of my questions based on a questionnaire (see Appendix) and the answers were taped with the consent of the interviewees. The interviews took place between the years 1998 and 2000.

In the following pages the interviews are reproduced as faithfully as possible sometimes in the words of the speakers themselves and at other times summarized when they tended to go off the main point and repeated some ideas for emphasis; very often there were some digressions as well. If these digressions did not steer one too much away from the main topic they have been retained. Not much of an editing has been attempted as, in spite of digressions, they all relate in one way or another to the topic at hand and in no way has the intention of the interviewees been modified. My hope is that the readers will also enter into the spirit of the interviews and not be unduly concerned with matters of style and expression of the speakers. Before the interview itself is presented, the name of the person interviewed is given at the start of the text as heading.

G.C. PANDEY

Professor Pandey, a renowned scholar in the field of Sanskrit Studies and equally well known as a historian of religion, culture and philosophy, started his comments with some general observations on the concept of *saṁnyāsa* itself. He was of the view that the preservation and progress of Hindu spirituality would not have been possible without the genuine efforts of so many of the renouncers (*saṁnyāsin*s). It is very good to be religious or spiritual to a certain extent compatible with our lives, as all religious-minded people are, he said, but you need professionals also, people who have dedicated their entire lives in search of the ultimate spiritual Reality like the renouncers in the Hindu tradition. Drawing upon his experience in Burma he emphasized this same point by recounting a Buddhist example:

> One day way back in 1937/1938 as a young man, I saw a person standing on the road stopping a Buddhist monk walking on the road and started asking him questions on the doctrines of his faith. Later I learnt that if the monk failed to satisfy the questioner it may lead to the monk being disrobed. Ordinary people need some others who are visibly representing something better and greater than themselves, to clear their doubts and act as leaders in things ethical, moral and spiritual.

Just as the Buddhist monk who was necessary to satisfy the spiritual needs of the commoner, the Hindu *saṁnyāsin* was also an important spiritual instructor and served the need of society, according to him.

Another point brought out by him was the question of the residence for a *saṁnyāsin*. The *saṁnyāsin*, he said, can stay at home instead of roaming around the country and he should also keep up the study of the sacred texts like the Veda (*svādhyāya*). Furthermore, the religion was not averse to their engaging themselves in social activism or *lokasaṁgraha*. Prof. Pandey believed that the sacred texts and tradition approved the activities of *saṁnyāsin*s like Swami Vivekananda who started charitable institutions like schools, hospitals, etc. He dismissed the criticism that the *jīvanmukta* concept which the *saṁnyāsin* is supposed to achieve, would allow a *saṁnyāsī* to behave in an amoral manner, as he is supposed to be above good and bad, as irrelevant. His training in moral virtues as a *brahmacārin* will not desert him even after he attains *jīvanmukti*, he added.

On the origins of the institution (*saṁnyāsāśrama*), he expressed his disappointment in not getting any reliable historical material on the subject of the origins even from the *maṭhāmnāyas* (chronicles) of the Śaṅkarācārya *maṭhas* all over the country, though there was mention of Śaṅkara's setting up of *āśrams* in his biographies. He despaired that even these biographies were written very much later than Śaṅkara's period and very many records were also destroyed systematically by the continuous invasions the country had suffered. In fact, Buddhist monasteries like Takṣaśilā and Nālandā in which students from China, Korea and other foreign countries stayed for a number of years were destroyed along with the documents, not by Śaṅkara's advocacy against the Buddhists but by the physical destruction carried out by foreign invaders. There has been a lamentable lack of material, he added, to write a proper historical record of the country including that of the *saṁnyāsāśrama* in a continuous fashion. The *maṭhas*, however, have served a useful purpose by preserving and producing enormous philosophical literature in their respective traditions, which would have been lost otherwise.

While decrying a number of corrupt practices that have crept into the system of *saṁnyāsa*, he also condemned the extreme views of some, that they are parasites and a heavy burden on society as they do no work. There is also the misconception that they are beggars as they survive by accepting alms from *gṛhasthas* (householders). On the other hand, they have been a very useful part of the community by actually acting as unpaid counsellors/shrinks, he said; he added with a smile that shrinks, as is well known, are highly paid psychiatrists of modern-day society. He added that, with many counterfeit *saṁnyāsins* roaming around the countryside it was very difficult to make out who is genuine and who is not. It is here that the broader aspect of freedom in Hinduism comes into play and even the charlatans are allowed to roam around and exploit society. As you never can tell who a real *sādhu* is, everyone wearing the *geruā* (ochre robes) is honoured in society, hoping that the genuine ones are not left out which would be the case in a general proscription. He pointed to the example of Kamla Nehru, Pandit Jawaharlal Nehru's wife, being an ardent devotee of Anandamayi Maa with whom she had long conversations throughout her life, indicating the counselling role that these *saṁnyāsins*/*saṁnyāsinīs* fulfil in society.

He went on to emphasize the same point through an anecdote. Hridey, a disciple of Ramakrishna Paramahamsa, once asked whether he (Ramakrishna) could show him a true *jīvanmukta* (liberated person). The great sage told him to go down to the river Gaṅgā and look out for him after the *āratī* to the Goddess Kālī of Dakṣiṇeśwar. When Hridey went down, he saw a man fighting with a dog for some left-over food. The credulous Hridey asked him whether he was a *jñānī* (one who knows the highest truth). The man in turn abused him and threw a stone at him. Hridey ran away and went to Ramakrishna and told him what happened. Ramakrishna replied: "They don't let people like you come near them!" Pandey then went on to cite the example of Karpatriji whom he had personally known and believed was a perfect *saṁnyāsin*. He was a very learned man and a fervent *upāsaka*, he added.

On the question of *mokṣa* he said there were two views: Firstly it was not something that belongs to man after his death. In fact, *mokṣa* is indifferent to life and death. Secondly at a minimum, it means giving up the sense of ego, *rāga* (attachment) and *dveṣa* (hatred). Comparing the concept in Mahāyāna Buddhism he mentioned how for the Mahāyāna Buddhists, *mokṣa* or *nirvāṇa* is useless after death. Their aim is to become the Buddhas here and now so that they can do something for the world. To become a Buddha you certainly have to attain this kind of *mokṣa*, freedom from the attachments that bind you to these worldly things. Before you reach *mokṣa*, you must resolve that you have to continue afterwards serving humanity. At the end, one becomes a *bodhisattva*, which is the higher ideal. This actually is the fact of spiritual life, in fact of all *sādhanā*s.

According to Pandey, the philosophical systems generally have made a mistake regarding *mokṣa* because they have drawn the picture of the ultimate in a speculative manner. Using Sāṁkhya as an example, he pointed out that the Sāṁkhya school mentions the final stage or *mokṣa* as *kaivalya*, which is a state totally detached from *prakṛti*. Since *prakṛti* is the one who acts, according to Sāṁkhya, *kaivalya* would be a stage which is freed from all actions. It will be just being; consciousness without anything else. Supposing that is true, then, he cannot be an *āpta* (a reliable source of knowledge), one who can impart any instruction which is the third *pramāṇa* in Sāṁkhya, through which knowledge is gained. Since the one who has attained *kaivalya* cannot be an *āpta*, the doctrine of *kaivalya* becomes the doctrine of speculation alone. All the other *tattva*s are proved by perception and inference (*pratyakṣa* and *anumāna*) but *kaivalya* can only be proved after *āptānumāna* (inference from the instruction of one who has attained *kaivalya*). So the third *pramāṇa* to be valid requires the capability to be able to instruct and that is what the tradition maintains when it declares that Kapila (presumably one who has attained *kaivalya*) gave the instruction to Āsuri. He then said:

> For *mokṣa*, in my opinion, *saṁnyāsa* is not necessary. However, *saṁnyāsin*s who have vowed to take the path of *mokṣa* are necessary to train individuals and make them qualify for liberation; they also instruct society to keep on the right track, on the path of *dharma*, by their discourses and example.

Regarding (women) *saṁnyāsinī*s he went on to say that there were *saṁnyāsinī*s in the Vedic times and in later times as well. *Brahmacāriṇī*s and *brahmavādinī*s are mentioned in the Vedas and the *Brahmasūtra*. But the continuous invasions of the country by foreigners and also from the time when Hindus started arranging marriages for girls at a tender age, put a stop to their becoming *saṁnyāsinī*s. They therefore were unable to acquire or pursue any education or experience in the spiritual field.

> When you are not literate, you cannot study the Vedas. As a result women were not fit to take the formal life of *saṁnyāsinī*s. From the Tāntric perspective, in the Śrīvidyā system, they are the highest manifestation of divinity so how can they be barred from anything, except when they don't want to follow that kind of life. I am aware that women are initiated into *saṁnyāsa* by Muktananda, Sivananda and others in modern times.

Expressing concern for the future of the organization he went on to say:

> To preserve and ensure the survival of this *saṁnyāsa* institution, we should follow the excellent example of the Roman Catholic system. For two thousand years they have meticulously maintained the *brahmacarya* aspect of their priests through a number of seminaries throughout Europe and elsewhere. Through these institutions they have survived every kind of obstacle. They are stronger than ever before and I have a high respect for them. They do have a closed mind with respect to the idea of conversions though. They, however, have produced a number of scholars and thinkers not only in the field of their

own religion but they have attempted to learn about some of our own literature."

LAKSHMITHATHACHAR

An erudite scholar belonging to the Viśiṣṭādvaita Sampradāya, Professor Lakshmithathachar traces his descent from Anantācārya who was a direct disciple of Rāmānuja, the founder of the school of Viśiṣṭādvaita. Thus, in the course of this interview, he was able to throw light on a number of points related to the *saṁnyāsa* concept and the institution according to Viśiṣṭādvaita.

While *mokṣa* or liberation is meant for everyone, whether he is a *saṁnyāsin* or a *gṛhastha* according to Rāmānuja, *saṁnyāsa* in Viśiṣṭādvaita is meant mainly for the propagation and preservation of *dharma*, he said. It is because of this that one sees that Rāmānuja appointed 74 *siṁhāsanādhipati*s most of whom were *gṛhastha*s. He qualified that by saying that if the *gṛhastha* stage is not conducive to maintenance of *dharma* then a person can adopt *saṁnyāsa* and thus *dharma* is not exclusively the goal of a *saṁnyāsin*. He added that this way of looking at *saṁnyāsa* has led to a misconception that in Viśiṣṭādvaita there is no scope for *saṁnyāsa*; but that is not the truth as Rāmānuja's adoption of *saṁnyāsa* is itself a vindication of what he believed in. There were also many *saṁnyāsin*s after Rāmānuja and the institution continues to the present day.

The reason that Rāmānuja himself took to *saṁnyāsa* was primarily because his wife was not supportive of his beliefs and philosophy which, as the legend goes, was illustrated by her insulting behaviour towards his Kāñcī *guru* who was a vaiśya (non-brāhmaṇa). Thus the role of a *saṁnyāsin* is not primarily for seeking *mokṣa* for oneself but the maintenance of *dharma* in society. *Mokṣa* comes automatically when one follows the path of *dharma*. This was an important difference between the Advaita and Viśiṣṭādvaita schools regarding *saṁnyāsa*. It is therefore with this in view that the *saṁnyāsin*s are invariably attached to the temples, he said. In this tradition it is only brāhmaṇas who are entitled to take to *saṁnyāsa*. The temple-*saṁnyāsin* has no family to look after and no distractions from his chosen vocation of serving in the temples. They are completely dedicated to the administration of the temples and see that services are performed in a proper manner and at the proper time. However, Lakshmithathachar added that this rule of service in the temples only applied to the Teṅgaḷai Vaiṣṇava *saṁnyāsins* and the Vaḍakaḷais, the other division of the Vaiṣṇavas, do not serve in the temples as Teṅgaḷais do. One did not get a satisfactory reply as to why this difference is there amongst the followers of Rāmānuja. Rāmānuja, himself, chose to stay at the Śrīraṅgam temple as is well known and serve there as a regular priest most of his life.

He cited what Perumāḷ Nāyanār, brother of Piḷḷailokācārya, both prominent Vaiṣṇavites, states in support of the role of the *saṁnyāsāśrama* in the *Ācārya Hṛdayam* a Tamil work written by him:

> *Saṁnyāsāśrama* is not considered as a superior *āśrama*, if the person does not have any *bhāgavatajñāna* or realization of *paramātman*. It says that only if a *saṁnyāsin* has realized *parabrahman* will he be respected. He might have studied all the four Vedas but if he has not realized *paramātman*, he is like an ass. So *āśrama* does not become important for the realization of the Supreme which has been set as the goal of everyone.

Because of the importance attached to the *gṛhasthāśrama*, *saṁnyāsa-dīkṣā* or initiation is given only after the candidate has gone through married life. Only then, after experiencing the world, will he be able to realize the importance and duties connected with the *saṁnyāsa-dharma* which is to protect and preserve the *dharma* of everyone and the society as a whole. The procedure of initiation is laid down in the Yatidharmasamuccaya and a tradition has developed based on its principles while the common practice is for a *saṁnyāsin* of a renowned *āśram* to initiate an aspirant. He mentioned that certain *gṛhastha* (family) members were also given the authority to initiate eligible persons into mendicancy in the Vaiṣṇava tradition. He himself belonged to a family known as Āṇḍavan Piḷḷais and they were specifically authorized by the great Rāmānuja himself to initiate *saṁnyāsins*. In fact, he declared that "only two days earlier to this interview I gave *dīkṣā* to eight people. They undergo *pañca-saṁskāras* and the initiator recites the relevant *mantras*."

Talking about his family, he said that many generations of them have had a long studentship in the Sanskrit language right up to the Vedas and have also become well versed in the Drāviḍa Veda, i.e. *Nāḷāyira Divyaprabandham*, the four thousand verses of the great saints called Āḻwārs and many other works in the Tamil language:

> We have specialized in Vedānta studies especially Viśiṣṭādvaita. We are traditionally located in Melkote, the place to which Rāmānuja came and spread Vaiṣṇavism. Our forefathers were closely associated with Rāmānuja and his followers in this very place and therefore we are very well known for scholarship and adherence to the tenets of our religion. As mentioned, one of our important duties given to us by tradition is to initiate *saṁnyāsins* as well.

The Vaiṣṇava *saṁnyāsin,* after initiation, is generally attached to a well-known temple for the rest of his life. He worships and performs *pūjā* to the deity and caters to the devotees with their requests to perform *pūjā* on their behalf. Or in temples like Tirupati he assists the *pūjārī* in his *pūjā* to Lord Veṅkaṭeśvara. In many cases the *saṁnyāsin* also goes to a *maṭha* to study under the leading *saṁnyāsin* of the place to qualify further in his pursuits. There are many famous centres of such learning for Viśiṣṭādvaita *saṁnyāsins* called *maṭhas* like Ahobilam in Andhra Pradesh, Melkote, Śrīraṅgam, Tirupati, Yadugiri Yatiraja Math and many others. The head of *maṭhas* and prominent *saṁnyāsins* are given the title of Jeers (Jeeyars). The Jeer thus becomes the supreme personality and there is no hierarchy as such.

Lakshmithathachar was closely associated with Melkote and he mentioned some facts about that *maṭha.* Dattātreya is the originator of the Melkote tradition and he was a *tridaṇḍī saṁnyāsin.* He is held in high esteem even today at Melkote and other Vaiṣṇava centres. Lakshmithathachar added that Dattātreya stayed in Melkote and there was a shrine associated with him and that was duly honoured by Rāmānuja when he came there as an exile. There was also a *maṭha* called Dattatreya Peeth. It is interesting to note that both Vaiṣṇavas as well as those belonging to the Śaiva *paramparā* consider Dattātreya as one of their saints.

More on Viśiṣṭādvaita Saṁnyāsins

Maṭhas which house the *saṁnyāsins* are headed by *maṭhādhipatis* who wield considerable influence in society. They were also called *Chātrādinilaya* catering to the education and initiation of students and *saṁnyāsins.* They are given theoretical and practical training including administration of temples, etc. They also help administer important shrines dedicated to deities of the pantheon of Nārāyaṇa and his consorts. One important function of the Vaiṣṇava *saṁnyāsin,* not generally known, is also to participate in *śrāddha* rituals (death rituals) and partake the consecrated food kept specifically for the deities.

All *saṁnyāsin*s wear ochre robes of various styles to differentiate between sects. The *maṭha*s may run educational institutions and hospitals, though that is not their primary function. They are financially sound as they have rich disciples who contribute generously.

Lakshmithathachar came back to the topic of the *gṛhasthāśrama* and quoted many an authority to assert that the *gṛhasthāśrama* is the *āśrama par excellence* as it supports and maintains all the other *āśrama*s like the *brahmacārin*s, the *vānaprastha* as well as the *saṁnyāsa*. All the *āśrama*s are for the propagation and preservation of *dharma* and the main object of the *saṁnyāsāśrama* is also the same besides striving towards *mokṣa* at the same time. In the Vaiṣṇava system the *saṁnyāsin* can never separate himself from society. He stressed the importance of initiating *saṁnyāsin*s only after they have gone through the *gṛhasthāśrama*, as even the senses have to be satisfied.

K.T. PANDURANGI

A renowned scholar of the Dvaita school of philosophy, Professor Pandurangi was still very active in the fields of teaching and research at the time of this interview.

We started to talk of the *saṁnyāsin* and the *āśrama* and he said: The general frameworks of a *saṁnyāsin* and *saṁnyāsāśrama* are more or less the same in Sanātana Dharma. All these are sub-cultures of a big culture, the Sanātana Dharma. But, the philosophies of Dvaita, Viśiṣṭādvaita and Advaita differ considerably in the procedure of initiation, selection of the persona and the career and purpose of *saṁnyāsa*. For instance in the Dvaita tradition, there are two ways of giving *saṁnyāsa* — one is to a *brahmacārin* and the other is to a *gṛhastha*. Inside the Udipi Math for instance, on the western side of the Sahyādri mountain range, only a *brahmacārin* will be given *saṁnyāsa*. There are other *maṭha*s in Dvaita Sampradāya in Karnataka, Andhra and Maharashtra, on the eastern side of Sahyādri, such as Raghavendra Math, Uttaradi Math, Rasaraja Math, etc., where even *gṛhastha*s are also eligible. Majority of the *pīṭhādhipati*s, so far, right from Madhvācārya down to the present Swamijis are *gṛhastha*s in these *maṭha*s. As the *pīṭhādhipati*s have to give regular discourses to the public, it is incumbent on them to gain sufficient amount of scholarship before taking up *saṁnyāsa*.

In Udipi there are eight *maṭha*s all having only *saṁnyāsin*s who are *brahmacārin*s. They are traced to Madhva. His brother started the Subramanya Math. Madhva's Guru's *maṭha* also continued and that was called Bhandarigiri Math. There are in all 23 Madhva Maths. *Maṭhādhipati*s are all given *saṁnyāsa* invariably. This is done when the incumbent enters Vrindavan (i.e. at the time of death the *saṁnyāsin* is supposed to go to Kṛṣṇa's abode). *Saṁnyāsa* is also given to anyone, including *gṛhastha*s and *brahmacārin*s, when they expressed a desire to completely renounce the world goaded by *vairāgya* (dispassion). The practice of giving *vairāgya saṁnyāsa* is much more in Advaita tradition than in the Madhva Sampradāya. Humorously he added: "The reason is possibly the tendency for men to take *saṁnyāsa* when they quarrel with their wives and so on. So, the Madhvas being conservative do not allow an easy way out to these people. The number of *bidi-saṁnyāsin*s, stray *saṁnyāsin*s, non-*maṭhādhipati*s in Dvaita is much less, practically nil." However, Pejawar Swami has recently started giving *saṁnyāsa* to many people. This is because he wants them to propagate Hindu Dharma and Sanātana Dharma and Vaiṣṇava Dharma.

When *saṁnyāsa* is given there is a procedure. The procedure starts with *praṇava upadeśa*. *Praṇava-mantra-japa* is to be done a thousand times everyday by a *saṁnyāsin*. *Oṁkāra* represents the Supreme Being, Mahāviṣṇu — Viṣṇu is *ananta kalyāṇa guṇa pūrṇa* (embodiment of all auspicious qualities), and also *sarva veda pratipadya* (accessible through the entire Veda) — both these statements are interrelated as each word of the Veda conveys an attribute. *Pīṭhādhipati*s have to do this *japa* and his chief responsibility is to propagate Viṣṇu *sarvottamatva* (the supremacy of Viṣṇu). In addition he has to do *pūjā* to the *mūrti* in the temple which is part of the propagation of the supremacy of Viṣṇu. *Pūjā* with *tulasī* to *śāligrāma* (*śālagrāma*) is considered very important even more so than *mūrti-pūjā*. It is the saṁnyāsin's responsibility to make others also do the *pūjā* to *śāligrāma* as well, which is an integral part of Vaiṣṇava theology. He has to continuously give discourses on Madhva Śāstra. This should also be done by *saṁnyāsin*s in general but it becomes obligatory on the part of the *pīṭhādhipati*s. Performing austerities is another integral part of the life of all Madhvas but it is especially so in the case of *saṁnyāsin*s and *pīṭhādhipati*s as they have to set an example for others of the faith. The main austerities are *ekādaśī-vrata, Viṣṇu-pañcaka-vrata, kr̥cchra-cāndrāyaṇa-upavāsa*, etc., but observation of *ekādaśī* is the most important.

The Madhva *saṁnyāsin* is supposed to wander and he should not stay in one place for more than three days as a rule. He has to propagate Viṣṇu *sarvottamatva* all through the year, and only in *cāturmāsya* he can stay in one place, because of the rainy season. That is when the Vaiṣṇava *saṁnyāsin*s go and perform *pūjā*s and receive *pāda-pūjā* in the houses of the disciples. They go and take their own deities to the homes of the disciples and perform all the worship which they would normally do otherwise. One is familiar with *śiṣya*s going to the *guru*, but in the Madhva Sampradāya the *guru* goes to a deserving śiṣya's house as part of his duty.

Another sanctioned activity in the propagation procedure given to *saṁnyāsin*s and *maṭhādhipati*s is to spotlight the supremacy of Viṣṇu worship by criticizing those who worship other deities. They should not only declare Viṣṇu's *sarvottamatva* but they should frankly condemn those who do not follow their beliefs. Those who preach other philosophies like Advaita must also be taken to task as vehemently as possible. Since Madhvas believe that there is a distinct separation between *jīva* and Brahman they are particularly averse to those who do not agree with them on this and they are allowed to express their criticisms in an aggressive way. They feel that it is their responsibility to tell people what is right and what is wrong according to their own understanding.

There is a belief that when it is a matter of spirituality, one should not follow the normal attitude in civil life by politely letting others disagree. They say: "Knowing fully well what is wrong and what is right, if I don't tell the other what he believes is wrong, I will be doing a great disservice. I will not be helping an ignorant person. To help an ignorant person who has distorted knowledge is my responsibility as much as to propagate." Pandurangi added that this may be in response to the earlier aggressive faiths that were in vogue before the advent of Dvaita, such as the Śāktas, who were prone to spread their faiths by forceful means.

Discussing the role of women he said that in this *sampradāya* it is forbidden to give *saṁnyāsa* to women. But Pejawar Swami gave *saṁnyāsa* to Uma Bharati (who was a central minister at that time) and that was not according to tradition. This was entirely the Swami's discretion.

As to the origin of the *saṁnyāsāśrama* Pandurangi felt that, even before Śaṅkarācārya, individual *saṁnyāsins* coming down from the Himalayas and going round and propagating *dharma* and religion was very much part of the tradition. He added that the establishment of *āśram* is on the Buddhist model; some also say that the Jains started it. In his view, even at the time of Śaṅkarācārya the *pīṭhas* or *maṭhas* as such had not taken shape. Śaṅkara started the *pīṭhas* to bring back Sanātana Dharma. Only later, when Viśiṣṭādvaita and Dvaita came on to the scene, Śaṅkara's teaching was classified as Advaita and till then it was just Sanātana Dharma. Historically, in Karnataka, Jainism was aggressive and claimed a number of converts. Śravanabeḷgoḷā and other places spread throughout Karnataka are testimony to that. The Buddhists did not come into Karnataka as such. There were also many Śaiva sects in Karnataka to contend with, six to eight of them. These were united by Basaveśvara into one group. As Śaṅkara took the lead to save the Vaidikas, Basaveśvara did the same to unite the Śaivas. Rāmānuja and Madhva had to come to save the Vaiṣṇavas. When a big culture wants to eat up a little culture, some leader will come up out of the little culture and he will try to save it. This is inherent in human psyche. Indians also do not want cultures to go out of existence but want every culture to survive. Thus Indian society is like an organic body which wants all its parts to survive.

Maṭha as an Institution

Maṭha is an institution that has certain jurisdiction and rights and also has disciples. It is the responsibility of the head of the *maṭha* to take care of the disciples, property, and tradition. There are also *mūrtis* which are kept there. Whenever any dispute arises regarding rival claims to an *āśram*, each one claims that the *maṭha* is his as he possesses the *mūrti*. The case invariably goes to court. The court may have to decide on the basis of tradition, which is primarily based on the possession of the *mūrti* besides others. While an *āśram* can be formed by anyone, the head of an *āśram* is a *saṁnyāsin*. *Maṭha* is a long established institution with a tradition, and an *āśram* is started by a particular person to run it in his own way. Thus he drew a distinction between the traditional well established *maṭhas* and *āśrams* that just spring up because somebody starts them.

The discussion moved on to the ostentation visible in *maṭhas* to which Pandurangi said, "*Vairāgya* or dispassion characterizes the life of a *saṁnyāsin*, inmates of an *āśram*, head of an *āśram*, *pīṭhādhipati* etc. It is an internal state of the mind and even when dressed in finery or sitting on a silver *pīṭha* or outwardly having all the grandeur of a *pīṭhādhipati* cannot prevent his inwardly *vairāgya*. Sitting on the throne Janaka was a *virakta*. He ceases to be a *pīṭhādhipati* only if he uses that property for his relatives, for his friends etc. It is like a religious trust. As a trustee, to keep up the dignity of the institution, he has to keep up a certain way of life and presentation, that does not affect his *vairāgya*." All *maṭhas* of all the sects start off without property and wealth and as long as the *maṭhas* had no property, there was no problem. Gradually they acquire ownership of many places spread over vast areas, bank accounts, etc., and then the problems of administration and finances begin. Nowadays the finances are taken care of by donations from wealthy people as well as from NRIs (non-resident-Indians) who crowd the *āśrams* in large numbers.

Some special features of Madhva practice mentioned by Pandurangi are interesting to note. "Mādhvas have to put the seal of their faith on their bodies — the *mudrās* — besides other signs. *Mudrās* such as the *śaṅkha, cakra, gadā* and *padma* are imprinted on the bodies using devices heated by fire and are called *taptamudrās*. It is a kind of medical treatment, this burning with copper on the parts of the body. One of these is done before *upanayanam* and after *upanayanam* five are done. Women have only two *mudrās*."

The conversation shifted to the theory of the eternal *tāmasika-jīvas* (*nitya-tāmasikas*) who have no hope of *mokṣa*, that Dvaita philosophy believes in. Pandurangi tried to explain it and I have tried to give the gist of it to the best of my ability. He said: "According to Madhva the *jaḍa* and *jīva* are classified as *sāttvika, rājasa* and *tāmasa*. We know by our experience that all are not *sāttvikas*. All *padārthas* are not *sāttvikas*. Also, scripture. Let us keep the scripture aside. In experience every *kārya* has a *kāraṇa*. So there is a *tāmasa padārtha* and its *kāraṇa* must also have *tāmasa padārtha*, this goes on and the basic *kāraṇa* must also logically have *tāmasa kāraṇa*. Good and evil are basically two independent principles. Therefore unless you consider them to have been there all along, you cannot introduce them at any stage. Therefore, with respect to external objects and *cetanās* we do consider that basically these two things are there eternally. When somebody's basic nature is evil, how can we allow him Vaikuṇṭha, or *svarga*? God has not created the evil source or *sāttvika* source. They are *anādi*. God cannot remove the evil nature of people because He has only to administer the whole world." He did not agree to the widely held belief that this could have been due to Christian influence.

When asked whether *saṁnyāsin*s have a role in politics he said, "Normally *saṁnyāsin*s should not enter active politics. But if Indian culture is in danger it is the responsibility of these *pīṭhādhipati*s and not *virakta saṁnyāsin*s to save Indian culture. To save it without joining any political parties would be impossible. If they advise the citizen about the rights and wrongs committed in society through political activity they will be fulfilling their responsibility."

R.K. SHARMA

Professor Sharma, a consummate Sanskrit scholar, began the interview with giving details of the four *āśrama*s in the Hindu way of life as presented in the texts. The four *āśrama*s are complementary to each other. The *summum bonum* of life was of course realized in *saṁnyāsa āśrama* which was meant for doing all that one could do to attain salvation. But before reaching that stage, he was required to attend to his worldly responsibilities. So all the four *puruṣārtha*s — *dharma, artha, kāma* and *mokṣa* — were required to be accomplished within this life, and *saṁnyāsa* was meant for the realization of the last *puruṣārtha* that is *mokṣa*.

Quoting from the Bhagavad-Gītā he added: The Bhagavad-Gītā again and again emphasizes that the role of a *saṁnyāsin* is not just to attain salvation for himself but he has to be active. He has to live in the society. He has to serve people in a detached and dispassionate manner and he is the best type of *saṁnyāsin* who maintains the spirit of detachment, the spirit of non-doership and the spirit of having no vanity or any egotistic feeling in himself while serving society. He serves society just for service sake, whatever he can do, whatever his intellectual and physical faculty permit him to do. He should serve society to the best of his capacity and ability and should not have any sense of vanity; he does it only for his inner satisfaction and as part of his social obligation. One of the best examples, he said, is that of Swami Vivekananda. Here he also referred to the greatness of Ramakrishna Paramahamsa and Sri Aurobindo.

How does a *saṁnyāsin* engaging in social work differ from a social worker elicited the following response: "A social worker will emphasize the physical needs of the population, eradication of poverty, diseases, etc. He will work for all that is gross, improvement of material welfare of people, etc. Whereas a *saṁnyāsin*, while not ignoring the gross aspects of society, will also try to create awareness about the spiritual aspect of one's life. Most of one's problems arise out of the fact that one is not in touch with that invisible aspect of life. The moment you connect yourself with that invisible aspect, most of your problems are immediately resolved and solved. So a *saṁnyāsin* will take care to ensure that the other invisible aspect is not ignored and that invisible aspect of life plays a very significant role in eradicating the existent gross social problems."

Deliberating on the subjects of how society views a *saṁnyāsin*, especially the one who is only a *saṁnyāsin* in name, Sharma compared the fake *saṁnyāsin*s to the imitation gold sold in the market. The very existence of fake *saṁnyāsin*s proves the existence of real *saṁnyāsin*s behind these imitations. But even today, society has that respectful attitude to real *saṁnyāsin*s and in fact there are some real *saṁnyāsin*s available in the world today. He had visited several times an *āśram* in New York state run by a brain surgeon. The name of that *āśram* is Ananda Ashram. This brain surgeon, Rammurti Misra, hailed from Uttar Pradesh and took *saṁnyāsa* as Swami Brahmananda. He was a lover of Sanskrit and considered it to be the language to convey "the best spiritual ideology." The talk of spirituality pervades the *āśram* he said. "Patañjali's *Yogasūtra*s in original Sanskrit were on everybody's lips. The Swami sang the *sūtra*s and made everyone of his pupils sing along with him. In fact, he was teaching them Sanskrit language through the *Yogasūtra*s. Unfortunately he is no more but the tradition still lives there. This Swami made it his goal to bring the United State of Atman (USA) in the USA! Even today all the spiritual Sanskrit texts are regularly recited and aspirants from all over New York state gather there especially over the week-ends and participate in all the activities institutionalized by this great *saṁnyāsin* Swami Brahmananda."

Comparing Hindu *āśram*s in the West with those in India, he said that what distinguished Western Hindu *āśram*s from their Indian counterparts, is the very secular attitude that prevails in them. In these *āśram*s all the festivals of other religions such as Christmas, Easter,

Passover, etc., are also celebrated. Singing Veda *mantras* every morning they do *āratī* to Jesus, Mohammad and Moses besides the Hindu deities as well. This is a real service they are doing in the USA and outside India and he is impressed by the spiritual climate they have created around such *āśrams*, wherever they are. He concluded by saying that "It goes without saying that the role and quality of leadership of the head of the organization has a lot to do with the atmosphere and success of these organizations."

SRIVATSA GOSWAMI

Srivatsa Goswami, a scholar priest, was associated with the Rādhā Ramaṇa temple in Vrindavan and traced his lineage to Sri Gopal Bhatta Goswami, one of the famous six Goswamis associated with Caitanya Mahaprabhu. Educated at Harvard University, he even did a short stint as a visiting professor of Religious Studies at that University. Talking about his Harvard days, he mentioned that he was quite miserable there. He found it difficult to fit into the stereotypical image of a Hindu priest. So he chose to leave the University.

Asked about the concept of *saṁnyāsa* he said "*saṁnyāsa*, as defined in the Śāstras, is a transcendental state of an individual in the world, and the *saṁnyāsin* is one who has no other desire except to realize divinity, and to realize the transcendental state of the individual." There are some rules laid down for him to follow. One such is the obligation for him to take permission from his family before he accepts *saṁnyāsa*. There are also rituals before initiating a person into *saṁnyāsa*. There is a *virajā homa* for instance, where a human form made of wheat flour is burnt in fire which also consumes his hair and *yajñopavīta* or sacred thread symbolically, denoting that this particular human being is dead for all practical purposes. Then, a new name is given to him. The *saṁnyāsin* is normally from the Brāhmaṇa caste, but it can also be taken by anybody who is fit for that stage of life. After the initiation ceremony, he puts his hand over the fire and vows that he will have nothing to do with any material objects in the world, he will have no contact with women (even women in the form of wood). Thus, there are certain vows which he takes and he is then given a new name and *kāṣāya vastra* (ochre robes) on the same day.

Referring to the Śāstric injunctions, viz., *na śāstram ārabhe* (one shall not begin any Śāstras), I will not start any *āśrama*, I shall not preach any philosophy, I will not have any *śiṣya*s, I will be alone, I will be following the *saṁnyāsa vrata* all alone, etc., Goswami said there are no *saṁnyāsin*s in that very strict sense of a *saṁnyāsin* these days. Neither is it possible to adhere to these rules. Today there are *saṁnyāsin*s just doing social service, and it would be a misnomer to call them *saṁnyāsin*s as they do not fit into the textual/Śāstric definition of a *saṁnyāsin*. Many *saṁnyāsin*s have also brought a bad name to the *saṁnyāsāśrama* itself. He went on to emphasize that, "*Saṁnyāsa* does not give license to lead a licentious life."

He felt that there had been a corruption of *saṁnyāsa* rules and the *saṁnyāsin*s were there for improving their own lot and had nothing to do with the Śāstric traditional view of *saṁnyāsa*. While conceding that organizations like that of ISKCON, Ramakrishna Mission, Sivananda Ashram are doing good work, he still felt that many *saṁnyāsin*s could not measure up to the standard set by the tradition. He then added: "There are a number of incidents here in Vrindavan alone where *saṁnyāsin*s are misusing their trust; for example, there are 15 or 16 banks here in Vrindavan and each bank has huge assets to the tune of two crore of rupees, and many of them are personal accounts deposited by individual *saṁnyāsin*s. Many householders here cannot claim to have much of wealth while a *saṁnyāsin* can write cheques worth 10-15 million rupees in one go. Therefore, *saṁnyāsin*s of the day do not maintain the spiritual traditions which they are supposed to be doing."

In his view: "It is the *ācārya guru*s who preached the tradition in the past and they were all *gr̥hastha*s. Any number of such examples can be given from the Vedas and other scriptures. For instance all the *r̥ṣi*s of the Vedas and the Upaniṣads were *gr̥hastha*s." He felt he was proved right by even the Purāṇas and *itihāsa*s for his view that present-day *saṁnyāsin*s are not adopting the strict code of conduct laid down by the Śāstras. As if to substantiate that he quoted from the Bhāgavata Purāṇa where it has been said that those who are not well versed in *dharma* will be the propagators of *dharma* in the Kaliyuga. He was also of the firm view that Śaṅkarācārya did not start the *maṭha*s all over India but it was done by his *śiṣya*s.

Goswami then gave a brief account of his own tradition which was established by Sri Caitanya. There are seven biographies written about the great saint — three in Sanskrit and four in Bengali. Living in the fifteenth-sixteenth centuries, Caitanya took *saṁnyāsa* to propagate his *bhakti* movement throughout the country. He gave up all his material attachments and desires and any kind of desire for fame and so he threw away into the river even his *Navyanyāya* treatise that he wrote when he became a well known logician. Caitanya has a large following today both in India and the West where it is known as the ISKCON or the Hare Krishna Movement.

GAUTAM PATEL

Professor Patel, an acclaimed Sanskrit scholar, preferred to talk about one particular *saṁnyāsin* and his *maṭha* in Gujarat rather than talking generally about *saṁnyāsa* and the institution. He spoke about the establishment of the *saṁnyāsāśrama* called Shankar Mandir with which he had a close association. It was in Nandyal about 60 km from Ahmedabad.

The Shankar Mandir, which Patel described, was a unique example of how individual *saṁnyāsin*s model the *saṁnyāsa* institution according to their own vision, even while keeping within the perceived boundaries of the tradition. Thus, even the name of this institution as Mandir is not the usual designation for an *āśram* and is normally just a religious place of worship in Hinduism. This also highlights the point made earlier that very often what we find on the ground is not a faithful representation of what is available in texts themselves.

Patel began by saying that the Sankar Mandir was established about 168 years ago by Sant Ramji who was a great saint. Sant Ram was an *avadhūta* and people visited him to get his blessings. His first disciple was Lakshmidas. In this lineage came other saints: Chaturdas, Jairam, Mukutdas, Manikdas, and Jankidas. The head at the time of the interview was Narayandas and, as a rule, he stayed within the temple. He had imposed on himself this rule and stuck to it. The greatest achievement of Narayandas was his influence in maintaining religious harmony between various communities in the vicinity of the Mandir and the nearby cities and villages. It is mentioned that whenever riots overtook many parts of Gujarat between Hindus and Muslims, this saint declared: "There shall be no riots in our city" and people have listened to him and according to Patel, harmony between the communities prevailed to this day. In recognition of his work, he was awarded the President of India's "Kabir Award." An evidence of this harmony was that people of all communities throng the temple and also donate generously to the Mandir. Also, everyone, without discrimination is given *prasāda* in the form of food, a full lunch or dinner in the temple. The temple also encouraged women to take an active part in its activities.

As for the rules of initiation into this Mandir he said that those who were initiated into the centre for the first time were called *dīkṣit*s. They then wore the orange garb (ochre robes). When one became the head of the institution, he had to wear white clothes and he was given special *dīkṣā* in the temple. This had been the practice right from its inception. This, as would be noticed is the reversal of what normally happens. A *brahmacārin* who is given initiation normally wears white clothes while the head of the *saṁnyāsāśrama* normally wears ochre robes.

After that introduction I was given an opportunity to ask some questions to Narayandasji who spoke in Gujarati. Prof. Patel acted as translator and interpreter:

Q : Why have people lost respect for *saṁnyāsin*s in modern times?

A : Firstly there is widespread deterioration in righteousness (*dharma*) among the people and secondly, some *saṁnyāsin*s are not cultivating enough virtues which produce respect for them.

Q : What about the future of *saṁnyāsa*?

A : There is good hope. People have regard for our culture and this culture is not going to die. *Kāṣāya vastra* is their *paramparā* (heritage) and here also white clothes of a *saṁnyāsin* is a respected tradition.

Q : What do you teach your disciples?

A : Two things — *guru-mantra* to be chanted constantly and they should have an equal regard for each and every God. There should be no distinction.

Q : Should a *saṁnyāsin* get into politics?

A : For the preservation of *dharma* there is no need for a *saṁnyāsin* to go there, but at the same time, looking at it from another point of view, when the politics of a nation deteriorates to a considerable extent then good people should enter it and improve it. Otherwise the politicians will go their own corrupt ways leading the country to ruin. So in my opinion it may be necessary for saints to get into the political field in order to reform it and set it right for the good of the people. There are very fine examples in our tradition. Vasiṣṭha, for instance, a great realized soul was in the court of Daśaratha advising him on the proper governance of the land.

Q : How can *mokṣa* be achieved?

A : *Anusandhāna* or *jñāna* is *mokṣa*. The moment you realize Viśvarūpa, the *jagat* becomes *mithyā*.

Patel then took over and added some facts about the Mandir. In theory the Mandir followed Advaita philosophy and yoga practice. In tune with the broad outlook of the Mandir, a Harijan had also been initiated into *saṁnyāsa* and he was accepted honourably into their fold. They hold a festival on the *mahānirvāṇa* day of Sant Ramji. *Prasādam* is distributed to all who attend and they all stay together inside the temple. There is no *dharmabheda, varṇabheda* and *jātibheda* in this place. This is in accordance with the tenets laid down by Sant Ramji who said: If anyone comes, regard him as my form and give him *roṭī* and *pānī* — food and water, and whatever they demand.

It is rumoured that Mahatma Gandhi visited this place and was impressed with the atmosphere there. There is no *mūrti* in this temple as in others. There is only a *jyoti*. It is said that when Sant Ramji took *saṁnyāsa* a *dīpa* (lamp) was put at the place he went into *samādhi* and when he attained *mahāsamādhi* a lamp was lighted and it is still going on.

Patel went on to add: "The ideal of service displayed in this temple is exemplary. You will find ladies from well-to-do families pick up brooms and sweep the place clean every time. Recent innovations were done to the buildings to cater to the increasing number of people. There was a Mahā-Viṣṇu Yajña, Veda Parāyaṇa and Bhāgavata Saptāha. One lakh of people attended the *saptāha*. They doubled the capacity as the crowds increased daily. They had to install closed circuit televisions numbering over 101 to accommodate the crowds."

Patel then talked about the role of *saṁnyāsins* in modern society. "In the past, the *saṁnyāsins* belonging to various sects, *akhāḍā*s, and denominations such as Daṇḍīs, Udāsīns, and Vairāgīs, etc., held many *dharma saṁsthāns*. However there was no unity amongst them and even one Śaṅkarācārya will not sit with another and would avoid meeting them. The present trend in Hinduism as a whole is an attempt to undo the damage done in the past due to widespread differences and disunity. In a certain sense one can point to the recent Ram Janma Bhoomi episode as bringing *saṁnyāsin*s of different sects together. They have realized that orderly conduct and survival is at stake in the face of danger. They are including even Jain monks in their deliberations to protect all ancient traditions. This kind of an unity is a good turn for Hinduism as a whole."

"Nowadays the Hindu *saṁnyāsin*s have also adopted the Christian Missionary methods such as starting hospitals, schools, dispensaries even in the interior areas and villages as was and is being done by the Christians. The Vanavāsī Pariṣad had been started to organize and co-ordinate efforts in this regard. All great *kathākāra*s/story-tellers like Morari Bapu, Ramesh Ojha and others participate in this effort. Morari Bapu and others like him, though not *saṁnyāsin*s in the strict sense of the term, go to the downtrodden people and recite *Bhāgavata-kathā*s on a regular basis. They have added musical instruments, orchestras, etc., to popularize Hindu ideas. All this is having a very good impact. *Saṁnyāsin*s have realized that they cannot be parasites in society so they have decided to do something for society. Schools, hospitals and other charitable organizations are also coming up in a big way."

On the question of whether charitable institutions can be listed as social work by *saṁnyāsin*s, he said: "There is a vast difference between a politician starting a school and a *saṁnyāsin* starting an institution. Schools started by *saṁnyāsin*s begin with a Vedic chant or other prayers and religion is taught as part of the curriculum. Of course, sectarianism does creep in as in the Swami Narayan temple, for instance. But, nevertheless, by and large the *saṁskāra* and *dharma* is kept alive. Take the work of Pandurang Shastri Athavale. In his institutions and temples etc., Harijans are doing *āratī* while brāhmaṇas sit behind and sing *bhajana*s. At his bidding thousands of fishermen have stopped eating fish and join in the common observances, worship and all spiritual activities initiated by Pandurang Shastri. Though he is strictly not a *saṁnyāsin* in the traditional sense, his activities qualify him to be called as such. Thus modern *saṁnyāsin*s have greatly changed the way they function in society."

As to the future of the institution and the culture of *saṁnyāsa* he said that he was very optimistic that it will continue to hold respect in the minds of people as it has survived through so many trials in the past.

CHRISTOPHER CHAPPLE

Professor Chapple is an Indologist with a wide teaching and research experience. Chapple was able to talk first-hand about the way the subject had been interpreted in America and he could also compare this with what he had learnt about *saṁnyāsin*s and the institution in India through personal contact, the media, TV, films, etc. Chapple mentioned how the Rajneesh episode in USA had left a bad taste in the USA, because of his followers going about as *saṁnyāsin*s and resorting to wearing red clothes or pink or orange clothes. They also spouted some phrases that came from their teacher and said that they were renouncing the world but behaved contrary to what he had seen of *saṁnyāsin*s in India. He had met some genuine ones in India, who exuded knowledge and devotion and were greatly venerable. On a lighter note he said that he had also learnt that people who have had fights with wives, families, etc., also decide to renounce the world for purely personal reasons having the least idea of the spiritual import of the step they were taking. One can meet any number of them during travels through the country and they are a common sight in many places. I pointed out that these may not belong, generally, to established *āśram*s and may not be those who would have received training for a number of years by staying in an *āśram* and then being intitiated into the *saṁnyāsa-dharma,* to which he agreed.

His association with the Jain community had provided good examples of Jain *muni*s and nuns (*sādhvī*s) in white clothes, with absolute minimum possessions, who wander about the countryside, except in the rainy season and who never stayed in one place during the rest of the year. He had been with *digambara* monks, who had taken the vow of total nudity and was impressed with their complete dedication to their vows of pure mendicancy.

In his view *lokasaṁgraha*/service for the welfare of society mentioned in the Bhagavad-Gītā had been practised in India as the notion of sacrifice for the sake of others. *Dāna*, etc., has been part of the Indian culture from time immemorial. The value of giving back to society and sacrificing one's own pleasures and comfort for the benefit of helping someone has been part and parcel of the ethos of India and hence that kind of chosen life would not be unusual for *saṁnyāsin*s as well to do something that is constructive in their own chosen ways. Many people who had been raised in the Gandhian era and those who follow Tagore and Aurobindo and other saints have also been inspired to involve themselves in social work with a feeling of renunciation. He continued: Drawing from my own personal experiences and interactions with different kinds of spiritual people in a variety of traditions which extol the "deconstruction of the self (theologically speaking)" where you stop worrying about your own particular self or situation, there comes about an awareness of the suffering of others. And it is this suffering that would prompt some sort of social action as the Buddha had said.

Turning to the future of *saṁnyāsin*s he went on to say that: "Contemporary Hindu society within India is very complex and on the one hand we have a very 'modern secular mind set' which is fostered by education and a great emphasis on science and technology and encouragement on the part of Indian parents for their children to go into professions that will generate income. Therefore, within that mindset, there is not a whole lot of value given to someone who just wants to renounce the world. And consequently we have a little bit of ambivalence here because there is cultural memory of an institution that is valued, as it is seeking after the highest truth and is considered to be very important. But yet there is also this inbuilt tension that you really want your children to be successful and to fulfil all of the wonderful things that life has to offer. This is also exacerbated by the fact that contemporary secular culture is very sceptical of any kind of religiosity."

As for the perception of the Hindu *saṁnyāsin* in America he said, "There is this romanticization of the idea of *saṁnyāsa* and many Americans are looking for a parental replacement figure or looking to have an oriental experience of something exotic and romantic. Also there's a history in America of the beatnik movement, where Allen Ginsberg, who recently died, was a tremendous influence on American culture in 1960s-1970s. He had come to India and wrote an extensive account of his trip and really introduced the idea of "dropping out" to American culture and this is something that has stayed with Americans, this idea of a rugged individual going off, living a hard life, doing his or her own thing. Again this is a romanticization, but at the same time there have been enough people who have been involved with Eastern teachers and have become disillusioned for one reason or another. Thus there is this counterbalance as well. Chapple felt that with the Beatniks and Allen Ginsberg, there was a sort of continuation of what was there with the transcendentalists and in particular with Walt Whitman who himself was like an American *saṁnyāsin*. The writings of Emerson and Thoreau on India were really quite extensive and there was a thread of this relationship of the USA with India which was historically well-grounded and was also continued when America came in contact with Swami Vivekananda and others."

Talking about (women) *saṁnyāsinī*s he mentioned one particular *āśram* started by a *saṁnyāsinī* in America. He stated how he was particularly impressed with this saṁnyāsinī's pioneering effort in founding the Yogananda Ashram in Amityville in New York. She was quite grounded in Patañjali's *Yogasūtra*s and she had come to study in America in the 1950s and 1960s. Her teachings were very much focused on self-discovery and making a space for each individual to bring out the best in himself or herself. But at the same time it was certainly part of her dream to make a spiritual option available for people so the world could be a better place. One of the important outreach activities of this *āśram*, according to Chapple, was the establishment of a vegetarian restaurant, in which he participated with pleasure. Even though the *saṁnyāsinī* was no more, the *āśram* was still functioning in its existence of over 25 years. It was offering a different kind of education and lifestyle to the public that would go to the improvement of society.

Stressing the importance of the leadership of an *āśram* he was of the view that a well kept *āśram* reflects on the quality of leadership and its success in society. He made reference to a book by Waghorne on this aspect of *āśram* leadership and its growth etc., entitled *Gods of Flesh, Gods of Stone*. It is sort of a historical narrative of what happens when a charismatic leader goes away. He also referred to Muktananda's Ashram whose present leader Swami Chidvilasananda was chosen because of her charisma after some rancorous controversy on the succession issue when Muktananda died. "Here is an instance where charisma was a sort of requisite for the title and for the office to pass on as it happens to be a large organization. Anandamayi Maa, Mira Bai, Ammaji are fine examples of charismatic *saṁnyāsinī*s who attract large crowds by their strong image for female renunciation."

In answer to the question as to what are the qualities that a *saṁnyāsin* should posssess he thought that a saṁnyāsin's defining characteristic should be his courage to think differently and even against popular mainstream culture as in the case of some Christian Monastic orders who had founded the Loyola University where he is working. He should be someone who takes on the responsibility of being a spiritual teacher prepared to do tremendous amount of dedicated work for society with a purely unselfish attitude. Fine examples are Swami Vivekananda and Paramahamsa Yogananda in Los Angeles.

Where does the support for these American/Hindu *āśram*s come from was my next question to which he said that "Besides the Hindu diaspora which is their main support, local populations also take part in the activities of the *āśram*s which has led to their success." Culturally most Indians would gather around a Swami more as a social thing, to get together to be reminded of their own culture rather than something that would be overtly or specifically religious. Thus, supporting the *saṁnyāsin* and the *saṁnyāsāśrama,* also becomes part of the culture whether in India or in other parts of the world where there are these *āśram*s. Today there are also *āśram*s/institutions like the Self-Realization groups, for instance, that are run by non-Asians as well.

What about the future of these institutions in America? That led him to talk about the The Vedānta Society started by Swami Vivekananda in Los Angeles which is still very active with a very vital community. However, while thinking of the future, he said that the monks and nuns were ageing and they don't seem to have as many young people coming in as they did in the past. He also pointed out that keeping in view the changing demographics of the USA they had also started teaching in Spanish. Mexico in some ways has returned to reclaim its territory and with that have come new populations many of whom are interested in Asian spirituality. There are ups and downs and one is not very sure as to the future of these *āśrams*, he said. On the other hand, "The Hare Krishnas (ISKCON)" have thrived in the USA and are still growing to some extent. He added that they (Hare Krishnas) follow strictly the principle of celibacy.

This automatically led to the importance of celibacy in the life of a *saṁnyāsin*. He found the whole notion of celibacy somewhat problematic because it is very difficult to find a truly pure example of this. The texts talk about it but there are also a number of Buddhist texts that nuance it and there are certain categories that one would not normally have thought to have existed in traditional times when people married very young and in arranged marriages. But within some Buddhist manuals there is this little provision that among the consenting adults, that is okay, mainly the vow was to avoid marriage. He personally felt that celibacy is a requirement for spirituality. He compared it to the Christian monastic order and said: On the Christian side there are very strict rules that people who enter the religious orders have to follow and the requirement for what you can do and what you cannot do in a seminary and they are extremely stringent as much as in the Hindu tradition.

He reminisced about the difficulty that monastic orders are facing to recruit monks and specially Christian nuns. Their orders are just ageing, diminishing and disappearing which in many ways is very sad because the nuns have done great service in medicine and great work in education. And their orders are not being replaced and schools are being taken over and hospitals are being taken over by lay workers, which has also made them more expensive, so that, in many ways, there is a sad loss of Christian institutions as existed in the past and let us see what happens in the future. In a spirit of comparison of the Christian and Hindu monk he further added that the community is very important for the Christian priesthood. This superseded the earlier practice of a cloistered life without any contact with the external world that the Christian priests lived in. St. Benedict, however, changed all that by saying that people should not be solitary, that they should live together in a group and orders. Therefore rules were developed governing the community life of these people and up to the present, this emphasis on community living is of paramount importance for the Christian monks. He felt that for the Hindu *saṁnyāsin* there was a far greater emphasis on individuality rather than the community.

3

Interviews with Saṁnyāsins/Saṁnyāsinīs

LET me start with the method I have followed in the arrangement of the *saṁnyāsins/saṁnyāsinīs* belonging to the many *sampradāyas* who have been interviewed in this study. There are *saṁnyāsins* who are part of the traditional *maṭhas* started by Śaṅkarācārya, Rāmānujācārya and Madhvācārya, then there are also a few who belong to *akhāḍās* and are Mahāmaṇḍaleśvaras. Then there are a number of independent *āśrams* started from the eighteenth century onwards professing to follow a particular traditional *sampradāya*. For instance the Ramakrishna Mission and *maṭha* started in 1897 by Swami Vivekananda states that its philosophy is Advaita and so do a number of other orders like the Sivananda Ashram started in 1926. There are also branches of these *āśrams* in foreign lands like the USA, UK, South Africa, etc. Some of these *āśrams* outside India are affiliated to the main headquarters in India like the Ramakrishna ones but some have no affiliation to the Indian headquarters even though owing allegiance to the founder like the Vishnudevananda Ashram in Montreal. It owes allegiance to Sivananda who was the *guru* of its founder Swami Vishnudevananda, but has its own branches throughout the world including India. Similarly Dayananda Saraswati of Arsha Gurukulam has his own branches both in India and abroad though he himself was the disciple of Chinmayananda, to begin with, who in turn was the disciple of Swami Sivananda. Then there are *maṭhas* which are strictly not Vedic like the Śaiva Siddhanta Maths. There are also sectarian *maṭhas* catering to a single community like the Shankar Math of the Sāraswat Brāhmaṇa community. Modern movements like the Hare Krishna and Swami Narayan orders also have their *saṁnyāsa* groups.

In order to bring in some method amongst the different *sampradāyas* of *saṁnyāsins*, I have first of all arranged the traditional orders like those started by the original *ācāryas* like Śaṅkara, Rāmānuja and Madhva first. After that a kind of chronological order has been maintained for the *āśrams* started from the eighteenth century onwards grouping those belonging to the same *sampradāya* in one place. This method, it is hoped, will enable one to easily detect the subtle changes in interpretation that individual Swamis bring within the specific *sampradāyas* they have chosen for themselves.

SWAMI SVARUPANANDA SARASWATI

Swami Svarupananda Saraswati was the Śaṅkarācārya of Dwaraka Peeth and Jyotish Peeth at the time of the interview. He has the traditional title of Jagatguru (world teacher), occupying this ancient seat of religion and philosophy founded by Ādi Śaṅkarācārya, looking after most of western and northern India which is under his jurisdiction. He gave this interview in Hindi at his Ahmedabad centre where he was camping. What follows is the translation of the interview.

Saṁnyāsa-Dharma in the Sampradāya

Swamiji was not keen to talk about his past and how he came to adopt *saṁnyāsa* but plunged straight into defining who a *saṁnyāsin* is. He gave the traditional definition of a *saṁnyāsin* as described in Upaniṣads like the Bṛhadāraṇyaka, i.e. one who is totally detached from the three *eṣaṇās* (desires) which are the desires for progeny, wealth and worldly fame. Swamiji had the good fortune to be in the company of highly learned people in his childhood and had an early exposure to sacred texts. This *saṁnyāsa* ideal appealed to him as he came to the conclusion that the goal of detachment or giving up of the *eṣaṇās* is "welfare of the larger society as well as attainment of individual *mokṣa*. According to Ādi Śaṅkarācārya the *ātman* is considered to be *nitya mukta svarūpa* (eternal and free). It has no attachments which is a form of *māyā*. Realization of this automatically elevates one towards training for *mokṣa*, liberation. In this Śaṅkara Sampradāya the *saṁnyāsin* is unmarried, i.e. he is a *naiṣṭhika brahmacārin*."

Role of a Saṁnyāsin

A *saṁnyāsin* becomes a role model for householders. People emulate the *saṁnyāsin* especially his quality of sacrifice. He becomes an example for all to follow. As a *sādhaka* he strives to attain *ādhyātmika* knowledge.

1. Swami Svarupananda Saraswati, Ahmedabad

He is a *vividiṣā saṁnyāsin* or one still in search of liberation. The one who has realized *mokṣa* is called a *vidvat saṁnyāsin*; he still lives in society and then, his entire life is sacrificed for the welfare of the society, as he then lives only for the society and not for his self.

Activities of his Āśram

This *āśram* gives ādhyātmic or spiritual education: "We run a Sanskrit academy, a college and Vedic school, an *āśram* school situated in Dwaraka, where tribal kids are taught. In Madhya Pradesh we have an *āśram* that teaches 50 students Sanskrit and which also feeds the children. It is also doing work among tribal population. Camps are conducted to teach Indian culture. For instance from Mathura, *Rāmalīlā* parties go there to stage performances for the tribes. As is our Indian custom, free food is given for all those who attend these folk festivals. They also participate in singing *kīrtanas*, etc. We have also built a big hospital where free medicine and treatment is given."

Saṁnyāsin in Society

When asked about how society views a Hindu *saṁnyāsin*, he said that Hindu *saṁnyāsin*s are treated with respect by all people. He quoted Tulsīdās who said that "there is no difference between a *sant* and Bhagvān." Sometimes due to the misdeeds of some *saṁnyāsin*s doubts about their authenticity are created in the minds of people. But a real *saṁnyāsin* is respected at all times in India.

On the question of rituals for a *saṁnyāsin* he added: "*karma* and *jñāna* are considered to be rivals according to Śaṅkara. However, I am myself caught in this trap and in spite of saying this, I do my *dharma*. Does it mean I am going against my own *siddhānta*? No. When *karma* is done as per the rules of that particular situation and is dedicated to God in his *saṁkalpa mantra*, it becomes *akarma*."

General Information

While Swamiji himself has not travelled abroad, he has no objection to it. He, however, added that "one should go only to countries where Vedic knowledge is appreciated." He was open to anyone to come to his *āśram*, stay and learn from them. About the future of the *āśram*, he said: "I cannot foretell my future. Man cannot forecast his future. But, our *āśram* wants to open a Sanskrit University where a lot of people can sit and learn. In addition in Badrinath, we are building a free tourist boarding and lodging for travellers."

Issue of Succession

The head will select the most able disciple as the next head. It is entirely the personal decision of the Śaṅkarācārya. The person selected should be in charge of protection and welfare of different *maṭhas*/*āśrams* and should fulfil the aims of the mission laid down by Śaṅkarācārya, i.e. to spread *dharma* and complete the work started by Śaṅkarācārya. In the text written on the subject of succession by the *āśram*, the qualities of the head of the *maṭha* are specified. Only a male *saṁnyāsin* can occupy this position and not a *brahmacārī*. Women cannot be given *saṁnyāsa* in this *sampradāya* and so they cannot be heads as well.

Women

Though women are not given *saṁnyāsa*, Swamiji has opened an organization exclusively for women on the banks of the Narmadā called "Ubhaya Bharati Mahila Ashram" in memory of Ubhaya Bhāratī, the wife of Maṇḍana Miśra, who presided over the debate between her husband and Śaṅkarācārya and declared that Śaṅkarācārya had won and her husband had lost. Any woman wanting to lead a spiritual life will be given a place in this *āśram*. A house has already been built. The area acquired is of 25 acres. Up to 15 women can stay there. Eventually 100 will be accommodated. Sanskrit, English, philosophy, etc., will be taught. It is near the place where Śaṅkarācārya took initiation from his *guru*. There is a beautiful cave nearby where it took place. The government provided the land for the project. The government also gave grants for the *maṭha* to run an old-age home.

In answer to the question as to whether unwanted persons have created problems for the *āśram* Swamiji said: "The *āśram* has had bad elements coming under its roof but, by and large, there has not been too much of a problem. It is not easy to discipline people and the *āśram* follows a policy of slowly coaxing people by giving them a chance to improve. Those who repent of their bad actions are taken back. Those who do not change are not welcome."

Initiation Rituals

"The initiation of a *saṁnyāsin* is by performance of *virajā homa*. During the *homa*, the Vedas are merged with *Gāyatrī mantra*, *Gāyatrī mantra* is then merged with *Oṁkāra*. When *Gāyatrī* is merged into *Oṁkāra*, all the different fires of *agnihotra* are internalized into *ātman* and they are merged into *ātman*. The only ritual is the ritual of *dīkṣā*. Then *pāpa, puṇya, sukha, duḥkha* are all sacrificed. This is the giving up of the *karma-kāṇḍa*. Then their hair and sacred thread (*yajñopavīta*) are cut. Then he goes and throws away the *śikhā*/hair and *yajñopavīta* into the sea after which he walks naked to the *guru*. The *guru* gives him his *daṇḍa* and *kāṣāya-vastra*. He delivers the *upadeśa* of *mahāvākya* to him and from then on he is declared a *saṁnyāsin*. The four *maṭha*s established by Śaṅkarācārya have their own *mahāvākyas*. Sarada Math in Dwaraka is for Sāmaveda and the *mahāvākya* associated with it is *tat tvam asi*."

Advice to Saṁnyāsins and Householders

The two significant features of a *saṁnyāsin* should be — detachment from his family and receiving *dīkṣā* from his *guru*. Nowadays self-proclaimed *saṁnyāsin*s retain their ties with their families and do not have any *guru*. They cannot be considered as *saṁnyāsin*s. Only simple *kāṣāya-vastra* (ochre robes) should be worn by *saṁnyāsins*. *Kāṣāya* is the colour of fire. Knowledge is fire. Symbolically the fire burns up all his *karmas*. That is the significance of the *kāṣāya* colour.

> My suggestion to householders is that they should sincerely carry on their duties. It is their *dharma*. There are two aspects to *dharma* — one simple *dharma*, and the other is *viśeṣa dharma*. The simple *dharma* has ten qualities — *ṛtam, kṣamā, dama*, etc. *Viśeṣa dharma* lays down the *dharma* of a brāhmaṇa, kṣatriya, vaiśya and śūdra; householder, *brahmacarya, vānaprastha, saṁnyāsin*, woman, man, father, brother, etc. The *maṭha* tries to propagate its message through its publications like *Naya Bharati* in Gujarati, and discourses by the reigning Śaṅkarācārya are also sometimes published.

SWAMI BHARATI TEERTHA

The *āśram* of Bharati Teertha in Śṛṅgerī is nestled in a picturesque spot in the plateau of the Western Ghats surrounded by hills on the banks of the river Tuṅgabhadrā. Surrounding hills are known as the Ṛṣyaśṛṅga Parvata named after the saint mentioned in the Rāmāyaṇa. It is about 96 km from the nearest railway station. We (my husband and I) travelled from Anandashram in North Kerala about 150 km away through very difficult mountainous terrain and at places very rough roads before we reached the place. But once we reached Śṛṅgerī all the troubles were forgotten in the beautiful surroundings.

We were fortunate enough to meet the Śaṅkarācārya of Śṛṅgerī, in view of the strange circumstances of our visit. The previously planned interview with the Swamiji, we found on arrival, had not been fixed. The administrator of the *āśram* had assured us in writing that he will do the needful. When we reached Śṛṅgerī, the administrator was out of station and the office was not aware of any arrangement to have a proper interview. There was obviously a breakdown of communication. Śṛṅgerī being one of the most prominent and historic *maṭha*s established by Ādi Śaṅkara himself, we did not want to lose this opportunity of having an interview with the Śaṅkarācārya himself. Somehow we managed to convince the management about the necessity of meeting the Śaṅkarācārya, and the office staff agreed to guide us. As a formal interview could not be had, we had to follow the long queue waiting for the *darśana* of the Swamiji and take our chances. When we approached him, we stated our purpose of the visit. He readily agreed to answer any questions and so I took the opportunity of asking him some questions however brief it was, in view of the tight situation we were in. The questions and answers were in Tamil at his request. What follows is a summary of the brief conversation.

Saṁnyāsin

First of all I asked him what his view was about *saṁnyāsin*s. He said that a *saṁnyāsin* is anyone who gives up all desires, who is selfless and who is not attached to the world. "As far as this *pīṭha* is concerned only a *naiṣṭhika brahmacārin* can be given *saṁnyāsa*. They are also not allowed to marry and they take up *saṁnyāsa* right from *brahmacarya*." He went on to say: "The unique feature of this organization is that it has preserved the ancient Vedic tradition in many aspects of its functioning over the centuries. We run a number of *pāṭhaśālā*s both here and elsewhere. The school here goes back to over 105 years. There is one in Bangalore which dates back to about 88 years. There are hospitals and clinics for the benefit of the public. But the main aim is to preserve and maintain the Vedic heritage."

2. Swami Bharati Teertha

Successor

I asked him as to how the head of the *maṭha* or the successor is chosen. He said that the person in charge, the present head will have the full authority to select the next one. "But there are a lot of conditions. He has to be a great scholar, he has to be one who has *vairāgya* or dispassion. But it all depends on the grace of Ambāl." Ambāl here refers to the presiding deity of the *pīṭha* known as Śāradāmbāḷ. We were informed that in this *āśram* they do not have a governing body, etc., and the head sets the guidelines for the day-to-day functioning as well as the general policies for the entire organization. As for the financial aspects: "The government does not contribute anything and the *āśram* is run by public donations." In answer to the question of women *saṁnyāsinī*s he said: "Women are not given *saṁnyāsa* here as the tradition does not believe in it." This short interview came to an end with the Swamiji giving us his blessings and asking us to talk to one of his followers in the *āśram* who was knowledgeable about the tradition of this *āśram*.

Information gathered from Inmate

We gathered from our conversation with this inmate that the Swamiji does not give *saṁnyāsa* to anybody other than the one chosen by him to be his successor which was also mentioned by Swamiji himself. There are other *saṁnyāsins* living in the *āśram* who have been authorized to initiate anyone aspiring to become a *saṁnyāsin*. According to tradition this is believed to be the first *pīṭha* established by Ādi Śaṅkarācārya and the present Śaṅkarācārya of the *pīṭha* is the 36th in line of succession according to their *āmnāya* (lineage). The publication of the *āśram*, affirming the Swami being the 36th in the line, states that he ascended the "throne" on 19 October 1989. "The Śṛṅgerī Math/Peeth/Ashram, is also known as the Dakshinamnaya Peeth and has had an unbroken succession of spiritual luminaries." He is called a *jagadguru*, world teacher, a title shared by all Śaṅkarācāryas.

Śāradāmbāḷ Temple

The temple of Śāradā is the main attraction for the pilgrims, besides the *darśana* of the Śaṅkarācārya. The temple "originally consisted of a *yantra* carved on a rock in the middle of the Tuṅga river by Śrī (Ādi) Śaṅkarācārya with a sandalwood image installed on it and covered by a thatched roof." The present golden image dates from the time of Śrī Vidyāraṇya, the famous *ācārya* of the Śṛṅgerī Peeth, also known as an empire builder, since he is supposed to have helped to consolidate the Vijayanagara Empire which ruled the whole of south India for some time in the fourteenth-seventeenth centuries.

The first head of the *pīṭha*, according to tradition was Sureśvarācārya, one of the first four disciples of Ādi Śaṅkarācārya. According to one legend Sureśvara was known as Maṇḍana Miśra who was married to Ubhaya Bhāratī and with whom Śaṅkarācārya held a debate in Mahiṣmatī. Legend also believes that Ubhaya Bhāratī presided over the debate between these two stalwarts, one (Maṇḍana Miśra) arguing for the supremacy of the path of rituals (*karma-kāṇḍa*) and the other (Śaṅkarācārya) for the superiority of knowledge over ritual. When Maṇḍana was defeated, Ubhaya Bhāratī is supposed to have disappeared from the world and regained her celestial form as Sarasvatī Devī, the goddess of knowledge. She, however, granted a boon to Śrī Bhagavatpāda Śaṅkara that she would be immanent at a place where he may invoke her presence. The goddess now is enshrined here at his behest and she is Śāradāmbāḷ.

Rituals in the Āśram

Even though Śaṅkara himself was against rituals we were witness to Swamiji performing *pūjā* the night we stayed there. The *pūjā* was quite long lasting from about 8.30 p.m. to 10 p.m. The next morning there were over 2000 people lining up to see him. There were a number of rituals going on — *pāda-pūjā*, people taking *tīrtha* from the hands of the Śaṅkarācārya, people asking for advice and so on. We were told that he does not travel much but preferred staying in the *āśram* and guiding the devotees. We ourselves saw him talking to a number of people and listening to their problems and advising them, thus acting as their counsellor.

Additional Information

Like *saṁnyāsins* in general, the *saṁnyāsins* here also wear the *kāṣāya-vastra*. The Śaṅkarācārya was wearing *vibhūti* (sacred ash), on his forehead. He also wore a *rudrākṣa-mālā* round his neck. We went round the *āśram* complex and noticed that there was a temple within the complex for Śiva represented by the *Śivaliṅgam* where daily worship is conducted. The temple is known as the Vidyā Śaṅkara temple. As their publication states: "No visitor to Śṛṅgerī can fail to notice it and be impressed with the grandeur of the conception and the architectural art of the times which made such a structure possible out of finely carved stones."

In common with the practice of all *āśrams* in general, this *pīṭha* also provided two meals every day for all visitors free of cost. Śṛṅgerī was established by Śaṅkarācārya to take care of the southern region and the *āśram* takes its task seriously. Even though Swamiji is not fond of much travel he undertakes visits now and then to other centres in south India and also up north to meet and speak to his devotees about Sanātana Dharma and Advaita Vedānta. The impression that one gained of this *āśram* was that it is more concerned with the preservation of Vedic Dharma and devotes considerable energy in that direction.

SWAMI JAYENDRA SARASWATI

Sri Jayendra Saraswati, the head of the Kāñcīpuram (Kāñcī) Śaṅkarācārya Ashram also known as the Kamakotipeetham was interviewed at his *āśram* in Rameswaram during one of his visits there. Swamiji gave the interview in Hindi and the translation is given below.

He briefly mentioned his background and his entry into *saṁnyāsa*. "When I finished my education, my *gurujī* asked my parents if I could join the *pīṭha*. Then everybody agreed. Accordingly I underwent appropriate education and at the age of 19 I took *saṁnyāsa*."

Saṁnyāsa and Saṁnyāsin

Swamiji started describing the many different kinds of *saṁnyāsins* as evidenced in the texts. He said it is already defined in the Bhagavad-Gītā in three ways: (1) *vividiṣā saṁnyāsin* who is well versed in the Vedas and other texts and who is engaged in an inward search; they do everything except *agnisaṁskāra*; (2) the second, who has no *karma* (ritual) is represented by the Daśanāmī *saṁnyāsin*; they do *upāsanā* and do service to the community; (3) the third is the *karmayogī*; he passes through *brahmacarya* and *gṛhasthāśramas*; he does all *karmas* and surrenders his deeds to God. Nowadays you find *vividiṣā saṁnyāsins* and the *sādhu* type, the Daśanāmī type. *Karmayogī saṁnyāsins* are rare; (4) the fourth type is referred to as *vidvat saṁnyāsin*. He is learned and is an *ātmajñānī*. He lives but does not function, he rarely eats and sleeps. He has neither a *guru* nor a *śiṣya*, he lives with *adhyātma-dṛṣṭi* and is forever blissful. So long as the body is on this earth, he lives. The moment the body dies, he unites with God. "Women are not allowed in our *sampradāya* to take to *saṁnyāsa* even today. Nowadays, however, many women are taking up *saṁnyāsa* in *āśrams* other than our own and there are women in the Daśanāmī Sampradāya." Even though Ādi Śaṅkara started the Daśanāmī Sampradāya, nowadays the Mahāmaṇḍaleśvaras and their *paramparā* have got together and started their own way of propagating the tradition." He seemed to suggest that the present-day Daśanāmīs were not true to Śaṅkara's tradition.

Śaṅkarācārya's Paramparā

In this *paramparā* right from Śaṅkarācārya to date a *saṁnyāsin*'s role is defined as one who surrenders to God and meditates on God to become a *jīvanmukta*. By being an example, he will automatically teach the society a way of leading a pure life. The other *saṁnyāsins* who run an *āśram* have to work towards their own liberation as well as do service for the society. Although community service is not obligatory, it is expected of a *saṁnyāsin* who runs an *āśram*. Swamiji seemed to make a distinction between a solitary *saṁnyāsin* and one who is in the *āśram* and especially the one who is the head of an *āśram*. He added:

> The objectives of a *saṁnyāsin* can never be attained to the fullest. Satisfaction is derived based on the input. As long as society exists, there is always a need for personal and social works. It depends on a person's own will. The Hindu *saṁnyāsin* commands a lot of respect from the people.

Śaṅkara Maṭhas/Pīṭhas and the Issue of Succession

"Śaṅkara did not start the *āmnāya* of the *pīṭha* but later Swami Vidyāraṇya started it. Śaṅkara established *pīṭhas* in four *dhāmas*, in four prominent places. In Śṛṅgerī he established the Śāradā *prāṇapratiṣṭhā* and established *pīṭha paramparā*. The final one is the Kanchi Kamakotipeetham. Later on saints have established *āmnāya pīṭhas* and attributed them to Śaṅkara. When the need arises, I will appoint one of my *śiṣyas* as the *pīthādhipati*. One of my disciples took *saṁnyāsa* in the year 1981 at the age of 13 years. He is 30 years now, and does *pūjā*, etc., very well. He is capable of being in charge of the *pīṭham*. Once a person becomes a disciple, he has two objectives to be achieved: personal

3. Jagadguru Sankracharya Jayendra Saraswati ji Maharaj

enlightenment through self-enquiry and being in charge of a *maṭha* in a dhārmic way. Both are essential. A *saṁnyāsin* should follow the *saṁnyāsa-dharma*; however, it is not necessary that one should follow exactly what is written in the texts, but it may vary here and there depending on the times, just as a human being does."

General Information

He offered some general comments on the institution. In this *pīṭham* a *saṁnyāsin* follows more or less the dhārmic path. He was confident that his *pīṭham* will certainly run for generations to come. The head of the *āśram* lays down the rules for running the *āśram*, he said. Donations are received to finance its activities. Until now they have had no need to establish checks and balances to weed out unwanted elements from the *āśram*. He went on to add that in Hindu Dharma nobody is an undesirable element. Only difference is some people think and carry on their duties and some don't. *Saṁnyāsa* initiation is done through the performance of the *virajā homa*, etc. "I will be giving initiation in future, but have not given any so far. The rituals, *homa*, etc., is done by priests."

Activities

The *āśram* celebrates all Hindu festivals. It has a Vedic *pāṭhaśālā*, a Sanskrit school and a Vedānta school in Kāñcīpuram. Every Thursday they have a conference on higher learning. Regular Vedic conferences are held here and elsewhere. On Swamiji's birthday a Vedānta conference is held. On Bālaswāmī's birthday a Mīmāṁsā conference is held. There is a university run on modern lines catering to students from all over. Hospitals are run by the *maṭham* in many places in India. They have a publication unit. Swamiji travels all over India and also recently visited Nepal. There are four *saṁnyāsin*s serving in the *āśram*. There are many more in other centres.

Other Information gathered at Rameswaram

We witnessed Swamiji going into the Rameswaram temple and were told that he would worship the *Śivaliṅgam* there. Tradition has it that he is the only person, besides the Nepal Rājā (king), authorized to perform the *pūjā* and perform *abhiṣeka* inside the *sanctum sanctorum* (*garbha-gṛha*) apart from the usual priests. We saw Swamiji walking all the way from his place of stay to the temple. Of course, questions as to the opposition between *karma* and *jñāna* in the Advaita Sampradāya did come to our mind at that point.

SWAMI MAHESHANAND GIRI

Swami Maheshanand Giri is a Mahāmaṇḍaleśvara of the Nirañjanī Akhāḍā of Hardwar. This interview took place in his Delhi *āśram* called Vishwanath Saṁnyasa Ashram. Maheshanandaji was heading the Nirañjanī Akhāḍā at the time of interview, which has been in existence for a long time probably from the time of Śaṅkarācārya in the eighth century CE. He was also in charge of a number of *saṁnyāsa* organizations or *āśrams* in Varanasi, Delhi, Mount Abu, Bikaner, Ujjain, Ajmer, etc. The headquarters of his organization is Dakshinamurti Math situated at Varanasi which was established 300 years ago by Mahamandaleshvar Ramgiriji. This *maṭha* is connected with the Nirañjanī Akhāḍā.

Daśanāmī Order

Swamiji spoke briefly about the *saṁnyāsins* who follow the Daśanāmī tradition established by Ādi Śaṅkarācārya. According to him, Ādi Śaṅkarācārya founded the Daśanāmī Sampradāya to maintain and propagate Sanātana Dharma throughout India. He constituted four centres as the four headquarters to spread Sanātana Dharma. In those centres the proper study of the scriptures take place. He had also instituted six other centres (*pīṭhas*), for worship of the five *devatās* (*pañcadevatā*) and Kārttikeya. Thus in his view the four centres along with the six *pīṭhas* constituted the Daśanāmī Sampradāya. The heads of the *pīṭhas* (the first five) are required to move about all over the country and preach philosophy and religion and so they are referred to, even now, as the *ramata pañca* (the wandering five). They are the preachers whereas the Śaṅkarācāryas at the four headquarters are required to stay in one *maṭha* and do most of the teaching.

Akhāḍā and Mahāmaṇḍaleśvara

Being himself a Mahāmaṇḍaleśvara he was asked about the origin of the institution of Mahāmaṇḍaleśvara. He did not talk about the origin of the *akhāḍā* nor of the coming into being of the institution of Maṇḍaleśvara/Mahāmaṇḍaleśvara and without elaborating on the topic he only said that "A hundred years ago each *akhāḍā* had only two Mahāmaṇḍaleśvaras. They were both called *ācāryas*: one of them was a

4. Swami Maheshanand Giri ji Maharaj

teaching *ācārya* and the other was a preaching *ācārya*. The other *saṁnyāsins* were junior to them. As the responsibilities of the *akhāḍās* grew, it became necessary to increase the number of Mahāmaṇḍaleśvaras and today there are over 80 Mahāmaṇḍaleśvaras."

Still on the topic of the Daśanāmīs, he pointed out that the ten names (Daśanāmī) are distributed amongst the *saṁnyāsins* of the Śaṅkara *maṭhas* at the time of initiation and they are as follows: *Giri, Parvata*, and *Sāgara*, are assigned to Jyotirmath in the north; *Bhāratī, Sarasvatī*, and *Purī* belong to Śṛṅgerī in the south; *Vana* and *Araṇya* are given to Govardhan Peeth in the east, and *Tīrtha* and *Āśram* were assigned to the Dwaraka Peeth in the west. He went on to say that in former times, there was a continuous contact between these centres. But, later on, during the Mohammedan period, the three *maṭhas* of north India were practically destroyed and there was very little contact with the *maṭhas* in the south. Later, as late as 1942-43, the north Indian *maṭhas* were again re-established but the close relationship with the southern *maṭhas* that should have been there is not there.

Origin of the Saṁnyāsāśrama

"Basically a *saṁnyāsin* belongs to the fourth *āśrama*, i.e. he gradually progresses from the first *āśrama* to the next ones. But the Upaniṣads have also laid down that a person who has *vairāgya* can directly go from *brahmacarya āśrama* to *saṁnyāsa āśrama*. There are also references to *saṁnyāsins* in the Ṛgveda itself." He himself is a *naiṣṭhika brahmacārin* and has been the head of the organization for over 42 years. But he added that the head of the Nirañjanī Peeth can also be occupied by one who had been married; the only condition being that he has to cut all relationships after becoming a *saṁnyāsin*.

Activities of the Āśram

Like all other *saṁnyāsāśramas* today, this organization also runs dispensaries and colleges. There is one college in Delhi, and another one in Varanasi where they train students up to the *ācārya* level. The success or otherwise of institutions run by *saṁnyāsins* is very difficult to assess, he said, as things have changed considerably over time especially with exposure more and more to Western ideas. For instance: We had a dispensary giving Ayurvedic medicines earlier and people were quite happy with that. But today they are not satisfied with that and so we had to engage an allopathic practitioner, a GP. As the cost of the medicines is also going up day by day, we find it difficult to cope with it as our resources are limited. These services however will hopefully continue. But in absolute terms the success or otherwise of an *āśram* cannot be quantified or measured by these services alone, as they serve a larger purpose in life.

Personal Sādhanā and the Future

The *saṁnyāsāśrama* is the place for spiritual training and seeking enlightenment. But running the *āśram* as a whole and keeping one's spiritual goal in view is getting to be more and more complicated, according to Swamiji. "The activities go on increasing and getting more complex. The amount of time available for individual training seems to be progressively limited." He was of the firm view that unless individuals are properly trained the future of the *āśram* is at stake and that is true even with regard to the *gṛhastha*s (householders) who come to the *āśram*. "They attend *sādhanā* camps for their spiritual training, meditation, recitations, etc. The student *saṁnyāsin*s also need more vigorous coaching into their duties and responsibilities besides having time for their own *sādhanā*s as *saṁnyāsin*s." His concern was for the personal spiritual *sādhanā*s of *saṁnyāsin*s in the *āśram*, which suffer because of the many responsibilities of the institution. As the head of the *āśram*, he has a tremendous responsibility in the day-to-day running and overall success of the *āśram*. Success also depends on the *saṁnyāsin*s and *gṛhastha*s and others who co-operate in maintaining the institution through their dedication.

Choosing the Successor

As Swamiji was primarily the head of the Nirañjanī Akhāḍā he talked about how a successor is chosen in his *akhāḍā*. The succession issue is tackled by the *akhāḍā*s in a properly laid-out procedure. The head of the institution chooses the next person to take over. But this choice has to be acceptable to other Maṇḍaleśvaras as well. We have also to choose people who can help the head in carrying out his duties. These procedures are also subject to change as it has been since the time of Śaṅkara.

Saṁnyāsinīs

Swamiji, while talking about the existence of *saṁnyāsinīs*, mentioned the Junā Akhāḍā which is in Hardwar. This unique institution comprises entirely of *saṁnyāsinīs* and "has been there from time immemorial." It is situated in Hardwar. There are a number of other *akhāḍās* as well catering to *saṁnyāsinīs* alone. There are about eight Maṇḍaleśvaras who are women. In the Nirañjanī Akhāḍā and other *akhāḍās* also there are a few *saṁnyāsinīs*. He was of the view that there is a strong tradition of initiating women into *saṁnyāsa* and they have been heading *āśrams* and *akhāḍās* since a long time. The *saṁnyāsinīs*, however, deal more with women than men.

Initiation into Saṁnyāsa

The initiation of a person into *saṁnyāsa* in so far as the *akhāḍās* are concerned is done by an *ācārya* at the time of the Kuṁbha Melā. They are called Ācārya Mahāmaṇḍaleśvaras while others are called just Mahāmaṇḍaleśvaras. The ceremony is conducted after the initiates have undergone three years of rigorous training. Kuṁbha Melās have been specially chosen to anoint the *saṁnyāsins* with a specific purpose. That is the time a large percentage of *saṁnyāsins* of India gather in one spot. "So, everybody will know, he is a *saṁnyāsin*. So there is a practical aspect to it as well."

Āśram Routine and Other Matters

The following routine is followed in the *āśrams*: Generally everyone gets up very early in the morning about 3:00 or 4:00 when they hear the ringing of a bell. At 5:00 we have the *āratī*. At 5:30 the *pūjā* starts which lasts up to about seven. Then there is breakfast. People assemble in the hall to listen to a lecture daily. After a brief rest period, food is served at 10:30. In the afternoon there are classes starting at 3:00 p.m. for the *āśram* inmates. The public can come after that to meet the Swamis. The *pūjā* is conducted by those appointed by the head who himself does not participate in them. Devotees give donations for the upkeep of the *āśram*. Government does not help except to levy taxes. Neither do they help nor do they stop hindering especially on the tax issue. There are about eighteen *saṁnyāsins* staying at present in the *āśram*. Strict discipline is maintained in their conduct and anyone observed not conforming to the norms has to leave. Any serious misbehaviour will result in disrobing the individual so he cannot take shelter in any *āśram*. *Vairāgya* is one of the important distinguishing features of a *saṁnyāsin*. He has to study the scriptures regularly. In this *āśram* everyone has to acquaint himself thoroughly with Śaṅkara's works.

Role of Saṁnyāsin in Society

A *saṁnyāsin* is in a position to guide persons both spiritually and materially also. He can, for instance, console an individual who has come for counselling after some calamity, he can also help needy persons materially. More importantly, as one trained in the sacred literature he is able to advise people on how to conduct *pūjā*s in general, and also special worships for particular occasions and other religious activities. These are not performed by the *saṁnyāsin*s themselves but they are authorized to give appropriate directions as per the scriptures, to householder devotees who have a need for it.

Swamiji was of the view that without the *saṁnyāsāśrama*s the entire Hindu tradition would have collapsed. Even today, the role of *saṁnyāsin* in the service of the Hindu population and its progress is indispensable. "Spirituality in India is connected with philosophy. Every sect has a philosophical background. Now philosophy has to be studied properly and the householder will be so busy that he will not be able to study it properly. Studying properly the scriptures is not studying as an observer. So whatever you study you have to practise. And unless there are *saṁnyāsin*s who are doing this, they will not be able authoritatively to say that this is what the scripture means. Because, unless it has become, part and parcel of your realization, it is a meaningless thing. Any pundit can talk about it."

Swamiji used to travel quite a bit; but now the one below him, Swami Punyananda, whom he had appointed, visits many centres connected with this *āśram*. He is not keen on going abroad like many other *saṁnyāsin*s who travel quite a lot abroad spreading the message of India's spirituality. He feels that unless India is completely cured of its ills it becomes a farce or hypocrisy to go outside and talk about these things. Very few *saṁnyāsin*s were so honest in stating this though.

Saṁnyāsins and Politics

Swamiji was not happy with the idea of *saṁnyāsin*s entering politics. He has been insisting that this is wrong and has to be rectified. "The ones in politics are not associated with any *pīṭha*; they might have been in it once but have left it for politics. The *pīṭha*s generally do not support any member to be active in politics. Even if a person is detached, politics is not the thing for us. Because the whole idea of entering politics is to exercise power and rule over people. This means you might not be true to the philosophy of say Advaita. The *saṁnyāsin*s and heads of *maṭha*s are there to give advice and not to order anyone, which is what politics is all about. Because then the whole structure falls." On that note the interview came to a close.

SWAMI BHOOMANANDA TIRTHA

Hailing from Kerala Swami Bhoomananda Tirtha has established an *āśram* near Trichur called Narayanashrama Tapovanam. This interview was recorded in Delhi where Swamiji comes twice a year to give a series of lectures in his *āśram* in Ghaziabad near Delhi and in a number of other places and institutions as well. He also travels abroad where he is invited to give talks on Vedāntic subjects.

Swamiji himself was attracted to this path because of three personalities — one is Rāma, another is Kṛṣṇa and the third is Ādi Śaṅkarācārya. "The Rāma affinity comes from Rāma's dhārmic renunciation; Kṛṣṇa inspired him with his jubilant happiness. He makes everyone happy with his tuneful flute and fills them with laughter. Ādi Śaṅkara was the only child of his widowed mother, but still wanted to become a *saṁnyāsin*. I was also inspired from the very first *darśana* of my *guru* Baba to become a *saṁnyāsin*." He did not make clear how he connected *saṁnyāsa* with Rāma and Kṛṣṇa.

Saṁnyāsa, Saṁnyāsin and Saṁnyāsāśrama

Swamiji started by saying that "*saṁnyāsa* represents the wholesome pursuit of wisdom termed by Śaṅkara as *kevalajñānaniṣṭha*. When Śaṅkara started his mission, Buddhism had taken roots and had widespread influence throughout the country. Only Buddhism inculcated *saṁnyāsa* and *saṁnyāsa* became popular and many were becoming *saṁnyāsin*s. Śaṅkara had to institute a new cult in Hinduism called *saṁnyāsa* and highlight it in order to subdue the ascetic influence of Buddhism. *Sarvakarmaparityāga* can be achieved only through *saṁnyāsa* according to Śaṅkara. Śaṅkara was able to stem the spread of Buddhism through *saṁnyāsa* and through the Upaniṣadic message.

He vigorously supported *saṁnyāsa*. He rejected rituals out and out. He himself did not do any rituals even at the time of the death of his mother. He just burnt her body. Only legend connects him with temple rituals. In Kerala they say many of the temple practices are instituted by Śaṅkara. When there is a great man, people have a tendency to graft all things upon him. I don't think Śaṅkara wrote Saundaryalaharī also. Śaṅkara has not accepted *tantra* as a practice at all. There is no mention of *tantra* in Vedānta. These are all peculiar concoctions."

A *saṁnyāsin* is defined by Swamiji as one who has attained *saṁnyāsa*; *saṁnyāsa* is an attainment and an accomplishment, a refinement which generally comes to you from enlightenment. When enlightenment becomes functional to dissolve egoism and possessiveness, one becomes a *saṁnyāsin*. *Saṁnyāsa* is the pinnacle and fulfilment of human life and it is acclaimed and accepted in Indian culture. Anyone who is either an accomplished *saṁnyāsin* or at least one who makes a wholesome commitment and pursuit towards that goal should be considered a *saṁnyāsin*.

Saṁnyāsa can be taken at any stage in life; after *brahmacarya*, *gṛhastha* or *vānaprastha* stages. "By *saṁnyāsa* alone is human life fulfilled. But there are some people who can feel an affinity to and take to it right from *naiṣṭhika brahmacarya*. They want to pursue wholesomely the concept of *saṁnyāsa*. By *saṁnyāsa* one gives *abhayam* (fearlessness) to the entire world. It is always for the benefit of others — *lokasaṁgraha* and *sarva-bhūta-hite-rataḥ*, the two expressions of the Bhagavad-Gītā. Under the canopy of *saṁnyāsa* anything can grow, but a sure gain is the growth of knowledge. A *saṁnyāsin*, however, is capable of doing anything in any sphere of life. Vālmīki looked after an abandoned, pregnant Sītā, Kaṇva brought up Śakuntalā a forsaken child. Therefore, any kind of socially beneficial act which others are incapable of doing is capable of being performed only by a *saṁnyāsin* as has been shown historically. Our minds are equally disposed to all. Others will make differentiation between one human and another. Only *saṁnyāsins* can transcend differences and do great acts."

General Information

Swamiji is heading two organizations called Narayanashrama Tapovanam and the Hind Navotthana Pratisthan. Apart from other activities for the benefit of society, Swamiji also runs an old age home which had 120

5. Swami Bhoomananda ji Tirtha

inmates at the time of the interview and is called "Vānaprasthanilayam." He gets many applications for this Nilayam. He is also engaged in village extension programmes like help for educational scholarship, treatment in hospitals, abjectly poor people who have nothing to eat, are given 15 kg of rice and some money every month. There is one tailoring unit, footwear unit, etc. What is unique about Swamiji's *āśram* is that it is fitted with modern innovations like refrigerators, generators, fans, filtered water facilities, etc.

Mokṣa

Enlightenment should always be a pursuit of the intelligence and it should be in pursuit of wisdom alone and it cannot be in pursuit of action. "Wherever bondage is prevailing, in that place *mokṣa* is down." Social work may bring expectation in them and they may be happy. But you will not get anything like the spiritual joy of freedom. Unless you do *sādhanā* and dissolve egoism there will be no enlightenment, *mokṣa*. If a *saṁnyāsin* gets too much involved in social work, he rarely gets time to do *sādhanā*, personal effort towards enlightenment. Swamiji therefore emphasizes the spiritual aspect of *saṁnyāsa* rather than the social aspect. He strives primarily for spiritual welfare of himself and of others and to be oriented towards wisdom constantly.

Politics and Saṁnyāsa

Saṁnyāsins in his view should not enter politics. They should not enter Parliament. They could however be consulted on politics. Stability is preserved by *saṁnyāsins*. The spiritual persons/*saṁnyāsins* were never consulted by politicians especially when formulating the Constitution. Because of this there are some defects which could have been avoided and which have led to avoidable suffering. "We don't interfere in politics. We must however have the power, if people go wrong, to correct it."

Women and Saṁnyāsa

"I personally think that women by their biological and psychological framework will not be able to take up the rigours of the wandering life of a *saṁnyāsin*. It is not normally suitable for them but there are instances where women can and do become *saṁnyāsinīs*, but they would always be supported and protected by somebody. Today, Ramakrishna Mission and others have started a women's wing of *saṁnyāsinīs*. I feel that they cannot take up the difficult disciplines of *saṁnyāsa* unless they are shielded and protected. They can definitely pursue the goal of *brahma-vidyā*. There is no doubt about that. A woman who delivers a man, is she not man plus? Or is she man minus? I believe that society has never been unfair to women. We have considered women to be the precious section of our society. You know we did not have any proper banking system in our society in early times. So the extra wealth, particularly separable wealth, was converted into gold and made into ornaments and women adorned themselves with it. Can you send such a costly woman unprotected?"

Swamiji has given *saṁnyāsa* to three ladies and two men. One more *saṁnyāsin* was Swami Krishnananda but there is no news about him these days. Swamiji has himself instituted a special ritual instead of the traditional *virajā homa* for the initiation of a *saṁnyāsin/saṁnyāsinī*. He has written a *saṁkalpa* in Sanskrit which they recite and become *saṁnyāsins*. There is no other ritual.

Functioning of the Āśram

As for the guidelines for the functioning of the *āśram*, Swamiji said that there are no concrete guidelines laid down for the functioning of the *āśram*. At present all the *saṁnyāsins* are trustees. There is a written constitution for the Narayanashrama Tapovanam and it has been registered as a trust. The constitution includes specific rules and specific objectives and operational practices also, like how the trustees should be appointed, what their functions will be and so on. There are four to five trustees. Swamiji lays down the guidelines for the day-to-day functioning of the *āśram*.

Daily Routine

The day in the *āśram* starts with a prayer, the Viṣṇusahasranāma. One or two chapters of the Bhagavad-Gītā are then read. This takes place in the Samadhi Mandir, where Mataji Sulabha Devi has been interred. She was Swamiji's first disciple and was given *saṁnyāsa* by Swamiji. Rituals are totally avoided. The *āśram* is maintained as a place of learning. There is no *devatā*-worship; the focus is on the *ācārya*. After the reading from the Bhagavad-Gītā, *puṣpārcana* is done to Swamiji after which he gives a talk, *ātmavicāra* (discussion) attended by some inmates. Before lunch, the 15th chapter of the Bhagavad-Gītā is read. Lectures by Swamiji on the Bhagavad-Gītā and other scriptures are recorded and some of them are published in their magazine and books. The *āśram* celebrates only *gurupūrṇimā* as the only festival in the whole year.

Message to Householders

"They should understand and evaluate their role as householders wisely. All *āśrams* depend on the householders for support. All *saṁnyāsins/saṁnyāsinī*s and *brahmacārin*s originate in households. They should understand that they are the sea that supports the rivers of the different *āśrams*. The birth of a child is not an accident but an incident. The kind of thoughtful begetting of progeny and proper bringing up of children are lacking these days. A spirit of *vairāgya* should be instilled from early life. If there is a false *saṁnyāsin*, the blame should go to the parents. Undue possessiveness is harmful. After the children grow they should develop an idea of detachment and dis-identification. Your responsibility is till they grow up and become adults. After they become adults, leave them to themselves. You remain at a distance. Attachment is affinity, detachment is divinity."

Social Work

The āśramites led by Swamiji are involved in social work in the nearby villages by building houses for the poor and digging latrines where there is none, providing money to the needy for hospitalization, operation, etc. Wells are constructed in nearby villages where there is no water supply. They go to the villages and give rice to the very poor households and give clothes. 1,500 to 1,600 families are served every year. The main distribution is done in the main hall of the *āśram* with Vedic chants, *āratī*, etc. This is done in July every year.

Note: Maa Gurupriya is a *saṁnyāsinī* who was initiated by Swamiji when she was about 50 years old. She has a PhD in physics. She was inclined spiritually from an early age. She worked in University of Delhi as a lecturer. She and her husband (Naya Swamiji), who was working as Professor at a leading engineering institution, both took *saṁnyāsa* from Swamiji and joined his *āśram* in Kerala about six years ago (recorded in 2000). They have been taking a very active part in all activities of the *āśram* and they also very often travel with Swamiji.

SWAMI ADVAITANANDA

Background

Swami Advaitananda is an independent Swami who has started his own organization to spread Vedic, Vedāntic knowledge and spiritual activities. He hails from Maharashtra. He was born of brāhmaṇa parents. "I chose this path because my *pravṛtti* was ādhyātmic right from age five. Even as a child I was involved in singing *bhajanas* and *kīrtanas*. My uncle was a religious saint and used to worship Bhagvān Viṭṭhal. He and other saints had a great influence on me. I had a serious quarrel with my father about my education. I left my house wandering around Anandi and Pandharpur as I lost interest in my family." At an early age he joined the Dwarkari Sikshan Samstha in Jalandi near Pune. It is here he read the life stories of most of the saints of Maharashtra like Jñāneśvara, Tukārāma, Nāmdeva and Eknātha.

He narrated how his life as a *saṁnyāsin* began: "After seven years of study and obtaining an in-depth understanding of famous saints, I had a desire to learn more about our culture. I went to Rishikesh and obtained an education in Pūrva-Mīmāṁsā and Uttara-Mīmāṁsā. In Varanasi I specialized in Vedānta especially in Śaṅkara's Advaita Vedānta and received the degrees of Śāstrī and Ācārya. In 1973 I received *saṁnyāsa dīkṣā* from Mahāmaṇḍaleśvar Ganeshanand Giri. This was 25 years ago and I am now 54. Since then I am engaged in teaching Vedānta and serving the needy. I belong to the Nirañjanī Akhāḍā. In the recent Kuṁbha Melā at Haridwar I was given the title Mahāmaṇḍaleśvara."

Saṁnyāsa

He defined a *saṁnyāsin* as: "One who is detached from worldly affairs and focuses on attaining *mokṣa*, is a *saṁnyāsin*. He treads the path of *mokṣa* by worshipping and meditating on the *nirguṇa nirākāra brahmatattva*. Learning Śāstras and Śrutis, and through *śravaṇa*, *manana* and *nididhyāsana*, he wants to merge with Brahman by following the Advaitic philosophy. His goal is none other than *mokṣa*. It is the attainment of eternal bliss after realizing the world which is transitory and full of sorrow." This was followed by a short exposition of the philosophy of Advaita.

He continued: "In this order we are not allowed to marry. It is not necessary that one should be a *brahmacārin* to become a *saṁnyāsin*. A householder can become if he is detached from the world. In order to tread the path of *mokṣa* it is necessary to be a *saṁnyāsin. Brahmacarya* and *gr̥hasthāśramas* are for *karma-niṣṭha,* and *vānaprastha* and *saṁnyāsa* are for *jñāna-niṣṭha. Vānaprastha* nowadays is both present and absent. In olden days there was not much population, so people could go to the jungle and build a hut and live there. So, when there is no conjugal relationship with your spouse and one is not very much attached to the children and always meditates on God's name, associating with learned people and detaching oneself from the world — then these are the qualifications for the *vānaprasthāśrama. Gr̥hasthāśrama* signifies child rearing, accumulating wealth, performing *yajñas* or partaking in religious activities, taking care of guests, serving the needy, etc. When you detach yourself from the world, and realize that this world is transitory, destructible and false, then whether he is a *gr̥hastha* or a *brahmacārī* or at the *vānaprastha* stage he is eligible for attaining Paramātmā."

Different types of Saṁnyāsins

He then went on to describe the different types of *saṁnyāsins*. "There are four types of *saṁnyāsins — bahūdaka, kuṭīcaka* (*kuṭicara*), *haṁsa* and *paramahaṁsa. Bahūdaka* is a *parivrājaka,* always roaming around the world. He teaches people by example about the righteous way. The *kuṭīcaka* serves by giving *satsaṅgas*. By staying in one place he is absorbed in God. *Haṁsa* is a *yogī par excellence.* He is always looking inwards to become self-realized. He has given up other *karmas. Paramahaṁsa saṁnyāsa* is analogous to a *jīvanmukta.* In his *dr̥ṣti* (sight) all are the same. He has no more interest in any activity. Both *haṁsa* and *paramahaṁsa* do not play any role in society. We fall under the category of *bahūdaka* and *kuṭīcaka.* We build *āśrams* and do rituals, give inspiration to people by either scriptural reading or by going out on pilgrimage. So we try to make people follow the path of spirituality. You choose the stage you like among the four."

"Although detached from society, the last two, *haṁsa* and *paramahaṁsa,* still contribute to the welfare of the society through their *ādhyātmika śakti. Bahūdaka* and *kuṭīcaka,* through dhārmic means and service, bring awareness among people and make them tread the path of spirituality. So whichever stage one chooses they all are for the welfare of the society. Some *saṁnyāsins* run hospitals and schools, etc., for societal upliftment. But we serve by disseminating spiritual knowledge through discourses on Upaniṣads, Brahmasūtras and other texts to students and the public. You cannot quantify our efforts as you do by measuring wealth, status, etc. These are not considered achievements by us. For us attainment of peace, happiness and detachment from the world through spiritual upliftment can be categorized as success."

Change in Oneself as a Saṁnyāsin

In answer to the question whether there was any change in himself after adopting *saṁnyāsa* he said: "Yes, both in myself and in others. I have noticed the change within myself over the years. If somebody dies, I accept it with a tranquil mind. If I feel pain in my body, I see it as pain caused to the body and not in me. The body is undergoing pain due to its *karma* and I am the witness. Enduring pain we do not blame anyone. Societal upliftment is our goal. But we are not in control to change the society, although we show the society the right path. Whatever one does is due to his accumulated *karma*. If failure is destined for you, you will undergo that *karma* no matter whatever you may do, nobody can change that. We are neither overjoyed nor feel sorrow for anything, we only do our job."

Saṁnyāsin and Society

How does the society perceive the role of a *saṁnyāsin*, is the question put to Swamiji. Here is the answer: "Hinduism is a Vedic culture, and the *āśram*s are the nuclei of this culture. It is the foundation for a Hindu irrespective of his caste. One can have a positive or a negative opinion about a saṁnyāsin's role, but the ultimate goal of a Hindu is to realize the absolute truth. I do not think a Hindu will reject a *saṁnyāsin*, based on my experience."

General Information

Swamiji has three *āśram*s, in Delhi, Rajasthan and Hardwar. Regular morning and evening *satsaṅga*s are held everyday. He has appointed administrators to run these *āśram*s efficiently. Up to 30 people come daily, some are *yātrī*s on pilgrimage. He will write down who his successor will be and a committee will finally select him. The committee is responsible to carry out the objectives of the *āśram* as laid down by Swamiji. "Nowadays there is a decline" said Swamiji when asked about the position of the *saṁnyāsins*.

"People's objectives are different, like making money, status, etc.; however, I would not say that all *saṁnyāsins* are the same. It is not the fault of the *saṁnyāsin* but the society in general and *gṛhasthāśrama* in particular. If this *gṛhasthāśrama* is crooked, all other *āśramas* are also affected by this. If there is a radical change in *gṛhasthāśrama*, then everything can be set right. When mother and father are on the wrong path, how can you dream that the children can be on the right path?"

Success of Āśram

"The success of the *āśram* is not dependent on the head, but on each and every individual's aims and dedication towards the betterment of society. If we don't mingle with people, give love to people, then they won't come. You see most of the daily proceedings do not take place without money. For example, if 100 people come over and I have only two rooms, then how can I accommodate 100. If out of 100 one is willing to offer some money, then in the *āśram* instead of two rooms, we can have four rooms. So, that way the purpose of the *āśram* is to serve the society better. Here the head of the organization counts. I have totally surrendered to God. I am an Advaitin, but I also believe in *Īśvara*. With His will and by mingling with people with love, we will be able to run this *āśram* successfully."

Women Saṁnyāsinīs

There are no *saṁnyāsinīs* in the *āśram*. Swamiji has no objection giving *dīkṣā* to one if she is detached from the world. "In fact I have not given *saṁnyāsa* yet to anyone" he says. "Even *guru-mantra* I teach for those who have been associated with me for more than six years, and only then I make him my disciple. I don't make anybody and everybody my disciple. I see that my objectives have some place in the scriptures, and I stick to them. Giving *saṁnyāsa* depends on a person's conduct. If a person is capable of following in the foot steps of his *guru*, only then will he receive *dīkṣā*, otherwise not. There is a three day ritual for giving *saṁnyāsa* in this *āśram*."

Rituals

"I do not believe in rituals. I am a Vedāntist. From the viewpoint of life, I preach to do *dharma*, but from God's viewpoint I consider *karma* as a transitory object. When I am within the social context, then I have no problem of performing *pūjā*. Then how can I preach not to do *pūjā*? So, if we do, our neighbours do, and our kids do which are all for the welfare of the society. Opening schools and hospitals, etc., are acceptable from society's viewpoint and not from a saṁnyāsin's. *Saṁnyāsin* is one aspect of society, so, in order to expand the society if a *saṁnyāsin* does that, it is like respecting one aspect of God. I will not just encourage, but actually do it."

General Information

"I am against publications. Because if I publish but do not practice, what is the use? By publications the ego is built-up, that's why I am against that. I go to Delhi during July and August, and in June to Hardwar, in September or April to Hanumangarh and rest of the time in Bombay. I have no objection going abroad as the sea is part of the universe, hence part of God." He explained his wearing stitched clothes as: "Robe is a mere thing. There is no impact of the robe on the *saṁnyāsin*. If a person wore a single cloth yet is full of anger, greed and attachment, then I would not consider that person a *saṁnyāsin*. I never went into the area of community service. *Sevā* is an aspect of God. It is an antidote to anger and ego, I am not against that."

SWAMI RANGANATHANANDA

Swami Ranganathananda was the President of the Ramakrishna Mission when I interviewed him in January 2000 at Belur Math, Calcutta. Swamiji was the recipient of a number of honours throughout the world including the Gandhi Peace Prize and the Indira Gandhi National Integration Prize. His publications are numerous and they are read worldwide, translated into many languages. He has had dialogues with famous scientists and spiritual leaders as well as political leaders, all along spreading the message of spirituality as advocated by Sri Ramakrishna Paramahamsa and Swami Vivekananda. He was born in Trichur, Kerala and joined the Mission in 1908. Thereafter he served the Mission in many capacities as a dishwasher, housekeeper, warden, librarian, secretary, head of many of the *āśrams* in many places like Rangoon (in erstwhile Burma), Karachi (now in Pakistan) and in many places in India, and eventually became its President.

The interview began with how he would define a *saṁnyāsin*. A *saṁnyāsin* is one who serves the people with dedication, he said. His

6. Swami Ranganathananda, Belur Math, Kolkata

goal is *mokṣa* which is realization of one's self (*ātman*) which is freedom from *saṁsāra*. While the old *saṁnyāsa* ideal as exemplified by Śaṅkarācārya was to serve householders to realize their spiritual nature, the new saṁnyāsin's role as defined by Swami Vivekananda is *ātmano mokṣārtham jagaddhitāya ca* (to work simultaneously for one's *mokṣa* and welfare of all humanity). In other words it is the service of God in human form that is the core of a saṁnyāsin's life according to him. To that end the running of schools, hospitals and other charitable organizations are well within the scope of a saṁnyāsin's life.

Swamiji responded to the question whether *saṁnyāsin*s should take interest in politics: "Any service is good and if politicians can serve truthfully their cause, there is no harm for a politician-*saṁnyāsin* to do so."

Saṁnyāsa can also be the objective of a householder, he added. In fact, he attaches a lot of importance to the householder whom he advises to give up the depressing feeling that "we are *saṁsārin*s or worldly people. Live in *saṁsāra*, or the world, but don't allow *saṁsāra*, worldliness, consisting of selfishness and exploitation and pettiness, to live in you." This is the teaching of Sri Ramakrishna and Swami Vivekananda. He told me to look up his booklet on the "Spiritual Life of the Householder" where he had expanded on his view of the householder. Swamiji calls a *gṛhastha* as a citizen of the country he/she belongs to in modern terminology. Such a one can be called a true citizen of his country only when he/she feels a sense of social responsibility along with freedom to act for the welfare of all. And that was the message which Swami Vivekananda preached. When *gṛhastha*s are imbued with a sense of responsibility and act with freedom selflessly to change the face of the country, this nation of ours will become a proud nation in the world, he says in the booklet.

One came away with the feeling that Swamiji was agonizing over the fate of the country where poverty and illiteracy were still looming large. In his view both *saṁnyāsin*s and *gṛhastha*s have to work selflessly towards the amelioration of these evils when the true culture of India for which she was renowned can be re-established.

SWAMI GOKULANANDA

At the time of the interview Swamiji was heading the Ramakrishna Mission Ashram in New Delhi. Swamiji had done his post graduation in philosophy from Calcutta University. While at the university, in February 1947, he came into contact with one of the great Swamis of the order, Swami Siddhesvarananda, who was the head of the Vedānta centre near Paris. He was at the time studying in the Christian Missionary College in Sri Rampur in West Bengal. As the secretary of the College Union, he thought it would be a good idea to invite this Paris Swami to the college, and did so. Swami Siddhesvarananda came and spoke on the "Influence of Ramakrishna and Vivekananda in modern times." While going back Swamiji told him, "You should organize such functions from time to time and go to the place of Ramakrishna for *sādhanā*." He was thus introduced to the Ramakrishna world and started reading "Letters of Vivekananda," "Life of Vivekananda," "Lectures from Colombo," etc. Vivekananda's statements on the conquest of the lower self by the higher self and the impermanence of life, etc., made him ponder over his future and he decided to take his *mantra-dīkṣā* in 1948 from Swami Virajananda, the then president of the Mission. He then took up a job in the Karimganj College in Assam. There he decided to devote himself to the search of the self and on 16 June 1954, he joined the Ramakrishna Mission and after nine years of training in various capacities was initiated into *saṁnyāsa* in 1963 by Swami Madhavanandaji.

Defining a Saṁnyāsin

Swamiji started with defining who a *saṁnyāsin* is: "A *saṁnyāsin* is one who has realized the impermanent characteristics of everything mundane. He is convinced that anything earthly cannot give permanent peace and happiness. The goal of human life is to attain liberation and preferably while in this life itself, become a *jīvanmukta*. For that one has to renounce the world and take up *saṁnyāsa*. We belong to the Daśanāmī Saṁnyāsa Sampradāya started by Ādi Śaṅkarācārya. We belong to the Purī lineage after Totha Purī, Ramakrishna's *guru*." As to the question whether married persons were eligible for *saṁnyāsa* in his order, he said: "In olden days, some of the direct disciples of Ramakrishna who were married were allowed to take up *saṁnyāsa*. For instance Swami Sivananda and Swami Yogananda were married. These may be exceptions. Nowadays I don't think it is allowed and the present-day trainees whom I come across are not married. After taking up *saṁnyāsa* one has to stay away from one's family but there is no bar from meeting the near and dear ones. We *saṁnyāsins* have a role to play in society.

We maintain a balance in society. If all follow the path of enjoyment, the world will be destroyed. Thus *saṁnyāsa* is a balancing force and we serve as guides to peace, happiness and contentment. For this people seek the company of *sādhus*."

Motto of the Mission

The motto of the Ramakrishna Mission is, *ātmano mokṣārtham jagaddhitāya ca* and is also the goal of *saṁnyāsa* in this order. Swami Vivekananda who coined this motto was so instructed by his *guru* Ramakrishna Paramahamsa, who chastized him for being selfish when he asked for permission to seek his own salvation. So it has to be not merely for one's *mokṣa* but for the welfare of the world. Vivekananda was told, "Try to see Brahman in everybody with eyes open to the illiterate, to the downtrodden. Know that service is the highest religion." Swami Gokulananda and other Swamis of the mission follow this instruction in their dealings with the public. He therefore has become a counseller to the devotees of his centre. He gave some instances of how this intervention helped some people resolve peacefully their family problems without seeking legal help.

Activities and other Information

"We have a youth wing and every Sunday some young people come and study some books under the guidance of a monk. They may or may not join the mission as monks but the aim is to make them become responsible citizens." Answering the question as to whether a *saṁnyāsin* is respected in society and by individuals he said, "The *saṁnyāsin* is still respected particularly in the north. In the north we have a tradition; when mother cooks food she keeps a portion aside for any *mahātmā* who may drop in. In Uttarkashi they say 'Swami Om' and not *namaskāra* or *maharāja*. They have a great regard for us. They are benefited by our guidance so they give donations." How about the West? "You see I went to the Benedictine Monastery in Rome. They wanted to have a dialogue with me. They wanted to know about my routine which I narrated to them in detail and they listened. They appreciate our leading a life of celibacy as they also do. I have been to Cleveland and other places. There is a great demand for our literature in Sanskrit and other languages. I can say with my personal experience that the West has a favourable view of Hindu *saṁnyāsins*."

Daily Routine

"I get up at 4 a.m. From 4 a.m. to 7 a.m. I have my own way, then after breakfast it is *karmayoga*, after evening I will be studying my scriptures. So it is an integrated yoga (*saṁnyāsa-yoga*) — *karma, jñāna, bhakti* and *rājayoga*. Morning we practice *rājayoga*: communion with God, the path of psychic control. Then we do *sevā*. In the leisure hours, we keep up our *vicāra* (contemplation) constantly. Everyday we come across many people, and we have this attitude that you are an *ātman* and anybody coming in contact with us is also *ātman*, 'worship of the spirit by the spirit.' Whatever you do you do it not with drudgery but with devotion and love. In any Ramakrishna Mission publication you will find the emblem of a coiled serpent, that is *kuṇḍalinī śakti*, the infinite power that lies dormant in us which can be aroused up in order to have the vision of *paramātman*. In the emblem there is a rising sun which stands for knowledge, a lotus which stands for devotion and watery waves stand for *karma*. It is nothing other than the synthesis of all the four yogas."

Success and Leadership

Swamiji is confident that he has been successful in carrying out the principles of the Mission in practice. "I have been here for the last six years. My role is to stress purity of character and devotion to God amongst all those who choose to come here. Even if you are in *saṁsāra* (the world), you have to lead a life of detachment, *īśvarānurāga* (love for *Īśvara*) and *anāsakti* (detachment). We also stress respect for all religions and *sevā*."

In answer to the question as to how effectively the *āśram* had discharged its perceived objectives, he said: "So far as the religious aspects are concerned we have ceremonial functions, initiations, discourses, prayers, spiritual retreats to cater to the large devotees to satisfy their religious and spiritual needs. A homoeopathic dispensary, a TB clinic, a mobile dispensary, a diagnostic centre and all such socially oriented programmes are effectively run for the benefit of the citizens of Delhi. Spiritually they get counselling, they learn to meditate, they also get benefits through different activities, not just social activities, but all types of activities because 'work is worship.' All this is in accordance with what Swami Vivekananda intended or rather Ramakrishna had instructed Swamiji. So he (Vivekananda) used to say: 'I am not telling

7. Swami Gokulananda, Ramakrishna Mission

you, it is Sri Ramakrishna who is speaking through me.' There was one Swamiji called Akhandanandaji who said: 'Put away meditation till the next flight. If you work for others you will be liberated right now.' So, in the Swamis of Ramakrishna Mission you will find a rare combination of work and contemplation."

Much depends on the head of the *āśram* for the success or failure of the *āśram* he said. He is the captain of the ship. If the captain gives the right leadership, then it is great. He has to get the co-operation from the members and he has to see that everyone follows his/her routine, take care of their personal need and spiritual life. It is a concerted action, not an individual one. One also has to get co-operation from lay devotees. Swami Vivekananda inaugurating the first meeting of the Mission in 1897 said, "We have left home in the name of Ramakrishna, you also saw Ramakrishna. We are going to start an organization in his name, you should come forward to serve the world." He went on to say that there were about 1600 *saṁnyāsin*s all over the world, and many more (lakhs) of householder devotees. He pointed out that in the Mission there are (women) *saṁnyāsinī*s, who also have their Sarada Mission and they follow the same structural pattern as their male counterpart. They also run hospitals, orphanages, etc., and have their own *maṭha*s both in India and abroad. The first order of nuns was created by Belur Math. The first *saṁnyāsinī* of Sarada Math was initiated by the then president Shankaranandaji. After that they themselves initiate their *saṁnyāsinī*s. Swamiji mentioned that there were also many foreigners as *saṁnyāsin*s in the Mission. In San Francisco and in Santa Barbara there were also nuns.

Administrative Information

A board of trustees runs the affairs of the entire Ramakrishna Mission with nineteen members. If there is vacancy at the head, they circulate one or two names generally between the ages 45 and 55. At present Swami Ranganathanandaji has been selected as the president. There is a general secretary whose term is for two years and again at the end of his tenure they select another. "I was in Arunachal Pradesh. A monk from Berkeley was sent there. He found it difficult to cope in that place. He was there for only eight months! I wanted to leave for six months as I wanted to go on a pilgrimage and do some *tapasyā*. But I was not allowed to go. I waited for two months and was wondering why I was not allowed to go. You come down to Belur Math they said. Meanwhile in Cherapunji one monk was selected and after only five months, he died of heart failure. So I was posted to Cherapunji."

"We are independent of the government," he said answering questions on administration. "Only when we apply for any grants have we to follow their rules and regulations. For instance for the Cherapunji centre we got 100 per cent grant for schools, buses and all that. We have ten *saṁnyāsins* in this (Delhi) *āśram* looking after the administration. For the initiation ceremony of *saṁnyāsins* in India, the President or the Vice President of the Mission comes. For Europe generally the head of the individual *āśram* is appointed to give initiation."

Moving on to finances he said: "We depend on donations to finance our organization. Sometimes we do get anxious and we have practically no grants. When I took over, I started an endowment system to look after our clinics, etc." In answer to the question of checks and balances for keeping out unwanted persons in the *āśram* he said: "To ensure proper functioning of the *āśram* and to get rid of unwanted elements, we do the following. If someone does not live his life correctly and we have reports that he has gone off the tracks, we ask for an explanation. Some monks may say they are on the right track and there can be difference of opinion. He may voluntarily leave the order. Some monks indeed have left the order. There are others who do not believe that the trustees have a right to expel. So there are legal complications. We write to them explaining the reasons why we will take action to remove them. Ramakrishna Mission is very strict. There are cases where their names have been removed from the register and some have left on their own. However there are not many cases."

Mokṣa

Explaining *mokṣa* Swamiji said: "The truth is that, we are all bascially, eternal free. We are *śuddha Caitanya*. But because of cosmic illusion, because of superimposition of name and form, we are not conscious of our divine heritage. Each one is *nitya, śuddha, buddha* and *mukta*. If there are clouds, the sun is hidden, but it is still shining. The *ātman* is *svayam prakāśa*, self-shining. We do not realize it, we have only to remove the clouds of ignorance and impurities. For that I have joined this order. We wrongly identify ourselves with name and form. You look at me as I have got a male body and you have got a female body. You are a householder and I am a monk. These are all superimpositions. The same *ātman* is in us all. Through *sādhanā* one can realize this truth and attain this stage in this very life and transcend the limitations of psycho-physical existence. A *saṁnyāsin* is one who lives on the plane of *ātman*, one who does not live in this physical plane and mental plane. He is a true *saṁnyāsin*. On initiation there is a *havan* and the ritual vow is "I am neither this body *svāhā*, I am *śuddha caitanya svāhā* — from Mahānārāyaṇa Upaniṣad. He gives up *loka-eṣaṇā, vitta-eṣaṇā, putra-eṣaṇā* and *sarva-eṣaṇā*; all desires are given up."

Message to Householders

The message to householders is that they should live a disciplined life as Sri Ramakrishna said: "After one or two children one should live like brother and sister. Householder's life itself is an *āśrama*. If one is married and has children, but if one goes on living like an animal going after sense enjoyments, then the real path of self-realization will be unfulfilled. There should be self-control. They should do Nārāyaṇa-*sevā, atithi sevā*. Children should be brought up in the right atmosphere and the parents should set an example for the children to follow. The householder's life is more important than a saṁnyāsin's as it is from the householder's family that *saṁnyāsin*s come. So from good householders come good monks."

Rituals

Swamiji added that they observe rituals in the *āśram*. "There are different stages in *saṁnyāsa* and some *saṁnyāsin*s do not need them as they have reached the highest stage. But most of the *saṁnyāsin*s are not at the highest stage of a *jñānin* and ordinary *saṁnyāsin*s take the help of rituals to outgrow rituals. *Āratī, bhajana*, etc., are done in the *āśram*. As Swami Vivekananda said, 'one should be born in a church but one should not die in a church.' Rituals have their effect. Even festivals have their effect. On Ramakrishna's birthday we go round the temple singing *bhajana*s; I give *arghyam* saying *namo bhagavate rāmakr̥ṣṇāya svāhā* and that has a purifying effect."

"As part of our *sevā* we run schools, hospitals, colleges and orphanages. During Nārāyaṇa-*sevā* we help with medicines, blankets, money, especially during time of famine, drought and floods. We publicize through the media, through our annual reports, etc. I am also invited very often for inter-faith conferences here and abroad. I have visited Montreal, Helsinki, etc., to attend international peace conferences. This 30 January I visited Birla House and the *āśramites* recited the Bhagavad-Gītā. We wear the common ochre robes and there is no *tilaka*. Some of our south Indian monks put *vibhūti* after bath."

Mission Hierarchy

"Our supreme spiritual head is our president. There are two vice-presidents. Then there is a general secretary, and he is administratively helped by four assistant secretaries. There is a treasurer to look after the finances and there are trustees. These are controlling bodies from Belur Math who do the postings, transfers and all that. Here I am the head. I have an assistant secretary; in some places there is a monastic assistant secretary but here he is a householder. I have a treasurer. I have one monk in-charge of the TB clinic. I have one monk in-charge of the library. I am totally responsible for this centre and have full freedom to run the centre. I started the Cherapunji centre and it is engaged in good work in helping tribal welfare. In the school run by the Mission we give job-oriented education, bee-keeping, carpentry, computer and many other courses; it is a co-educational institution. There is a girl's hostel a little away from Cherapunji. We have a number of books in Khāsī language."

"The Christian missionaries tell the Khāsīs, you have no religion and therefore you go to hell. This is not good. We tell them that you have a religion of your own. You stick to your faith. We have Christian teachers and students, boys and girls. Our door is open to all; there are some who come from abroad and they try to preach something which may have some denaturalizing effect. But, during the few years that I stayed there, I came across a number of very liberal Christians and they helped us a lot. Professor G.D. Swell, who died the other day, Deputy Speaker of Lok Sabha, was a product of the Ramakrishna Mission, Cherapunji. He would say Cherapunji is my second home." And the interview ended on that positive note.

SWAMI DAYATMANANDA

Background

The Ramakrishna Ashram in the United Kingdom is situated near

London and is headed by Swami Dayatmananda. As a young boy, Swamiji was deeply impacted by reading biographies of Sri Ramakrishna and Swami Vivekananda. Swamiji recounts his early life: "Then I wanted to study medicine. I joined the first year, I didn't like to continue, so I ran away from home because my parents would not agree and then I joined the Ramakrishna Mission at Hardwar. Later on I happened to come to Delhi and we have a procedure. They send us to the training centre for two years. Then I was posted to Cherapunji and I took *saṁnyāsa* in 1973. I joined in 1963 and ten years later I was a *saṁnyāsin*. Swami Yudhistharananda initiated me. He was the vice-president then. After that I happened to go to Hyderabad for some months and then I was transferred to Bangalore where I stayed from 1974 to 1991. Later, in the *āśram*, I assisted Swami Bhavyananda. He was my predecessor. He passed away in 1993, then I was asked to take charge."

Do you have any definite views as to why you really joined? Swamiji gave his views: "The only thing I wanted to say is that I wanted to realize God. If that was my aim, then there is no point in getting married or in continuing studies. Better to use that time for spiritual practices. In Hinduism, we say man just doesn't decide suddenly; previous *saṁskāra*s must have been that. These incidents are only accidental, just happened and I strongly felt that I should join Ramakrishna order."

Who is a Saṁnyāsin?

"A *saṁnyāsin* is one who has no desire for worldly life, he has dedicated himself to God, and that is the simplest and the best definition. In Ramakrishna order those who are married are not allowed. They should have minimum qualification, at least matriculation. And they should not be beyond 25 years of age. A minimum of 30 if they are more qualified. We give a little allowance. After 30 it is virtually impossible to join. We join as *brahmacārins*. For women there is a separate organization called Sharada Math. We have nothing to do with that, excepting that the ideals are the same. But money-wise, legally and otherwise, they are a completely different organization. We have a form to fill that asks about the person's health, how many children your parents have, etc. If it is only one son, then we don't want that person to join, unless the parents come and say that they don't mind the son joining the *āśram*. Our philosophy is that, if it is one child, he should look after his parents. You see we are not against married people."

"The purpose of this organization is to serve society. The motto that Swami Vivekananda has given is realization of one's own self and also serving the world. If we have to serve the world, if an old man joins, he will be a burden to the order, we have to serve him instead of serving the people. That is the main idea. We belong to Śaṅkarācārya's Daśanāmī Sampradāya. Our spiritual *maṭha* is called Sringeri Math. Śaṅkarācārya established this monastic order. Incidentally this is the second monastic order. The first one was started by the Buddha — the Buddhist monastic order, the Saṅgha. In fact, Buddha's teachings are mainly meant for the *saṁnyāsins*, not for householders. Of course, he also encouraged everyone to lead a good life. Śaṅkarācārya established the four *maṭhas* in four corners of the country. He also created ten orders — *puri, giri, bhāratī, sarasvatī, tīrtha, araṇya, āśrama, vana, parvata* and *sāgara*. We are all followers of Śaṅkarācārya. These are the names meant to be given to *saṁnyāsins* at the time of taking *saṁnyāsa*. These are divided among the four *maṭhas*. Sri Ramakrishna's *guru* was Totapuri. So he belonged to the Purī Sampradāya. *Saṁnyāsa* means you give up all ties. At the time of initiation, we perform our *śrāddhas* as though we are dead to the world. Then only we are given *saṁnyāsa*. Saṁnyāsins do visit homes but only if they are invited. We have no rights over property; we are not allowed to have any personal property. For example, if the parents say this is your portion, we say, give it to the Ramakrishna Mission."

Saṁnyāsin in Society

How do you perceive the role of a *saṁnyāsin* in society? "Without *saṁnyāsins* I think the society will degenerate. There is no doubt about it. First of all, a *saṁnyāsin* can give encouragement to any spiritual aspirant. Many people aspire to be without *sāṁsārika* bondage but they may not have the courage. A *saṁnyāsin* stands as an example for such people. He is a happy person even though he is not a married person. This is a direct challenge to many of these so-called pseudo scientists who say that if a man is not fulfilled in certain ways, then he lives a morose or useless type of life. The sincere *saṁnyāsins* are also authorities of the principles enunciated in the scriptures so that they are able to instruct others about the necessity of striving towards the spiritual goal of self-realization. As he is leading the right kind of life, he is able to instruct people that there is a life superior to worldly life. While some religions do not have the monastic way of life, Hinduism emphasizes that *saṁnyāsa* is the ultimate goal of every Hindu. Whether he attains it or not is a different matter. But as an ideal it is there."

"To interpret the scriptures you need authoritative persons. Such authority is vested due to traditional sanction in the person of the *saṁnyāsin*. Scriptural truths cannot be understood by intellectuals, they can only be intuited. There may be pundits but you will not go to them for any doubts on spirituality. You will have to approach a reputed *saṁnyāsin* who is a complete renouncer. He is true to himself, that is what makes a *saṁnyāsin* different from a worldly person. Ramakrishna said that true *saṁnyāsa* is mental renunciation and not external renunciation. While external things like robes, etc., are also necessary to mark a *saṁnyāsin*, when I go out in public I put on pants, etc., as I don't want to be stared at; I want to be at peace and this way nobody notices who I am!"

Saṁnyāsin as Counsellor

"As the *saṁnyāsin* is the spiritual leader, he is approached for solutions of a spiritual nature when encountered with problems. For instance, a woman during periods is not supposed to be active in anything. In a country like England where she is to fend for the family, has a working husband, school going children, etc., she cannot but do house work; otherwise there will be a breakdown in the family. Our advice would be, "mentally you keep yourself clean and keep on thinking about God and physically keep on doing whatever you can." Such a solution is in accordance with Ramakrishna's practical way of looking at scripture. A man comes and tells that he cannot do *Gāyatrī Mantra* for one hour, but he wants a solution so that there is no transgression. If he goes to a priest, he will say you will go to hell. "But if he comes to me, I will tell him to keep his mind on God and repeat the *mantra* for as many times as he can. He is satisfied and he knows that he is not transgressing. This is the type of solution the society is looking for from *saṁnyāsins*."

"We undertake philanthropic works in India during floods, famine, etc. Our monks know better than contractors as to what types of houses are better and built cheaply for these people. In 1976 when there were floods in Andhra, the Mission Swamis found prefabricated concrete blocks for constructing houses. With these well-laid-out houses with kitchen, dining hall, etc., were prepared. Swamis are good not only for spiritual matters but in many practical aspects also for the benefit of the society."

General Information

"We have achieved here in the *āśram* many of our objectives, through the propagation of our religion, through our philosophy and by maintenance of this particular place. There is a beautiful shrine here, congregational facilities, publications, books, etc. People, when they come, they think it is a calm and peaceful place. The very atmosphere gives peace of mind. Here we emphasize that there is no peace of mind without spiritual discipline. You may have material things but they are all temporary. We conduct worship to Ramakrishna. We tell people that, according to Hinduism, God can be worshipped in many forms and names. We also do Kṛṣṇāṣṭamī, Rāmanavamī, etc., all Hindu festivals. We do it ourselves and not through a priest. That is yoga, not what one does but what it does to us."

"We do regular counselling to our devotees which gives consolation if not spiritual benefits. The success in spiritual efforts cannot be measured. All that we can say is that a lot of people are coming to us, and they are sincerely struggling and we help as much as we can. But I would say, in a Vedāntic way, all these people (the religious and spiritual workers) are rendering invaluable service to people. So there is a high regard for us *saṁnyāsin*s, both for our work to alleviate sufferings of people and also for the disciplined way of life we lead personally."

"The Ramakrishna Mission is also well regarded for the enormous publications it has produced on religion and philosophy, which is sought after and distributed throughout the world. Year after year the sale of this literature is going up even without any publicity and advertisement effort on our part. We sell about 25,000 pound sterling worth of books every year. Many also come here to read and take books from the library. We are highly respected here. They are not interested in our religion, but they know that the *saṁnyāsin*s are Vedāntic personnel and they have to be respected." There are cases of protests against other faiths being given shelter here in England, but there had been nothing against us. If you come to Mayden Haven and you say to the taxi fellow that you want to go to the Vedānta Centre, he will bring you here. Everyone in the town knows where we are situated. One very noticeable thing — whenever the government has problem concerning Hinduism, they

8. Swami Dayatmananda

write to us. They say: Write to Vedānta Centre, and whatever reply they give that would be the authority.

"Here we are registered as a charity under the Charity Act. Because ours is a public building we have to follow government rules concerning fire hazards, roads, etc. Internally there are regulations and adjustments for local requirements and practical needs. Some of these have already been made and I have added to them. Each affiliated centre of our mission is completely independent. Our governing body consisting of local devotees meets three or four times a year to look after finances, administration, etc. A maximum of fourteen members along with me make collective decisions. Funds are raised locally and devotees from all over give donations. We have permanent funds and these are kept in shares. Disciplinary measures are in place and they are implemented."

West and its Perception of a Saṁnyāsin

Regarding the Western perception of a *saṁnyāsin* he said: There are only two types of monks in the West, one is Catholic and the other is Buddhist apart from our Hindu monks. So Catholic monks are absolutely like Indian monks, in all the strictness, the only difference is in the ideal. They believe in Christ, they believe in dualism which is what our Rāmānuja and Madhva Sampradāyas believe in. The only difference is in the concept of goal. But insofar as the life a monk is supposed to live, there is no difference either in the Buddhist monk or a Christian monk. As people know a monk is a spiritual person, all monks are respected irrespective of who they are, Christian, Buddhist or Hindu. We have some *brahmacārins* here in this order. We are training them according to our standards. All are Westerners, excepting one.

"As a policy, we do not allow any Indian to join in the West. If he is a Hindu, he must join in India. We send them gradually to Belur Math for training and *brahmacarya dīkṣā*. We accept anyone who is sincere and wants to realize God. So people see this plurality of Hinduism which is our philosophy. More and more people are coming to join the Mission, though not in large numbers. Vedānta and Ramakrishna do not attract huge members in the West, because we are not charismatic leaders like Sai Baba. When Swami Vivekananda used the word Vedānta, he used it in the sense of real Hinduism which was universal and not sectarian; the true spirit of the Vedas are the Upaniṣads.

Successor

The successor to the *āśram* is chosen by the headquarters at Belur Math There are about 150 official *āśrams* affiliated to the order and there are thousands of unofficial ones. There is a difference with regard to the policy in India and here. In India any head can be transferred anytime. The trustees, general secretary and assistant secretary decide: "Because of the practical nature of our works, we are supposed to take six to ten years to be acquainted with the culture and language and how people think. So usually we don't transfer unless the Swami himself says that he doesn't want to stay here. Then the head himself will select a Swami. The policy is usually when a Swami becomes old and asks for an assistant to train so that they can take over responsibilities. The headquarters suggest names of younger monks for training for two or three years to take over eventually. They are the world trustees and those are for the entire order. There are about fourteen or fifteen members in the controlling body. They recently selected Ranganathanandaji as president on the death of Bhuteshanandaji. There is no difference between the way in which a monk lives in India and here. Only external adjustments have to be made. We adapt to the local people, local climate and our own bodily necessities. But there is no difference otherwise."

Success and Leadership

"The success depends on many factors. But the most important factor, if the head of the centre is sincerely leading a holy life, that has an enormous impact. Apart from that, the people who are living with that person, if they co-operate that is, they also try to lead a holy life. The head person himself is necessary because everything depends on him and if the head is loose then everything tends to be loose. I, as the head, have to adjust to the personality and background of any visitor either Indian or one from here. For a Westerner I wouldn't be using many Vedāntic words. It would be non-technical, a general way. The ambience and atmosphere and behaviour of those responsible matter a lot. We cannot have lavish decorations with gold, etc., then they may think that we are not leading a strict monastic life. We have to talk to every one with dignity and tact. We try to balance. In that respect we don't try to be a monk under a tree. The shrine and surroundings are simple and serve our purpose. Our garden is well kept. It need not be super. We are in close contact with many of the inter-faith groups. They don't belong to our circle at all. But they know that Ramakrishna Mission monks are very good monks. So it would be a good thing to invite them for inter-faith meetings."

"I have given talks many times. In fact, I am going to Bucharest this Saturday to attend a three day peace conference. Our Mission is going to grow in strength. Apart from leading a good life, ideology should also be universal, non-sectarian and ready to welcome anybody and everybody. Ideology-wise this Ramakrishna Mission maintains an absolute purity of Vedānta. Although Advaita Vedānta which says give up everything and go to Himalayas and meditate, we are not that type, though our philosophy is Vedānta. We accept all paths."

He went on to describe the main characteristics of a *saṁnyāsin* and a householder as: "A *saṁnyāsin* should be impartial, must be truly and sincerely detached. All the energy of a monk is supposed to be dedicated to spiritual life, only to God. To the householders I would say you may not take formal *saṁnyāsa* but mentally you should lead a monk's life. The ancient message is that you all belong to God. You forget that and that is why you are all caught up in a mesh of *saṁsāra*. Try to lead slowly into a spiritual discipline. Try to realize your own true nature and try to be free, and that is basically *mokṣa*. We preach only ultimate liberation."

"In the Vedānta centres in the West, we don't encourage too much of Hindu festivals. But we keep some. People enjoy them. We have quiet singing and elegant ceremonies. We don't have any educational facilities. I travel a lot. There is a hierarchy with the president on top and a manager and different heads of the departments. Somebody looks after the *pūjā*. Someone to look after the accounts and so on. We get up in the morning and go to the shrine, meditate for two hours, then attend to some correspondence or take classes for the boys, meet with the visitors. A lot of correspondence and preparing for talks — these are our routine. Giving interviews and giving talks on Vedānta when invited and answering questions like abortion, divorce, euthanasia, which are frequently asked in these parts, beside the routine work at the *āśram*. We don't have community services. With Ramakrishna's grace, Rukmani, you came and I am very glad."

PARIVRAJIKA VIVEKAPRANA

Background

Parivrajika Vivekaprana belonged to Sarada Math of the Ramakrishna-Sarada Mission at New Delhi. She was 63 years at the time of the interview. She was originally from West Pakistan but had to come to India during Partition of the Indian subcontinent. She was attracted to the philosophy of Swami Vivekananda and joined the *maṭha* in 1963 and was given *saṁnyāsa* in 1975. She held a masters degree in philosophy and a bachelor's degree in teaching.

Saṁnyāsinī

A *saṁnyāsinī*, she defined, is one who is traditionally a person who has left her personal life in order to achieve *mokṣa*. Quoting Swami Vivekananda she continued: A *saṁnyāsinī* is one who in order to achieve personal freedom works for the society in general. That becomes the path of service and the personal endeavour to make the path a spiritual one. Drawing a distinction between social service by others and by *saṁnyāsin*s/*saṁnyāsinī*s she said "usually social service is done as a part time job or as an extension to one's main life, like a householder life or professional life. For us service is a path to personal liberation. For us, on the other hand, it is the main reason for being in society. We have no other reason, we have no relationships and we have no other personal lives either."

Some General Information

Marriage is not allowed in this Sangha. The girls who join at an early age do not marry at all. In the early stages, perhaps, there were cases where people joined after marriage. Some who joined were also probably widows. After taking *saṁnyāsa* what is enjoined is total renunciation and there is no contact with their families whatsoever. They follow the Ramakrishna Mission motto coined by Swami Vivekananda: *ātmano mokṣārtham jagaddhitāya ca* — Service to society becomes a spiritual path. There are centres all over and everyone who joins gets training and are employed in various activities. These activities are non-paying and are taken as the spiritual path. This is different from what Arjuna got as advice from Lord Kṛṣṇa, viz., keeping a personal life and living a spiritual life. "But ours is renouncing personal life and making the service

9. Pārivrājikā Vivekaprana, Sarada Math

of society as a spiritual path. You can say it is a new kind of *karmayoga*. But it is a little different from the one that is given in the Bhagavad-Gītā."

Everyday there is a time set-up for personal study, training and meditation. At the same time there is the usual routine which involves one in public activities and both have to be carried out side by side. This has been maintained from the very inception of the organization: "The very sense of having meaningful life is the way you judge whether it is successful or not. There is tremendous meaning in this life. It is a very hard life, it is not easy. It definitely gives you a sense of evolution and a sense of being useful to the society. It gives you personal satisfaction. The societal response is tremendous and is shown by the large number of requests we receive from all over India and even from the world at large."

Saṁnyāsinī in Society and Success of the Order

How does the society you live in view a *parivrājikā*? "I am afraid there is a lot of confusion today, because people are becoming less and less aware of *saṁnyāsāśrama*. I don't think there is any pointed desire to understand what we represent, but those who come in contact with us intimately — by attending our classes and becoming a part of this centre offering their service for society — view us with tremendous respect, regard and affection." Overall she felt the awareness regarding *saṁnyāsa* is increasing in society. She contrasted that with the Westerner's perception and said: "The Westerner is more conscious of what the Hindu *saṁnyāsin* represents than the Indians are. In India *saṁnyāsin*s are taken for granted. But in the West the response is single-pointed and focused and they connect with the spiritual work done by *saṁnyāsin*s. They expect the *saṁnyāsins*/*saṁnyāsinī*s to give them ideas connected with personal evolution as, in general, people who come in contact with *saṁnyāsin*s are looking for that personal evolution."

The head of any organization plays an important role and for this young organization in particular, a leader plays a large part in successfully galvanizing people for progress. It is very crucial and, therefore, the person who leads any centre has to have tremendous capacity for organizing, leading and guiding those who want to join towards the main objectives that the *maṭha* represents.

Management and Activities

There is a managing committee and a board of trustees. They choose the head depending upon the merit, qualifications and capacity of a candidate. There is no lifetime election. This organization is still in its formative period and has not become very rigid. Service and dissemination of the philosophy popularized by Swamiji (Swami Vivekananda) is the main function of this *āśram*. "Ladies from outside the set-up are chosen as members of the managing committees. Schools and colleges run by it are maintained by the fees charged. Donations keep the institutions going. Fortunately there is no dearth of funds. People come unexpectedly and volunteer funds. There is no outside, foreign income for the centre."

They practise and propagate spiritual methods based on the traditional yogas — *karmayoga*, *jñānayoga*, *bhaktiyoga* and *rājayoga*. However, since *rājayoga* is not practised scientifically nowadays, it is not being given much importance here. The other yogas are meticulously taught and followed by the *parivrājikā*s of the Sarada Math. Specific ancient scriptures — Upaniṣads, Brahmasūtras, Bhagavad-Gītā, lives of Ramakrishna and Vivekananda, etc., — are followed in great detail for teaching the students and aspirants. Instruction of Sanskrit takes place through somebody who knows the subject. Sometimes *puṇḍit*s are employed and those *parivrājikā*s who have undergone a thorough study of these subjects become the teachers for the next generation. Many colonies in the capital invite them for regular lectures and these talks are joined by both devotees and lay people who are interested in spiritual philosophy. "Every Saturday I take classes for youngsters. Now I am going to start teaching the Bhagavad-Gītā. Many come to the *āśram* to learn and there is a growing interest all around."

Women

There is a great need, she said, for people in general and women in particular, to understand their position in society by referring to their spiritual heritage. Society has changed to a great extent and now women have a special status and responsibility towards their families and others in society. It is very crucial that this awakening is canalized towards greater awareness of ethical, moral and spiritual education and pursuits. "I do not personally know any of the *saṁnyāsinī*s heading organizations. There is Daya Mata (a follower of Yogananda) I understand. But I know women have always been the guardians of culture and especially spiritual culture. Because they are mothers and they have to pass it on to the next generation. I will not be surprised if in future women do become leaders in spirituality. I think it is high time. They have to take up a new role, give a new turn, a new perspective."

Women may not have had this role as *saṁnyāsinī*s in the past, but modern-day *ācārya*s like Swami Vivekananda have given the lead in encouraging women to come forward and plunge into the spiritual field. This movement is a unique kind of movement in the world and bound to succeed. "We are not obliged to any other outside authority — spiritual or secular to manage our business or manage our spiritual concerns. There is no outside authority excepting our own women who are trustees and who run the show. We are absolutely independent of Ramakrishna Mission or anybody else."

She added that the girl inmates were under strict supervision as to their conduct and training and also their welfare like health, etc. If there was a case for disciplinary action, the parents were brought in and things were settled without any fuss so as to protect the girl's future. Everyone was dealt with sympathetically and with love and persuasion. There were no tight and rigid rules. In all matters the committees were involved and there had never been any intractable problems.

Relation with Government

The government periodically examines the donations received and checks that they are spent for the purposes for which they have been given. The government has exempted payment of income tax on the donations received. Every year the *āśram* has to show their accounts to government inspectors. With the help of the secretary and her assistant, the head of this institution lays down the rules of governance and their implementation.

Parivrājikās

Defining the characteristics of *parivrājikā*s, Vivekaji said, "Individual *parivrājikā*s should be very sure of renunciation as well as the ideal of service. These two are very important. Unless one is capable of forgetting oneself, service is not possible. If you cannot renounce your personal selfishness, you cannot serve. As we all come from different backgrounds, it is necessary for everyone to be accommodative. There are five *parivrājikā*s here at present. There are also two *brahmacāriṇī*s and three probationers. There is a two year probation in the centres and two more years at headquarters. At the end of ten years, they are made *parivrājikā*s. The president initiates them. The initiation ceremonies are sacred and secret. They do however correspond to the procedures laid down in the texts, just as for men."

Rituals

The place of rituals has become controversial even in society, where people under the influence of Western ideas feel that the rituals have degraded our society. But Sri Ramakrishna has proved that rituals done in the correct spirit do not degrade but they are actually of tremendous help. Because human life cannot be lived without rituals — even eating is a ritual, taking a bath is a ritual. "We have consciously organized ritual of *pūjā* and celebrations. We celebrate the birthdays of not only *avatāra*s and *ācārya*s but also celebrate the birthdays of Jesus Christ and others. We relate to these greats through our ceremonies. It is of great help. We follow the *pūjā vidhi* as practised traditionally. Even though the texts forbid rituals, I find there is no contradiction. It is a necessity in a particular stage in life; you gradually graduate out of them in due course."

The centre publishes books. A magazine is produced here. There are 23 Sarada Maths in India. They all do their work without much publicity. She herself (Vivekaji) is invited abroad every year to give lectures. There is no rigid hierarchy in the centre. Older *saṁnyāsinī*s are respected and looked after. All have their work laid down and the head has special responsibilities like meeting the public, etc. Some are involved in running the school, others attend to administration in general, some do accounts and so on. They also run tuition schools which are attended by a large number of students. There are four schools run by the *parivrājikā*s where there are 250 children. There is also a school for the poor underprivileged children. Here they are given food, clothes, etc. They also run a Sunday school for local children for religious and cultural activities. For the ladies there are many classes in English, Hindi and Bengali. In Dum Dum area in Calcutta there is a college for girls. In Arunachal Pradesh there is a residential school for tribal children.

SWAMI SARADANANDA

Swami Saradananda, 43, was the head of the Ramakrishna Centre of South Africa founded by Swami Nischalananda in the year 1942. The centre was not affiliated to the Ramakrishna Mission of India at the time of the interview but has since been affiliated and Swami Vimokshananda from the headquarters was posted on 27 March 2007 as president of the Centre in Durban, South Africa. It has 18 branches all over South Africa. The interview with Swami Saradananda took place in the *āśram* premises which has a newly-constructed beautiful temple to Ramakrishna Paramahamsa.

Background

Swamiji decided to take to the monastic order after reading Ramakrishna-Vivekananda literature borrowed from the school library, at the early age of 16. What inspired him especially was the biography of Swami Vivekananda by his Eastern and Western disciples. Following the principle laid down by the Ramakrishna order, he did not marry and cut off all worldly ties. "One does not look down on one's own family but one accepts it as part of the world family implying an expansion of consciousness," he said.

Defining Saṁnyāsa

In Swamiji's opinion a *saṁnyāsin* is one who has renounced the world and who sees God and God alone everywhere. Swami Vivekananda's motto was being followed in the centre by all *saṁnyāsins* — personal spiritual development coupled with service to society especially the disadvantaged; to carry into society the ideas to inspire it and be inspired by it in turn. Interacting outside as an extension of the Self as enunciated in practical Advaita Vedānta, one aims at God realization or *mokṣa* through service to the people. *Saṁnyāsa* vow enjoins on the incumbent to renounce the pleasures of the world, all the three pleasures together (*putra-eṣaṇā, vitta-eṣaṇā* and *loka-eṣaṇā*) for the achievement of Brahman/*mokṣa*. Swami Vivekananda had expressed it as — *ātmano mokṣārtham jagaddhitāya ca* — "for the liberation of the self and for the welfare of humanity" which also forms the motto of the Ramakrishna Mission in India.

One should be involved in the practice of *brahmacarya*; practise regular meditation, adhere strictly to *dharma*, study of the scriptures, voluntary adoption of poverty — these must be meticulously maintained. Personal spiritual development comes foremost and as an extension of this endeavour is the welfare of humanity. But the welfare activity need not take one away from one's spiritual effort. Emphasis is on *sādhanā* and one should be firmly established in it; that is why there is a regular continuing practice so that the final goal is not lost sight of.

The centre builds schools for educating the local population and then hands them over to appropriate authorities for running them. About 6000 children in schools are served food daily. Agricultural education is also given. There is a medical wing to help a large number of people. Many medical programmes help treat people suffering from chronic diseases and they are also educated as to how to prevent infections. The magazine published by the *āśram*/centre gives out information about the constructive works being done periodically. Swamiji travels whenever the necessity arises. He wears the robes of a *saṁnyāsin*. If the place and context demands he is not averse to wearing clothes other than the *saṁnyāsin* clothes. There is no hierarchy in the centre; however, the president takes decisions as and when the occasion arises. All monks enjoy equal status. There are no popes or archbishop type of hierarchical posts. According to Swamiji, *mokṣa* can be defined as knowledge of the Self, *ātman*, Brahman in the ultimate objective sense and service is a means to achieve that. It is an integrated approach to all yogas, *karma*, *jñāna* and *bhakti* as shown by Swami Vivekananda, with a particular yoga dominating, depending upon one's personality.

Visible Success and Activities

The success of this centre could be measured by the huge organization that has been built up in the last 60 years through the unstinted efforts of Swamiji and his volunteers in all parts of South Africa. It has great potential to do considerably more constructive work, spiritual and temporal, for the people of South Africa. Education, medicine, agriculture and spreading spiritual and cultural knowledge has been the primary focus of its activities. It is also concentrating on nation building activities such as finding common ground between various religions especially between Hinduism and African traditional religions. The centre is strictly non-political.

10. Swami Saradananda

Clientele

The clientele of the centre are mainly diasporal Hindus but it also works with all the other communities; particular mention must be made of the largest thrust made towards disadvantaged blacks. During the apartheid regime, communities lived an isolated existence without any interaction whatsoever.

Swamiji made the point that the isolation process will take some time to overcome; it is in the minds of people. It is not legislation that will take it away. There are some stirrings of it. Even though it is not completely removed, right now enormous changes are taking place in society for the good of all and the Ramakrishna centre is fully involved in bringing all the communities together. There is a steady stream of youthful members who come to the *āśram*, those that were drawn to the earlier Swamis bring their families and they in turn bring others and so on; thus there is a regular supply of youth without break. Swamiji's message to the householders is that they should be constantly engaged in *sādhanā* and should continue their dedication to the ideals of the mission.

Saṁnyāsin and Society

The Hindu *saṁnyāsins* are looked upon with respect by all in South Africa. In a foreign land the Hindu *saṁnyāsin* has to adapt himself to the conditions prevalent locally while, at the same time, following the spirit of the Hindu *saṁnyāsa-dharma*. Only then very effective changes can be brought about, according to Swamiji.

Besides Swamiji, one more *saṁnyāsin* was with the centre heading the branch at Johannesburg. An *āśram*, called Sri Sarada Devi Ashram, exclusively meant for ladies, exists affiliated to the centre in Durban. It is headed by a *parivrājikā*, a Hindu nun, initiated into the monastic order by Swamiji. It is largely autonomous and is far more fruitful to the women devotees.

The Centre and branches are governed by a written constitution and a managing committee consisting of all member trustees only from the monastic order. There were four members and one had passed away a while ago. The centre is meant for monks and a monk always will be the head. The lady *āśram* will have a lady monk as its head. The trustee monks will choose the head of the centre by consensus or by election, from among themselves only.

Apartheid Days

During the oppressive apartheid regime various indignities and vicissitudes had to be faced by the Indian community in South Africa. The centre, headed and manned by dedicated *saṁnyāsins*, brought solace by bringing the message of God-consciousness through the teachings of Sri Ramakrishna and Swami Vivekananda to the people and brought them the much needed feeling of security. The sense of belongingness to a spiritual community built up the morale and was sustained by the various spheres of activities affecting people's lives. Sense of security, strength, optimism and vision became the hallmark of the effect of the work done by the *saṁnyāsins* to members of the community; this is something that cannot be quantified.

Swamiji became a *saṁnyāsin* for his own attainment of the great goal of liberation set for a Hindu, but was inevitably drawn into the troubled situation his people faced, which then became a by-product of this chosen way of life. A *saṁnyāsin* in his personality became the harbinger of hope in the brutal, uncivilized, racially dominated white rule through a spiritually and religiously-oriented approach to bring peace and stability to those who came to him; he also went out to meet their problems of all kinds. During those dark days, while working with the community of which the *saṁnyāsin* was also a part, the propagation of the ideas helped in a big way to bring sanity to a stricken population of an enslaved country.

It is interesting to note that even today, according to Swamiji, 70 per cent of the congregation, consisted of youth between the ages of 15 to 40: "In those tyrannical days the *saṁnyāsins* of this organization brought hope to the depressed community by transmitting the great message of the scriptures of the Hindu Sanātana Dharma as exemplified by Sri Ramakrishna, to the tormented people and after the end of apartheid, this order is poised for greater things like building bridges across commumitites in South Africa."

Relationship to Government

The centre is free from governmental interference in its day-to-day activities. The main features of the new South African Constitution such as human rights, equality of the sexes, etc., have been taken into consideration into the functioning of the centre. The previous regime created many difficulties in the way of progress; they wanted to move them out of this place imposing increased rates, etc. The new people's government gave its ready approval for this being a regular religious centre. The government's attitude is very helpful and the centre is now free to function in pursuing the goals without hindrance from other quarters. The centre on its part adheres to the norms laid down by the government in building the structures and fully co-operates with it in all such matters.

Daily Routine

The daily routine in the *āśram* has been laid down by Swamis Nischalananda, the founder, and Sivapadananda his successor and it is being strictly followed. Rising early, the morning meditations from 4:30 to 5:30, the *āratī*, prayers in Sanskrit, *pūjā* with flower and food offering, and similar evening prayers and meditations are the daily routine of religious life in all the *āśram*s. Major Hindu festivals are observed. Youth and adult spiritual retreats, retreats specially meant for ladies, regular classes on the Upaniṣads and the Bhagavad-Gītā, reading from the *Gospel of Sri Ramakrishna*, special Sunday prayers, discourses, many of them led by the head *saṁnyāsin*, are the important activities of the centres all over South Africa. Readings from the Scripture are also one of the main features of the spiritual practices.

Finances, Initiation and other Information

The income of the *āśram* is largely from members, also there are donations for particular welfare projects from business houses and other sources. There is no doubt in Swamiji's mind about the successful continuity of the *āśram*s as the momentum is very much there. There are sufficient checks and balances instituted for the running of the *āśram* based on the Hindu *saṁnyāsa-dharma*. Those who do not confine themselves to the rules will be asked to leave whoever they are, *saṁnyāsin*s or otherwise. The capability to enforce discipline is there but there has been no breach of discipline so far.

"We do not encourage people to become *saṁnyāsin*s. It is a purely voluntary choice of the individual concerned. We generally prefer matriculates or those who have higher educational qualifications. The volunteer once chosen is expected to continue his studies for his betterment and utility to society. The initiation ceremonies are conducted in accordance with the procedures laid down in the Hindu *saṁnyāsin* system. *Brahmacarya* vow is taken by an entrant to this order and he undergoes rigorous training for eight years before taking *saṁnyāsa*. Proper *virajā homa* sacrifice is conducted as part of the initiation ceremony; training still continues even after the ceremony." Swamiji's initiation was done by his *guru* Swami Sivapadananda in the *āśram* itself.

Contribution of Saṁnyāsins

In the opinion of Swamiji the *saṁnyāsin*s have made the greatest contribution in maintaining the highest traditions in Hindu society. They have taken this up as a full-time occupation. The two great ideals of service and renunciation laid down by the Ramakrishna order have uplifted the people who come to them while they themselves scaled the heights of spirituality. Tremendous amount of social service has been made possible only because of the high integrity shown by these monks. This is a unique contribution of the order. A *saṁnyāsin* engaged exclusively in secular activities, sacrifices truth to the detriment of the spiritual progress of society. Whereas *saṁnyāsin*s following the Ramakrishna–Vivekananda philosophy have been able to maintain the high standards set-up by sages of the past, even while contributing to the welfare of humanity at large.

Hindu Saṁnyāsins and other Monastic Orders

The Hindu *saṁnyāsin*s did not have the opportunity to interact with monastic orders of the other faiths because of the pernicious system of apartheid earlier. But things were improving and recently Swamiji was invited to a leading Roman Catholic institution where he had occasion to address over 100 monastic members of their order. They listened attentively to his talk and were duly impressed. But when he started detailing his daily *sādhanā* they felt very inadequate in comparison as they found the Hindu practices are more detailed and severe and very meticulously carried out. They were inspired to ask a number of questions.

"Many monks and religious heads of other faiths have been regularly visiting the *āśram* to learn and practise our meditations and know more about the philosophy, etc., indicating that the globalization process is on. As the Ramakrishna order has a universal outlook in the religious field, it can contribute towards this process." He is keen to organize seminars with others on matters such as monastic practices, mysticism, areas of theology, etc., especially amongst Catholics, for mutual benefit, now that the door has opened at the end of apartheid.

SWAMI SAHAJANANDA

Background and Apartheid

It is pertinent to refer to Swamiji's life during the infamous apartheid regimes that were inimical to civilized life in general. He was called V.S. Srinivasan in his pre-*saṁnyāsa* days and was a young school teacher. During that time, like all those suffering under apartheid, Swami Sahajananda was having a restless mind and was vehemently opposed to the very principles of the pernicious order under which they had to face great difficulties. Even then, he was very much drawn towards the spiritual path. While at school, he happened to glance at a book by Swami Sivananda on yoga titled *Practice of Karma-Yoga*. Then and there he knew that Sivananda was the *guru* he was searching for and decided to give up his academic pursuits and fully dedicate himself to yoga *sādhanā* having been convinced that it is the only way to achieve the goal of God-realization. Once he started getting absorbed in yoga and religious literature, his interest in academics lessened and he abandoned the idea of furthering his studies. His attitude towards apartheid changed, in fact, his whole attitude towards life changed as he started to look on everyone as God including the European. The change came in a flash, overnight and after that there was no looking back.

After a year of being a teacher, he gave that up also to pursue full-time occupation as a spiritual seeker. He was certain that he was saved by the Divine Grace of his Master Swami Sivananda as without the guru's blessings nothing could be accomplished. Whatever he had accomplished, he said, is in accordance with his Master's instructions and his spiritual and temporal guidance from afar. He had visited Rishikesh thrice, twice when Swami Sivananda was alive, and in 1963 when Swamiji had passed away. It was during his second visit in 1956 that he was initiated into *saṁnyāsa* by Swami Sivananda himself. He had already started a branch of the Divine Life Society in Durban in 1949, even before he became a *saṁnyāsin*, through the inspiration of Swami Sivananda.

Defining Saṁnyāsa

A *saṁnyāsin*, according to Swamiji, is one who strictly adheres to the rules laid down in the *saṁnyāsa-dharma*. He is a man of strict discipline who is particular in observing the vow of celibacy. Swamiji himself felt very embarrassed when in the initial stages he had to deal with women closely. According to him, *saṁnyāsa* can be taken by married men, but only after renouncing all desires, family, relations, etc. The *saṁnyāsin* has a role in society in developing and advancing the spiritual aspirations of its members. Sivananda, his *guru*, asked his *saṁnyāsins* to get involved actively in socially-oriented programmes even though the ultimate object of a *saṁnyāsin* should be *mokṣa*. Swamiji himself is particular in leading a strictly disciplined life while engaged all the time in *āśram* activities, at the same time emphasizing the same spirit of discipline in his disciples.

Yoga and other Activities

Swamiji showed us the latest printing equipment he had installed to produce literature based on the sayings and writings of his *guru*. Many of his publications have become famous throughout Africa and elsewhere. They are all printed in bright eye catching colours and convey lessons of moral discipline which are very popular in educational and religious institutions. Swamiji has taken the initiative to build schools in many parts of South Africa especially for African students in remote areas who have no resources whatsoever. After building these schools Swamiji hands them over to the appropriate authorities to run them.

Following the great example of Sivananda who has propagated the practice of yoga worldwide, Swami Sahajananda has done the same in South Africa. Regular classes of *haṭha-yoga* for all age groups, especially for the very young, are conducted in all centres. He encourages them to take part in all other physical activities as well like swimming and other games. Character building has been his constant emphasis in all of his youth programmes run in his *āśram*.

Another important routine in all his *āśrams* is group singing of devotional songs which are conducted in all solemnity and earnestness by young and old alike. People of all classes and creeds and of all walks of life give wholehearted active support for all these activities including physically taking part in voluntary building activities at various centres.

11. Swami Sahajananda, South Africa

This is entirely due to the personal example set by Swamiji himself through his lifelong selfless devotion to his ideals.

General Information

A managing committee of six members looks after the running of the different *āśrams*/institutions. Forty closely knit dedicated workers are available at all times to partake in any undertaking the Swamiji is engaged in. After his time he has made sure the committee will take over and run these smoothly in accordance with the principles laid down by him. The members have been chosen very carefully after years of training and close observations as to their conduct and character and there is no doubt in his mind that they will not fail to carry out their duties and responsibilities. Swamiji is confident that his gurudeva's unseen presence will guide the running of his institutions for the present and the future.

Another important aspect of his management technique is to entrust the responsibilities of the *āśram* to one chairman of the committee for a few months and after that to transfer the work to somebody else who is equally capable, so that a number of people can gain experience in shouldering the heavy responsibility. He has thus made sure of a band of trusted people who have leadership skills. Swamiji feels this work can be done not merely by *saṁnyāsin*s alone but by others as well. It is noteworthy that many of the committee members are women and he wanted women members of the society to be equally equipped to handle matters connected with his work which is primarily bringing spiritual and temporal help to people. Full-time lady members are resident in the society premises in Reservoir Hills, downtown Durban, South Africa.

Personal Sādhanā

In answer to the question of his own *sādhanā* amidst all these secular activities he is engaged in constantly, he said that he believes in the ultimate achievements of an earnest seeker and absorption in *samādhi* as indicated in the Śāstras. "One has to pursue this through regular daily meditations and prayer without fail which I never miss even while looking after the affairs of the institutions. This means a complete transformation of one's life to meet the challenges posed by all the activities. *Mokṣa* is obtained when one is absorbed wholly and solely in God." Swamiji repeatedly emphasized the importance of divine grace in the path towards one's spiritual progress. His routine is to get up at 4:30 in the morning which sometimes gets upset due to emergencies like floods etc., when the *āśram* is engaged in wholesale rescue efforts. His regular spiritual practices however continue non-stop including meditation in the afternoon, evening and at night.

Success of the Āśram

The *āśram*'s success can be gauged by the popularity of the *āśram* publications and distribution of spiritual literature which has changed the lives of many people. Even though the society is engaged in constructing school buildings in ample measure as part of its social work he feels that the printing and distribution of books are more important. Spiritualization of society which is of utmost importance for Swamiji can come about through reading good books, he believes. Christian churches have shown keen interest in his books and they have bought them in bulk for use in their schools and churches. A Muslim divine called the books next only to the Koran and commends its introduction in all the Islamic educational institutions. His printing work over the years has made a palpable impact on both young and old of all classes and persuasions. Their universal appeal is due to the fact that Swamiji has included saying from all religions, saints and sages besides those of Swami Sivananda. His books are also vibrant and lively with excellent representations and photographs in colour of animals and birds, wildlife and nature from all over the earth. Swamiji is personally involved in designing the entire process of printing and publication which includes the format, cover, photographs, colour, actual operation of the machinery, binding, etc.

Interaction with Government and other Information

The *āśram* had obtained from the government permission for the *āśram*'s fund-raising bodies, school construction activities, etc., and there is no official interference in the day-to-day functioning of the organization. They have not issued any guidelines also for the running of the *āśrams*. Swamiji and the committee are solely responsible to lay down the rules governing the set-up and no one else. He is open to suggestions from everyone including children. It is a complete democratic system that is meticulously followed. The income the society gets is very high which includes donations and sales of books. Very thoroughgoing open accounting procedures are followed and supervision is enforced at every step so that the entire procedure is above board. Swamiji is very particular in seeing that every penny spent or acquired is used properly. As a *saṁnyāsin* he is against accumulating money and he gives generously whenever there is a demand. He had given substantial sums of money to the Ramakrishna Centre of South Africa in Avoca, Durban for their very constructive activities in the field of education in remote areas of Natal Province, South Africa. Over 30 more institutions both in South Africa and many in India also receive financial assistance regularly from Swamiji. Needless to say that such a transparent meticulously controlled highly charitable set-up attracts many donors who give large sums of money unhesitatingly to be spent on such worthy causes carefully chosen by Swamiji who is by nature very shy to ask.

Some Additional Information

Some of the other points made by Swamiji are given below in his own words: "Generally I admit only people of about 35 years of age as members. I rarely take people who are fifty years of age or above as we do not have volunteers to look after old people. I do not accept the property of those who come to stay permanently as they must have something to fall back on, if they decide to go back. Only persons with high ethical principles of life will be taken as members. This organization gives the highest respect for ladies. We do not keep *mūrti*s of deities as it would be a sin to keep them without elaborate rituals laid down to propitiate them. We do only the *āratī* to Gaṅgāmāī (the river goddess, Gaṅgā) in the *āśram*. We have printed pictures of *gurudeva* and Hindu deities for distribution and we display them at some places in the *āśrams*. We keep our *āśram*s spotlessly clean. We celebrate all the Hindu festivals in which there is large participation. No conscious publicity is done but our publications do it for us. I do very little travel. I had been to Val Morin in Canada which had been set up by Swami Vishnudevananda, a close disciple of Swami Sivananda. An odd trip is made to Europe/ Germany looking for printing machinery and very rarely to India. I travel in saffron clothes. I do go sometimes to clean squatter colonies in Durban along with my members."

Main Characteristics of a Saṁnyāsin

"Celibacy and detachment towards property should be the two main characteristics of a *saṁnyāsin*. I expect householders to strictly follow Hindu *dharma* at all times. We follow the rules laid down by my master and interpret them in accordance with the circumstances of any situation or occurrence suitably adapting it by using our own common sense. The *saṁnyāsin* is the best counsellor Hindu society has. I firmly believe Hindu *saṁnyāsin*s like Swami Vivekananda, Swami Sivananda, Aurobindo and others have upheld Hindu *dharma*. I believe in *mokṣa* but I want to come again and again to serve my master. *Mokṣa* is the attainment of *samādhi* and God-realization. I have had spiritual experiences in my path towards *mokṣa*. *Mokṣa* can come after intense *tapasyā* which was the hallmark of lives of our *ṛṣi*s and sages right from Vedic times. My master gave me the bliss of God. I can throw away these *āśram*s, etc., just for the sake of this great blessing my master gave me. However, one has to pay a very heavy price to get to the final stage of liberation from this māyic existence. To attain it one has to do a lot of *tapas* but to retain and maintain it this unstinted effort must be continued constantly. To an ordinary seeker there are many distractions. I have dedicated myself for other's *mokṣa* which gives me greater satisfaction than my own. It is my great good fortune that I have had the privilege of having *darśana* of many great saints of Hindu religion such as *gurudeva*, Ramaṇa Maharṣi, Anandamayi Maa, Krishna Bai, Swami Ramdas, Sri Aurobindo, Sadhu Vaswani, Swami Muktananda and others who are self-realized souls. One can detect a spiritually perfect being through their personalities which has a great impact on the observer."

SWAMI MAHADEVANANDA

Background

To begin with, Swami Mahadevananda was asked what motivated him to take to this path. His reply was: "Peace of mind. As a youngster I was very ambitious, very pushy, but was never happy doing what I was doing. I was trying to expose myself to different levels of society and different teachings, to different people, to different countries, different cultures. But I never was satisfied. I rejected various positions offered to me in life. I was born in Italy, but I also was educated in Switzerland, France, Germany, and England. So, I had many changes in my life. But

12. Mahadevananda, Val Morin, Montreal

at the last moment for one reason or other whenever I wanted to go through a particular door, that door was shut completely or I couldn't do it. And there were stalemates. Until eventually I found yoga; I felt that peace, nothing mystical I would say, but I found what I wanted, and then I understood subconsciously, why either that door was closed 100 per cent shut or why I myself couldn't go through that door. One day I was doing *śavāsana*. When I was relaxing, the idea came very clear in my mind that yoga was my life. When the idea came, then I felt that that is what I want. That is what I want to do."

Hailing from Italy, Swamiji entered *saṁnyāsa* under the tutelage of Swami Vishnudevananda, a close disciple of Swami Sivananda of Rishikesh who was one of the great *guru*s responsible for spreading yoga/*haṭha*-yoga and Vedānta in many parts of the world. Swami Mahadevananda came to study with his *guru* in Val Morin, in the Laurentian Mountains of the Quebec province of Canada. This interview took place in his *āśram* in Val Morin.

Definition of Saṁnyāsin

A person who renounces the world and tries to find spiritual knowledge is a *saṁnyāsin*. A *saṁnyāsin* can marry before taking up *saṁnyāsa*. Great saints were married and had children, but when the time came they just dropped out, and became great saints. Suppose if I am married and had children, and suddenly I met Swami Sivananda and got a call. What am I going to do? The call can come any time. There is no question of staying with the family. There should be a lapse of at least twelve years after taking up *saṁnyāsa* and visiting one's birthplace as such. He should maintain and help in spreading spiritual values. Social work is not similar to a *saṁnyāsin*'s work. Social work is needed, but the main purpose of a *saṁnyāsin* is to look for truth and give knowledge of truth to those in need.

A Hindu *saṁnyāsin*, in Swamiji's opinion, is more of a genuine spiritual person than the parish priest. Here he was comparing the Eastern and Western systems from personal example: "That society which has a certain amount of knowledge of yoga, respects the *saṁnyāsin* a lot. This is true both in India and here in the West. Serious people here in the West appreciate the work and worth of a Swami. They see a living example of what he is talking about. We have been able to survive even during the reign of the communists who are opposed to our spiritual yogic work and did create problems." (This was with reference to the atmosphere in Kerala where Swamiji worked.) "Otherwise in India in the north as well as in the south, there is general acceptance and veneration of a *saṁnyāsin.*"

Personal Sādhanā

It is very important, in his view, to maintain personal *sādhanā* constantly, all the time; time lost in not doing the daily routines as taught by the *guru* is a very serious drawback in one's spiritual advancement. Swamiji took to *saṁnyāsa* 30 years ago (in 1968). He detailed his *sādhanā* which has been taught to him and other disciples by Swami Vishnudevananda. One should get up before 5:30 in the morning. At 6 o'clock there is *prāṇāyāma* and meditation. Then all get together for *bhajana* and *kīrtana* and then the *guru* gives a talk. After this daily spiritual practice, one gets involved in *āśram* work which is part of one's selfless service. Depending on one's capacity one gets the work assigned towards running the set-up. In the evening the spiritual practice is continued with meditation, *satsaṅga*, followed by one's personal *sādhanā* including studies to improve spiritual knowledge. Basically a period of *āsana*, *prāṇāyāma*, meditation, study, etc., is necessarily included in the *sādhanā* of all members of the *āśram*.

There is a stress on acquiring spiritual knowledge leading to the practice of meditation and *samādhi* through scriptural lectures based on Vedānta. Swamiji considered Vedānta as the highest philosophy. The great Swami Sivananda called himself a practical Vedāntin. The necessary grounding towards this end is made through *karmayoga* and *rājayoga*, which are quite effective in bringing about the development of a *yogī* to arrive at the Vedāntic goal.

Activities

The social work undertaken by the *āśram* is mainly in India in the form of running schools; they even had a driving school, a mechanical school, but they were all secondary to the main work. If one gets bogged down in running hospitals, etc., then it is not considered an *āśram* but only as a hospital. Social institutions should not form part of an *āśram*. A person goes to the *āśram* in order to find one's self. These activities can form only a subsidiary part of a spiritual institution's work and should not become the main purpose. It should not become the main part of the life of a *saṁnyāsin*.

Success of Objectives

Swamiji was contented with the achievements of his objectives. However, he acknowledged that whatever comes out of it is not in his hands, "and that is also the very thought of yoga and Vedānta." Here comes the famous quotation from the Bhagavad-Gītā. "The right is to work wholly, let the results be in the hands of God. The more one realizes this the more one is firmly on the spiritual path. We try to surrender our own thoughts, words and deeds. These three because it doesn't matter how clever, how intelligent and how educated one is, it is eventually His will that will prevail. So surrender is the word and the result will always be contentment."

"It is hard to say," said Swamiji when asked how much of change he has effected in people. "Because, we are talking about spirituality, and you know personally I have been teaching for so long, I would say that thousands of people have been given this spiritual knowledge. Now how these thousands of people have been affected, only God knows! The impact of a lecture, the impact of a reading on the behaviour of a person at the moment, or even ten, fifteen, twenty years later will be difficult to assess. Unless you are a great saint, how are you going to detect that? Very few people have really come forward to take up *saṁnyāsa* inspired by our talks, say five per cent do come and join the organization. I am absolutely certain and very satisfied that I have been able to bring about the desired change in some of these people."

Perception of the West regarding a Hindu Saṁnyāsin

In answer to the question: "How do you perceive the role of a Hindu *saṁnyāsin* here in the West over the past three decades you have been working in this field?" he said: "Human beings are the same wherever you go because the soul is the same; the hunger for spirituality is the same." People come here and tell me that, "I am divorced from my wife," "My child is taking drugs," "I am in the turning point in my life, what to do," and so on. It is the same questions that they ask. These people at a certain point in their lives want to have a higher and wider answer to certain questions. And spirituality is able to give them the answers; so they come to the *āśram*.

Youngsters also want to find out what life is all about. The problems that affect them are the same as in India — dissatisfaction, drugs, finding a better world, looking for guidance and leadership, lack of confidence, etc. In the past 30 years this trend has increased. Consequent to this the need and demand for someone like a *saṁnyāsin* who can help them has increased. Present-day society is creating more and more stress and strain; there is acute competition, etc.; and so they all want to find out avenues of relief. The *āśram* serves that purpose.

Swamiji, comparing the monastic order in the West and East, remarked: "The *saṁnyāsin* is more of a genuine spiritual person than the parish priest." As he is a person born and brought up in his formative years in the West, that is a significant observation.

General Information

Swami Vishnudevananda started the *āśram*s around the world to teach spirituality through yoga. He had built up a very viable set-up here in Val Morin and elsewhere which are running successfully. He had instituted a number of measures, rules and procedures to keep the institutions running smoothly. One such is the body called the Executive Board Members (EBM). Policy matters in the organization are decided by the EBM consisting of seven members. If one leaves for any reason the other six will decide in the future. All were selected initially by Swami Vishnudevananda here in Val Morin, Canada. "There are five *saṁnyāsin*s at present in our *āśram* and some *brahmacārin*s."

This *āśram* is a beacon of light to the society and encourages people to adopt a healthy and spiritual outlook in their lives by practising *sādhanā* as laid down by Swami Vishnu for the benefit of mankind. Swamiji elaborated further: "I see quite a bit of change through the years in the environment in the social, economic and mental activities of people around the *āśram*s. In Kerala where we have a very vibrant *āśram*, I see the great difference it has made to the lives of the people who participate and those around it as well. Swamis Sivananda and Vishnu emphasized the goal of self-realization that would be achieved by following their great examples and these precepts have been imbibed by the Yoga Vedānta Centres throughout the world. If one man or woman gets self-realization, they can do more benefit to the world than thousand social workers. They need not physically go and address from the platforms or the pulpit but by just being in society, they have the power to transform the world."

Women and Saṁnyāsa

There are women who have taken to *saṁnyāsa* in the Sivananda Yoga Vedānta organizations. Many *āśrams* are headed by *saṁnyāsinīs*; one in Val Morin, another in London and so on. "Our society is still a very macho society, but we definitely need (women) *saṁnyāsinīs*. They are very sensitive, very emotional, not in a bad way, but in a positive way. Well, in India they are not perceived in such a role. Traditionally *saṁnyāsins* there have been male. We do not have such a tradition here. It is easier for Western women to be *yogīs* and *saṁnyāsinīs* as they have more freedom and are not so much tied to tradition." The role of a *saṁnyāsinī* is the same as that of a (male) *saṁnyāsin* as far as self-development is concerned. Here they have common names such as Saradananda, Karttikeyananda, etc., which are given to both male and female *saṁnyāsins*. In fact, when Swamiji went to Tiruvananthapuram *āśram* it was headed by Swami Vishnu's mother who was a *saṁnyāsinī* and was 85 years old."

Festivals

Their *āśrams* celebrate all festivals such as birthdays of saints like Śaṅkarācārya, Śrī Rāma, Śrī Kr̥ṣṇa, Jesus, etc. They run schools for small kids in Kerala. *Āśram* brochures are issued from time to time. Swamiji travels extensively in India and abroad. He has been busy opening new *āśrams*. There is one in Rome, Italy, as there is a great demand for yoga there. He visits all the *āśrams* in India such as Gangotri, Delhi, Chennai but stays most of the time in his headquarters in Tiruvananthapuram. The *āśrams* all over the world run courses on *haṭha-yoga* for both beginners and adepts, teacher training courses, symposiums and many more. Swamiji mentioned that they have to struggle to be viable. The *āśrams* all share the expenses as the work in each *āśram* is on a periodical basis.

SWAMI CHIDANANDA

Background

Swamiji was the head of the Chinmaya Mission and *āśram* at Mumbai,

Maharashtra at the time of interview. When he was a student of M.Tech. in Chennai, in 1980 he was first exposed to lectures on Vedānta from Brahmartaparama Chaitanya of the Chinmaya Mission. Later he heard discourses from Swami Chinmayananda himself in 1981. He says: "There was a great joy and great sense of belonging. And in 1982, after finishing M.Tech. I went to Delhi to work there in a private company. I worked there for two years in Hindusthan Computers. In 1984 I joined this *āśram* with the idea of enriching myself but not to become a monk. Accordingly, after doing this regular programme for two and a half years I did go back to the regular life and taught as a lecturer in a private college in Bangalore for three years. However, after some more reflection I found there is no need to sail in two boats. Personally, in my family, nobody depended on me materially for financial support. So in 1989 after serving for three years as a teacher in a secular college, I made over to this Chinmaya Mission. From 1989 to 1999, ten years I have totally dedicated to learning and teaching Vedānta."

Saṁnyāsa Dīkṣā

Saṁnyāsa dīkṣā is a very serious matter. The rituals and *mantras* are like a death ceremony. *Antyasaṁskāra*, symbolically indicating the demise of the ego, will also be done, so it is on a higher plane. *Virajā homa*, etc., are performed. *Gṛhasthas* can come over, study for a while and then if *gurudeva* or the present head decides, they can receive *saṁnyāsa*. Once they receive *saṁnyāsa*, family is renounced. A *brahmacārin* taking *saṁnyāsa* cannot marry.

Gross and Subtle Definitions of Saṁnyāsa

The gross definition is, one who is not married, who is devoted to god, who likes to spend all his time in pursuit of Brahman. He wears the orange or saffron robes, etc.; the gross definition has more to do with one's social and marital status and dress, some uniform that has a place in society. Then comes the higher and subtler definition. In Ramaṇa Bhagavad-Gītā, Ramaṇa Maharṣi says, *saṁnyāso nirmalam jñānam*, which means one who has pure knowledge, therefore rising out of that knowledge is a spontaneous detachment from pleasures and he is a true *saṁnyāsin*. The higher definition that has more value has its own place. But for society both these definitions are needed and "I respect them both." As for *mokṣa* it is possible when there is clearest knowledge.

When there is the purest *ātma-jñānam*, liberation ensues. The role of a *saṁnyāsin* in society is primarily to influence society spiritually, to arouse in them love of God, love of truth. He exemplifies the great values of detachment and renunciation. A *saṁnyāsin* is the custodian of *nivṛtti-mārga*, the path of withdrawal. In today's world he is directly involved in social services like setting up hospitals, nursing homes, colleges, etc.

Activities

There is a science college in Hardwar and an international school for Indian and Non-Resident Indians' children in Coimbatore. "It is one of our prestigious projects. We have little schools called Harihar schools, which are vocational; even in villages children are given some vocational training instead of going to cities in search of white collar jobs. They can do some carpentry or such things and improve the village economy. We run old age homes, *vānaprastha saṁsthāna*s in Andhra Pradesh and Himachal Pradesh. Swamini Sharadapriyananda, she is a phenomenal person, has built low cost homes in a village for a number of families. She has given them as gifts to people. The place is not very far from Tirupati at Yelliahpalli Chinmayaranyam in Andhra Pradesh."

Chinmaya Mission's work has been successful to a large extent in spreading the message of the Bhagavad-Gītā and Upaniṣads and other scriptural knowledge to people. Whereas in social services they had achieved lesser success, it being a secondary objective. Job-oriented Harihar schools have also not been very successful and have not taken off in earnest.

Saṁnyāsins and Society

Have *saṁnyāsin*s contributed a lot in the maintenance of Hindu spirituality? Swamiji: "I do not think we would have lost our spirituality as God probably would have shown some other way. It is a fact of history that *saṁnyāsin*s have protected, preserved and spread the spiritual message." How does the society you live view a Hindu *saṁnyāsin*? "It is divided in the light of so many waves of change. Half the society respects and the other half looks either with indifference or even with some suspicion. As in any field, here too there are genuine cases, there are fake cases. So the genuine cases have aroused faith and devotion in people, some fake cases, some raw cases have put them off, that is the cold fact."

Hindu Saṁnyāsin and the West

He was questioned about how the West views the Hindu *saṁnyāsin*: "The Western man I would typically imagine is straightforward and he wants to see how spirituality helps him to get over stress or have peace and so on. Yoga has become popular there and meditation has caught on well. The Westerner does not care so much for the detailed philosophy as it is difficult to understand our texts which are mainly in the Sanskrit language. So Chinmaya Mission has not touched the Western man so much. Moreover, it has only served the Indian community in the West. One reason is because we explain the scriptures and every ten minutes or so, we will be citing typically a Sanskrit *śloka*. The Western mind is very much open to pure Vedānta but not so much to Hinduism with its variety of rituals and variety of gods; it becomes a bit perplexed. Though I should admit Swami Muktananda, Mata Amritanandamayi, Mahesh Yogi and Satya Sai Baba are well received there. These masters who have succeeded have shown some miracles. Swami Chinmayananda, whom we believe had great spiritual powers, avoided exhibiting any miraculous powers. He focussed on teaching philosophy. He himself was well received by Westerners. But his organization has not been able to make much of an impact, and frankly the Chinmaya Mission has also not made it as its objective. In order to serve all sections of society, their doors are open for all, but their focus has been on the Indian community. The Indian community has so many demands and needs and the Mission got very busy catering to their needs. When I was there in the West for five years, I was fully occupied with the Indian community which had so many needs. Once in a while I thought, why not teach the Westerners, but there was no time. We were overwhelmed with (our own) clientele."

Appeal to different Groups

"Educated *saṁnyāsin*s affect the upper middle class; uneducated *saṁnyāsin*s have an appeal for the lower middle class. The learned Swamis of Śaṅkara *maṭha*s through their personality, influence the elite and the upper middle classes and to some extent the lower middle class. The last mentioned, however, go more for the *darśana* of *mūrti*s at the great temples like Śṛṅgerī Śāradāmbāḷ, the Kāmākṣī Temple at Kāñcī, Jagannātha Temple at Purī, etc., but less to the *mahātmā*s themselves. We are not taking care of the poorer sections and are letting them down. We come from different backgrounds, we speak English or use Sanskrit half the time, not intentionally but because we have been serving the educated classes for so long. *Saṁnyāsin*s also come in many colours catering to different clientele."

Future of the Āśram

How do you see the role of your *āśram* in the next five years?: "It has been five years since the founder passed away. This mission started in 1953, but the *āśram* in Mumbai started in 1963. The organization will complete fifty years by 2001, but this centre will complete only forty years by then. In the next five years I foresee a great amount of stabilization of all our programmes. We shall be tying up a lot of loose ends and systematize things and so on."

Succession

He next tackled the succession issue: "It is like this. The present head nominates his successor during his lifetime. In the case of only one transition that took place so far, *pūjya gurudeva* Swami Cinmayananda made some hints but nothing very explicit, and so there was some vagueness about who should succeed. However, the central body called Central Chinmaya Mission Trust with eight or nine members dealt with this selection. Once the head is decided, the head appoints everyone else."

Changed Times

How does the modern *saṁnyāsāśrama* differ from the old ones started in Śaṅkara's time?: "It is just a matter of degree that some *āśram*s are more orthodox and some are more liberal. So, in today's world, science and technology have made conveniences available to all *āśrams*. It is one side of the story — phones, fax, television, etc. The other side is the conduct, rules for one's personal life. There again if you see some organizations such as Swami Narayan they are extremely orthodox, even today their *saṁnyāsin*s do not have any contacts with women, whereas missions like Chinmaya Mission are very liberal. Śaṅkarācārya himself was very orthodox but by the standards of his own time he was liberal. By our standards we do adhere to a number of norms. *Saṁnyāsāśrama*s also have to change according to the times. The success of an *āśram* will depend half on the head and the other half on other factors. The other factors are — how it is organized, what is the quality of the members/devotees, etc., which play a major role. The *saṁnyāsins* have to deal with both devotees and non-devotees. *Saṁnyāsins* do go to places where they are invited and they encounter both. For example, in this very interview you are not a devotee of the *āśram*. We have met for the first time and I am giving you the information. In the West also I went to many universities. They were not devotees, most of them did not know anything at all about our religion. I lectured in community colleges in San Francisco Bay area. It is a very cross-cultural group who wanted to know about Hinduism."

Women

Swamiji made an interesting observation about the number of Hindu *saṁnyāsinīs* being more in the West than in India after I remarked that in many *āśrams* I had visited in Canada, USA, England, Europe, West Indies, etc., *saṁnyāsinīs* outnumber male *saṁnyāsins*: "I too have visited a convent of Ramakrishna Mission in Santa Barbara. There too there are nuns. That may be more reflective of greater freedom women enjoy in the Western world in contrast to what you have in India. There are the Brahmakumārīs who are all women only, as you know. You also probably know that Ramakrishna Mission has a sister body, the Sarada Muth. Today in India Mata Amritanandamayi is a rising star. There are many like that. We have twenty *saṁnyāsinīs* and we have sixty or seventy monks. Out of them one fourth are women. Some of them head *āśrams* also. There is a young lady of my age, Swami Nirmalananda in Coimbatore, a very dynamic lady. Right now she is in Africa on a lecture tour. An architectural engineer before, she is making an impact on the youth in colleges and so on. The roles of both male and female *saṁnyāsins* are the same. In Chinmaya Mission there is no discrimination based on gender. However, let me add, that, frankly, this society here is not really out of it. As a backlash of the society not really being mature, we do think of it while posting in (certain) areas. In centres where no devotee's house is nearby, we would rather put a man in charge than a woman. The order itself does not make any distinction."

Ācārya versus Saṁnyāsin

He was asked to explain the difference, if any, between an *ācārya* and a plain *saṁnyāsin* in the organization. He said that the *ācārya* position, in the order, had been held by about seven or eight so far and all have been men: "*Ācārya* is the chief teacher and he could very likely be a *saṁnyāsin* as well. Occasionally a *brahmacārin* also has been an *ācārya*. So Chinmayananda, Dayananda, Harinamananda, Swaroopa Chaitanya, Purusottamananda, Tejomayananda, Chidananda and Anubhavananda — these eight *ācārya*s have held the post here. We have conducted eleven courses, one or two have done double courses. This is the eleventh *brahmacārin* course going on. The duration of each course is for two and a half years. It is really an intensive course covering the teachings of the entire Advaita *paramparā*."

General Information

The Mission is a charitable organization. In the West it is called a non-profitable organization. It is registered as the Central Chinmaya Mission Trust (CCMT) and to run the *āśram*s there is a second trust called Para-cultural Trust. The CCMT is a worldwide body and the second one is a local body. The CCMT is housed here, but this *āśram* is run by the Para-cultural Trust: "So we all have registered under what they call as Charity Commissioners, government officials in different big cities, which enables us to receive donations and get income tax exemptions called ATG. We are planning to have a seven storeyed structure here and we have gone through a lot of legal aspects with the municipality. We thus follow the set government guidelines."

Guidelines for Running the Āśram

Who sets the guidelines for running the organization? "The *ācārya*s with some consultations with the head of the organization. Swami Tejomayananda (the head) has to be consulted on the rules governing any set-up. He keeps visiting the centres. His rules over-rules our rules. Donations are the source of income for the organization. They come from all over the world. There are some amounts in fixed deposits and they will also run out. The proper functioning is ensured by the management committee, by the *ācārya*s and other trustees. We periodically meet once or twice every month. There is an executive body with a chief executive and a deputy executive. If there are unwanted persons in the *āśram*, we try to help them by transferring them to some other place or ask them to go to one of our retreats to calm down and so on. After such measures, if disturbances still continue, we do expel them. We have expelled some members and sometimes these people themselves get out. The system is able to take care of itself. Eventually it all depends on the head. I have some powers too and I can myself decide at the lower levels. At the higher levels the head has to decide."

Specific Guidelines for Saṁnyāsins and Householders

At the grosser level a *saṁnyāsin* is spending all his time in God-related activities and is a celibate. At a higher level there is only one criterion of unconditional love for God and total disinterest in material pursuits. The *saṁnyāsāśrama* where *saṁnyāsin*s live is characterized by activities which has renunciation as the main feature. Scriptural studies, meditation, prayers and so on and not activities where some earning is involved. That is not a characteristic of the *saṁnyāsāśrama*.

He talked about the responsibilities of the householders as: "Householders should not ignore their material pursuit in a rightful manner but they should also learn the spirit of love of God from *saṁnyāsins*." In Ramakrishna Paramahamsa's words: "Householders have to work with one hand and have to hold on to God with the other." He continued: "*Saṁnyāsins* are holding to God with both hands. Householders have to work and also keep their religious goal in mind. In the case of *saṁnyāsins* much missionary activity is not good. *Saṁnyāsins* who are not truly very evolved, may have to pay a price when they teach too much. Too much teaching means you miss meditation, so you succumb to lust and greed, anger or jealousy. If I write too many books, then I am worried that nobody is buying my books!"

Festivals

Swamiji mentioned that in this centre Śivarātri is the greatest festival that is celebrated: "Over two thousand people come that day from early morning till late in the night. It is a huge affair. The temple's two priests and the Swamis also participate, to a lesser extent, by chanting and so on. We also celebrate Janmāṣṭamī, Ayyappa festival, gurudeva's birthday, Swami Tapovan's birthday, Bhagavad-Gītā Jayantī, Rāmanavamī and also Christmas when there are Christian students."

13. Swami Cidananda ji Maharaj,
Chinmaya Mission, Bombay

Teaching about Hinduism

The mission of the institution is to teach about Hinduism. So the Swamis go out to teach people about Hinduism. "We identify with Hinduism. Vedānta is universal, but we serve it on the plate of Hinduism." Publicity material consists of audio, videos and publication of books. Numerous newsletters are published, and there is an international newsletter from Chennai called *Tapovan Prasad*. There is also the *Chinmaya Mission West Newsletter*, published from California. It is specifically for North America. "We have plenty of newsletters both in India and abroad in countries like Australia, Hong Kong, South Africa, etc. Sometimes there is a confusion because two different centres, without realizing, have named their newsletters by the same title. Thus there is a *Chinmaya Jyothi* in Kerala and another one in Uttar Pradesh. Mumbai has two centres, this one and at Mulund. The English Newsletter is published from here and the Marathi one from the other centre."

Regarding the dress, Chinmaya Mission Swamis normally wear the *kāṣāya vastra* but there is no hard and fast rule about the *tilaka*. The daily routine consists of getting up at 4.30/5.30 a.m. and start with a Vedic chanting class. Swamiji does meditation regularly: "I do several sittings of 20 minutes each. I try to do 3-5 sessions. Sometimes, I fail, as I try to do missionary work, and lose on personal study and meditation. I go at least a few times a week to the Vedic chanting class. At 7.00 a.m. and afternoon I give my main lectures, Upaniṣads in the mornings with Śāṅkarabhāṣya. Afternoons it is Bhagavad-Gītā and other texts also. Right now Kenopaniṣad is going on and in the afternoon *Pañcadaśī*. In between, typically, four hours a day I spend time with visitors or counselling someone in need and similar duties. I am the only Vedānta teacher here. I teach only Advaita. So periodically the head himself helps out, sometimes others also come. For teaching Sanskrit there is a lady who comes here. Then we have about 6-7 hours of programme for these students."

SWAMI DAYANANDA SARASWATI

Swamiji heads the Arshavidya Gurukulam near Coimbatore, Tamil Nadu, India which he established in 1985. He has *āśrams* in other places including one in Hardwar in India and another in the USA. He specializes in textual analysis and exposition of mainly Advaita Vedāntic texts. He has travelled widely and gives well attended lectures all over the world. His Bhagavad-Gītā *pravacana*s all over the spiritual talking circuit is sought after and have become very popular. Swamiji's interview was recorded at his *āśram* in Coimbatore.

Saṁnyāsa

Prefacing his talk on defining *saṁnyāsa*, Swamiji said: "A *saṁnyāsin* is one who has undergone a certain discipline, living with a teacher for a length of time and studying Śāstras and then initiated into the *saṁnyāsāśrama* when the *guru* is satisfied. The very word *āśrama* is a stage of life. So in fact it is the last *āśrama* in life. There are exceptions which allow a man or woman to quit *saṁsāra* whenever he or she is ready to quit and to take to *saṁnyāsa*. We encourage *gṛhastha*s who are retired to take up *saṁnyāsa* and not from *brahmacarya* stage. Thus *saṁnyāsa* is meant for *mokṣa* or *saṁnyāsa* is a means to self-knowledge. The source of this knowledge is Vedānta Śāstra. There is teaching before *saṁnyāsa* and after it too. You are freed from all obligations familial, national, even divine obligations. You free yourself from all those *karma*s. He drew a distinction between a *sādhu* and a *saṁnyāsin* as "While the life of a *sādhu* is to renounce, the life of a *saṁnyāsin* is more Vedic." According to the Bṛ. Up. you free yourself from all *eṣaṇā*s and pursue the path of *mokṣa mārga*, so one who pursues *mokṣa* is a *saṁnyāsin*."

He seemed to suggest that the *saṁnyāsin* has a method laid down by the Vedic tradition whereas the *sādhu* may not be bound by that.

Mokṣa is a *puruṣārtha*, continued Swamiji. Like *dharmārtha*, *kāmārtha*, *mokṣa* is a *puruṣārtha* — that which is sought after. In fact, all human beings seek *mokṣa*, whether they know it or not. Because, they all want freedom from *saṁsāra*. Birth and death, in between both are the struggles. *Mokṣa* is freedom from all this. If I am a limited person, I am limited for good. If I am not limited, then I have committed a mistake, taking myself to be limited. So if I am free from limitation, I should know as such, and for which Śāstra becomes important here. *Guru* becomes important, teaching becomes important. *Jñānaniṣṭha* is then undertaken after the teachings of the *guru* which is *saṁnyāsa*. Yājñavalkya in the Upaniṣad calls his wives after his long years of teaching, divides his property fifty-fifty, gives it to them and departs to take *saṁnyāsa*. After taking up *saṁnyāsa* you give *abhayam* protection/ fearlessness to all. All the *devatā*s are called in so many ways and told hereafter they need not be afraid of him. That is the biggest vow.

Saṁnyāsa is absolute *ahiṁsā*. No life form is disturbed. You become a non-competitor. It is a very deliberate life of non-violence and this makes for saints.

Opening hospitals and running them, schools, etc., comes under *karmayoga*. These are work of service organizations. These activities are not meant for *saṁnyāsins*. It is not real *saṁnyāsa*. You don't take *saṁnyāsa* to do that. *Saṁnyāsa* is the outcome of that life. You do all that and then become a *saṁnyāsin*. But a *saṁnyāsin* may inspire people to take up that kind of work.

Background

Swamiji comes from a brāhmaṇa background and had had regular Vedic training, *mantra* chanting, etc. While working as a journalist, he happened to hear lectures by Swami Chinmayananda. He started editing the *Chinmaya* magazine and at the same time started studying Sanskrit in Bangalore Sanskrit College. Chinmayananda gave him *saṁnyāsa* at age 32 while he was still a *brahmacārin*. He assisted Chinmayananda in public teaching work. Later he organized teaching Vedānta through courses designed by him to suit the various aspirants. In the ashram the main job is teaching and no other work; he even teaches Pāṇini. The entire course which should have taken nine years is finished in three and a half years. The aim here is *mokṣa* through scholarship, "not to have degrees. So, I don't have exams, and no degrees, purely *mokṣa*. We create *jijñāsā*. We create a love for knowledge." Swamiji is one of the very few *saṁnyāsins* who openly declared that his *gurukulam* is meant exclusively for spreading knowledge.

Stage of taking up Saṁnyāsa

At what stage should one become a *saṁnyāsin*? To this question Swamiji gave his views as follows: "Śaṅkarācāryas are chosen from their boyhood as *brahmacārī*s which I do not approve. They simply choose a person, a young boy who does not know what he is taken into. They give him *saṁnyāsa*. So I find a lot of problems. People have problems. Problems in the sense there is always a feeling inside, something they miss out. I do not like a child being pushed into *saṁnyāsa*. We encourage married people getting into this."

In Buddhism they have a different framework for selecting a Dalai Lama. They say every Dalai Lama is reborn. He is already born, he is a

Dalai Lama. "So on what basis do you select? You follow some norms, thinking that this is what it is. That also is not very correct. According to me, *saṁnyāsa* is a very responsible way of living. It is not easy, and therefore it is better to discourage *saṁnyāsa* and encourage *karmayoga*. That is the correct way. You snap the religious connection. After *virajā homa*, *aṣṭaśrāddha* is performed for yourself and for some generations. You are completely free from any religious rights. A saṁnyāsin's job is that of a therapist. He is a person to whom others can come to talk about their problems. The role of a *saṁnyāsin* is that, even if he sits quietly, he is teaching something. There he is an example. The Śaṅkarācāryas are maintaining *dharma* and therefore they are for teaching *karmayoga* and not *saṁnyāsa yoga*. Only *paramahaṁsa saṁnyāsin*s teach proper Vedānta as is done in this *āśram/gurukulam*. Such *paramahaṁsa*s are still there in Rishikesh, etc." It is here that he had a lot of praise for the *akhāḍā daśanāmī paramahaṁsa*s/*ācārya*s who made it their mission to teach and spread knowledge rather than engage in spreading of just *dharma*. He said that Daśanāmī *sādhu*s alone teach; no Śaṅkarācārya teaches as he has the responsibility of the *maṭha* which leaves very little time for teaching. Whereas the Daśanāmī *sādhus* have made it their mission to spread knowledge. Swamiji wanted to perpetuate that tradition of *paramahaṁsa*s in his *gurukulam*. Therefore the emphasis is totally on the spread of knowledge.

Politics

A *saṁnyāsin* should be non-political. It is not correct for *saṁnyāsin*s to do political work. Help them and advise them. A saṁnyāsin's advice is objective and impersonal. He does not want anything in return. He is dispassionate and so he can fearlessly give counsel. In India the *saṁnyāsī*s get a lot of respect. As for the Western perception of an Indian *saṁnyāsin*, he went into some detail and explained how there is no slot in which the Westerner can fit the Hindu *saṁnyāsin*. Thus when the Westerner asks questions like whether the *saṁnyāsin* has a job, a family, an inheritance, etc., and gets a negative reply to all those questions he concludes that he is a hobo (a vagrant) to begin with because "they do not have a 'slot' for our kind! Here, in India, we have a slot for a spiritually dedicated person." When the Indian gets a negative reply to the standard questions he would conclude "Oh so you are a *sādhu*?" So there is a slot in which the *saṁnyāsin* fits into the Indian society. The

14. Swami Dayanand Saraswati, Arsha Gurukulam

saṁnyāsin tradition here is a learned tradition. That is slowly waning. This is very unfortunate.

Saṁnyāsinī

Three *saṁnyāsinī*s have been initiated by Swamiji — one was there in residence at the time. She was from Staten Island New York. She was a microbiologist but had taken full-time study of Vedānta. Two more were in Rishikesh. He agreed with the idea that invariably women become members in large numbers and even become heads of *saṁnyāsin* and spiritual institutions that have sprung from Hindu origins in the West. In the West, he said, it was easier for women to come forward and take to *saṁnyāsa* as they are more free compared to the Indian women. They are professionally equal or excel men and are more advanced than here; they are free to take up any job or role in society. In India even though women have advanced professionally in recent years they still harbour a sense of protectionism *vis-à-vis* the menfolk. Indian men also do not freely give *saṁnyāsa* to women. However, he added there are real *sādhu*-women within the homes.

General Information

The *āśram* is run by a board. Swamiji disclaimed "being the head or anything." He said he is just a *guru*. "There are three or four *saṁnyāsin*s here. A few PhDs, a brilliant scientist and a Sanskritist well versed in Vedānta and so on. We do not have a laid-down procedure for choosing a successor. Swamiji may 'encourage' somebody to be the head. Otherwise everyone including the *guru* is equal. The funds are limited and students are not asked to pay anything but they do give. People who attend courses in Sanskrit, Vedānta, etc., help the *āśram* with funds. It is not a very rich *āśram* but is able to manage with sufficient resources." Swamiji takes classes in Bhagavad-Gītā and other Vedānta texts. He has trained students who teach all over India.

Swamiji does not take new *saṁnyāsins*. The students while attending his talks may develop a desire to become *sādhus*. Out of these students some are already *sādhus*, some *brahmacārins*. They want to teach and they do not want to get into any other kind of life. And the *āśram* helps them to teach. After they teach for some time, they feel they can take *saṁnyāsa*. So they come and ask to take *saṁnyāsa*. If Swamiji is convinced, then he gives *saṁnyāsa*. Without teaching, *saṁnyāsa* is not given. They have to teach for 4 or 5 years and they are observed for 6 or 7 years. Then the final decision is taken. In other words it appeared that Swamiji gives *saṁnyāsa* only to those who have taught in his *āśram* for a long time and proved their mettle as teachers with the other qualifications of a *saṁnyāsin*.

Initiation of Saṁnyāsins

Initiation is done by the person who is the head of the institution, in this case Swamiji himself as the head. Only his students are chosen. He does not give *saṁnyāsa* to anyone other than his students. "They should also be 'some kind of *sādhus*.' The ceremony of course is *aṣṭaśrāddham*. They do 2,400,000 times Gāyatrī *mantra*, each syllable for one lakh times, before becoming *saṁnyāsins*. There are 24 syllables, so they have to do this 24 lakh times. Then they go for a nap. Then we call them and give them new clothes. To ward off negativity, we give them proper names. This is the difference between what others do and what I do."

Guidelines for Saṁnyāsins

"A *saṁnyāsin* is devoted to *ahiṁsā* and *aparigraha*. He should not gather. He should not have anything which he cannot give up. You cannot have a thing which you cannot give up. I never had in my life anything which I cannot give up. *Saṁnyāsāśrama* is a place where whoever comes, should feel at home. Whoever comes is welcome. You invite them; you should not feel that they are taking advantage. There is no 'I', there is no judgement. It should have a learning environment, otherwise it will decay. You should never lose sight of your vision as Kṛṣṇa says *tattva jñānārtha darśanam*" (Bhagavad-Gītā, 13.11). Swamiji's institutions are all focused on teaching and creating teachers to go out and inform society. There are already his disciples like Paramarthananda and Sraddhananda teaching in other places in India. His disciples are spread out all over India. He would definitely endeavour to have more *saṁnyāsins* doing this work with dedication and service.

SWAMINI PRAMANANDA

Background

Swamini Pramananda is a disciple of Swami Dayananda Saraswati, residing at the time of interview at Arshavidya Gurukulam near Coimbatore in Tamil Nadu. She took *saṁnyāsa* from Swami Dayananda and had been actively engaged in all the spiritual activities of the *āśram* complexes founded by the Swami. She had met Swamiji at a very young age when she was about eleven. "I always saw him as a person with all the values that I was taught to have and I wanted to imbibe all those values — care for people, sensitivity, compassion, which is what I saw in him. He was a great teacher of the Śāstras and my interest in Śāstras started at a very young age after talking to him and influenced by him. I met him in Bombay. He was there at that time, 1971-72. Then I wanted to study with him, because I saw in him the embodiment of the values of Indian culture. Fortunately my parents who considered Swami Dayananda Saraswati as their *guru* also supported me. My father always backed me up but he wanted me to go through my education to the degree level. When I finished my BSc, I went and joined his *āśram*. That was 20 years ago and I was 19 at the time probably the youngest in the course. In fact, I studied there for three years then went to New York and did my graduate studies there."

"I worked as a microbiologist in Brooklyn for eight years. I have a Masters degree in the subject. I used to teach Vedānta to adults and children even while studying and afterwards when I started working. After a few years I felt the urge to give up everything; I got the feeling that I had done enough working and seen enough. One thing about the USA is that it teaches you what affluence can do and what it cannot do. I felt I had been on top of my career and I just wanted to give all my time to teaching Vedānta. I found that the other life was not for me. So in 1990, I resigned and went full-time by joining the *āśram* in Salisburg, Pennsylvania State. I started wearing only white clothes, stayed there a few years, and then came to Rishikesh and got *brahmacarya dīkṣā* from Swamiji. I became a *saṁnyāsinī* last year (1998). That was my life's fulfilment."

Saṁnyāsinīs and the Ritual of Saṁnyāsa

The ritualistic aspect of the *saṁnyāsa-dharma* is not emphasized when a woman is given *saṁnyāsa* in the *āśram*. The ritual is the *saṁnyāsa-dharma* itself that a person chooses to take up. The *aṣṭaśrāddha* and so on are not performed for women. Even in the *gṛhasthāśrama* one sees that normal *śrāddha* and *tarpaṇam* (rituals for the dead) are not performed by women. "So in my view, one need not begin to do something which was not there in society. When *karmas* (rituals) were not being done by women, there is no sense in talking about *karma-tyāga* which is not given by Śāstras for the women. *Saṁnyāsa* for the woman is more in the attitude. The *vastradhāraṇa* (adoption of ochre robes) is to confirm this attitude; and also for oneself and for the society. It is a very visible reminder of what that person has taken up."

"We (women) only take up the *mantra* given by Swamiji at the time for *anuṣṭhānam* (regular practice). Before *saṁnyāsa* is given we observe *upavāsa* (fast), stay up all night chanting. Then finally the ritual part is completed by *virajā homa* with the help of a priest. Then *saṁnyāsa dīkṣā* is given by the *guru*. We chant the *dīkṣā mantra*s and take personal vows. Whatever the tradition holds we honour and take up elements that are appropriate for women and those not necessary we don't. The ceremony takes a little more than one day. It starts the previous morning at 9 a.m., and the following morning is *virajā homa* done by the priest. Then on the banks of the Gaṅgā the *saṁnyāsa mantra*s are given. All this took place for me in Rishikesh on Śivarātri day."

General Information

Swamiji (Dayanandaji) used to say how difficult it is to give up whatever one is used to in a long life. He cited the case of a brāhmaṇa of 40 years who took the *saṁnyāsa vrata* on Śivarātri day. The next day after Śivarātri being *amāvasyā*, the new moon, it is obligatory for all brāhmaṇas to do *tarpaṇa* for their ancestors. This Brāhmaṇa who had taken up *saṁnyāsa* was perturbed at the thought that he could not do *tarpaṇam* which he had done for the past forty years. "The *śrāddha* commitment and diligence of ritualistic life this man carried out for forty years of life, suddenly disappeared from his ambit which took him a while to get used to. That is when I felt the cultivation of a certain type of paradigm shift that takes place when one becomes a *saṁnyāsin/saṁnyāsinī*."

Saṁnyāsins and their contribution to the Cultural Heritage

"I am of the view that *saṁnyāsāśrama* and *saṁnyāsa* have contributed greatly to the preservation of the Hindu heritage and Hinduism would not be what it is today had it not been for the *saṁnyāsin*s (which goes for the *saṁnyāsinī*s as well). A *saṁnyāsin* gives up his life for *vidyā* (knowledge). A *saṁnyāsin* imbibes the spirit of the great statements (*mahāvākya*s) like *tat-tvam-asi*, lives it and propagates it; that is where

15. Swamini Pramananda

his uniqueness lies. Even a *sādhu* who may not be that educated and trained, by merely leading a life of poverty and simplicity and looking at everyone with equanimity, is able to convey the very spirit of this heritage and thus help in its perpetuation for the good of humanity. All this is the legacy of the great *vaidika-dharma* and the ancient Śāstras which have come down to us over the ages. This is rare to find anywhere else in the world. Our culture has given sanctity to life and its divinity. While these principles, especially the *mahāvākya*s, are for everyone to follow and adopt in their day-to-day existence and work towards salvation, a sādhu's life has been specifically designed to exemplify these great principles."

She went on to add how this all-pervading divinity is enshrined in the cultural artefacts like art, music, language and in all walks of life in the day-to-day life of the people. "Unfortunately, today people are blind to this aspect due to an overemphasis on secularization of all aspects of life. It is therefore a necessity to bring awareness back into the psyche of the people through exemplary teaching and revival of our ancient heritage. This is not like setting apart a certain religious time, say a Sunday or so many times a day one should utter prayers, etc., but a culture that pervades all of life, every moment, permeated with the thought of the divine in all and every aspects of life, language, art, music, dance, food, clothing, etc. This was our earlier way of life and the *saṁnyāsin* tries to bring about this change into people's lives through living it himself and teaching it to others throughout his dedicated life, convinced, they will change their whole orientation."

Saṁnyāsinīs

About *saṁnyāsinī*s she started by saying that the East has always been a patriarchal society. "The whole of Asia has been like that. So there is a certain inborn masculine superiority. Even now women have no desire to see themselves equal to men." On the other hand, she felt that Indian women, in general, have held a well-nurtured place in society and had not been subjected to great pressure. In the Vedic vision, according to her, women were not less than men. She did not address herself to the present-day conditions nor to the deterioration of women's conditions over the years. On the positive side she felt that the women who took to *saṁnyāsa* took to *saṁnyāsa* pretty much for themselves. The difference arises between *saṁnyāsin*s and *saṁnyāsinī*s because: (1)

saṁnyāsa is not a long standing tradition for women. Society is less exposed to them than to *saṁnyāsins*; (2) the *saṁnyāsins* and the general public are not used to seeing so many women in robes. There is therefore an ambiguity as to how to interact with them. So very often they are ignored. She described her own experience in Tamil Nadu where people are sometimes amused on seeing her dressed in *kāṣāya-vastra*; they think it is some kind of a fancy dress!

But the whole situation changes when *saṁnyāsinīs* give *vidyā* she said. The people listen to *vidyā* irrespective of whether it is given by a *saṁnyāsin/saṁnyāsinī*, a person young or old, a man or a woman. "I find *vidyā* has *śakti*. There is great respect in our culture for spiritual knowledge." Contrasting the Westerner's approach to Hindu spirituality she said that the Westerner is seeking spiritual answers primarily and does not necessarily imbibe the cultural underpinnings within which that spiritual knowledge is embedded. This can lead to some imbalances as well, as they only strive towards intellectual understanding and miss out the nuances as compared to an Indian student.

SRIRANGAM ANDAVAN SWAMIGAL

The full name of Swamiji is Srirangam Srimad Andavan (Sri Mushnam) Ranga Ramanuja Mahadesikan and he was 65 at the time of the interview. At that time he was the head of the *āśram* started at Śrīraṅgam 400 years ago by Vazhutthu Andavan Swamigal. Swamiji belonged to the Vaḍakaḷai sect of the Viśiṣṭādvaita Sampradāya. He was based at the time of interview in Chennai in South India. He hails from Tamil Nadu and gave the interview in the Tamil language. What follows is a translation of the main points made by Swamiji.

Background

Swamiji had taught in schools, colleges and universities before taking up *saṁnyāsa*. He taught Sanskrit initially having passed Tarka Siromani, etc. When the government abolished Sanskrit, he became a Tamil teacher. He also worked at the Osmania University in Hyderabad in the Sanskrit department.

Origin of Vaiṣṇava Saṁnyāsa

The founder of the Vaiṣṇava Sampradāya was the great philosopher Rāmānujācārya. Rāmānuja himself did not establish any *maṭhas* but he initiated a number of disciples who were very close to him into the Viśiṣṭādvaita system. Besides he had about 7000 followers/*saṁnyāsins* devoted to him and who followed him all the time. The Vaiṣṇava movement split due to differing interpretation of the texts. The main divisions are called Vaḍakaḷai and Tenkaḷai (*Vaḍa* = north in Tamil *Ten* = south in Tamil).

Regarding the titles Āṇḍavar and Jeeyar used for *saṁnyāsins* in Viśiṣṭādvaita, Swamiji said that there is no difference between the two Vaiṣṇava *saṁnyāsins* called Āṇḍavar and Jeeyar. While Āṇḍavar belongs to the Vaḍakaḷai stream, Jeeyar belongs to the Tenkaḷai stream. There is however a difference in an outward sense; they wear different marks on the forehead called in Tamil *nāmam*. The tenkaḷais' *nāmam* is like a "Y" while the vadakalais' *nāmam* is like a "U". There are philosophical differences in interpreting the Vedas and Vedānta as well amongst these sects.

Advaita, Viśiṣṭādvaita and Dvaita

He next talked about the three main philosophies, Advaita, Viśiṣṭādvaita and Dvaita all based on the Vedas: "The north has taken up the Advaita and Viśiṣṭādvaita schools of south India and has set up various religious organizations. The Dvaita has not gone much out of Karnataka. The Viśiṣṭādvaita school was followed by Bhāskara, Nimbārka, Kṛṣṇa Caitanya and others even though they have their own interpretation of texts. Rāmadāsa also took up Viśiṣṭādvaita and his disciple is Guru Nānak. They later on became independent schools as time went by.

"Śaṅkara had to contend with the Buddhist and Jains who had prevailed throughout the whole of India and he was trying to bring back the Vedic culture along with Kumārila Bhaṭṭa. So he had to formulate his philosophy on the lines of these philosophies. But Rāmānuja purified Śaṅkara's ideas by bringing in Viśiṣṭādvaita. Rāmānuja did accept the Advaita contention that Īśvara is all-in-all, but did not agree when it was said that the world is not real. As it is a creation of the Lord, it has existence. Sāra/Brahman is responsible for the *cit-acit jagat* and as it comes into its own it has to be accepted as real, as it is the *pariṇāma* of Sāra. When the Advaitin says that it is only a mere reflection, they are assuming something apart from Sāra which enables the world to appear as the reflecting mechanism. When you believe in reflection, you have to see the truth of the phenomenal existence of the seen. So, it is the genius of Rāmānuja who masterminded both the Advaita and Dvaita thoughts into one of his own, i.e. Viśiṣṭādvaita."

The Vedas have many philosophical and theological statements — some assert the *bheda* argument, others the *abheda* argument. Śaṅkara spotlighted the *abheda* statements like *tat-tvam-asi* which proclaim the unity of *ātman* and Brahman/Sāra and more or less rejected the *bheda* ones. But Rāmānuja accepted the Śruti completely and declared that both *bheda* and *abheda* aspects are true. If somebody known as Nārāyaṇa is called Bāla (young) Nārāyaṇa, the *bāla* is an *upādhi* (limitation) that is attributed not to Nārāyaṇa as Viṣṇu who is *upādhi-rahita,* i.e. who is without *upādhi*. Difference is part of the real world while non-difference is that of Sāra. Otherwise the Advaita and Viśiṣṭādvaita systems are not entirely opposed to each other as it is made out to be. Rāmānuja just overcame the defect in the contention of Advaita and carried out the task of purification of Advaita.

Advaita and Karma

"It is a strange fact that though Advaita denies the efficacy of *karma* in liberation, the Advaitins are the people who are involved all the time in *karma*. We don't have such a problem. We (Viśiṣṭādvaitins) believe that *karma-mīmāṁsā* must be followed thoroughly before coming to *Brahma-mīmāṁsā* but there are very few who follow this amongst us. They do very little *vicāra* or *adhyayana* and adherence to the principles of their tenets. In fact, many follow in practice the Advaitic idea of giving prominence to *Brahma-mīmāṁsā*. While not keen to take up *karma*s as stipulated, they are eager to find out more about the metaphysical lore of the Vedas, i.e. *jñāna-kāṇḍa*, more than the rituals. They say one thing and do something else. The case of Dvaita *saṁnyāsin*s is a peculiar one. The Dvaitins on the other hand give prominence to only the differences, the *bheda* aspects of existence, and are satisfied with basing their arguments on this aspect alone. Dvaita *saṁnyāsin*s even create new Śruti passages to support their dialectic. All however accept the supreme authority of Śrutis and Smṛtis."

He went on to add that Śaṅkara's acceptance of both Viṣṇu or Nārāyaṇa and Śiva as two aspects of Brahman, made people follow him. But the Śaiva-siddhānta advent in Karnataka and Tamil Nadu made significant changes in the practice of the Advaitins. Before Appayya

16. Srirangam Andavan Swamigal

Dikshitar's time (seventeenth century), Viṣṇu was worshipped widely by the advaitins. But Dikshitar, a great scholar who wrote on all the philosophies revering them equally, himself leaned more towards Śiva-*pūjā* and his Śaivite *granthas* had great influence on the public. Due to his personality and scholarship, and influenced by the wide acceptance of Śaiva-Siddhānta principles in Tamil Nadu, Advaitins since then became more of Śaivites while retaining the philosophical approach of Śaṅkara.

Saṁnyāsa-Dharma

Saṁnyāsa-dharma is the most difficult *dharma* to follow. Two of the most important duties of the *saṁnyāsins* is to worship "Perumāḷ" (Lord Nārāyaṇa is called thus in Tamil) all the time with body and soul and the second is to instruct people of the *jñāna* enshrined in the Sanātana Dharma. They should not covet wealth, name or fame. "It is true that nowadays *saṁnyāsins* build hospitals and other social service institutions; but most of such activity is for obtaining *khyāti lābha* (fame) and accumulation of wealth which are both forbidden in the Śāstras. For instance, we should not travel by a vehicle. In those days one had to take recourse to a bullock cart or a palanquin. Paramācārya of Kanchi Kamakotipeetham used a palanquin. Then he abandoned it and started walking. Thiruvaḷḷuvar says in *Thirukkuṛaḷ* that *andaṇar*, a true brāhmaṇa or a *saṁnyāsin* is the most righteous and the most compassionate. Even though the term *andaṇar* is translated as a brāhmaṇa it meant only a *saṁnyāsin*. He should not cause any disturbance or injury mentally or physically to anyone including animals. Any transportation involves animals, dependence on others and trouble for them. So a *saṁnyāsin* should not use any transport. Nowadays I use a car. *Saṁnyāsins* now twist Śāstras."

Changes in life of Saṁnyāsin

"We have to adjust to the conditions dictated by the environment we live in, the requirement of the devotees, the area and the type of propagation required. Travelling by car, for instance, is not strictly according to the rules. They are to cut away from their families completely. But one finds *saṁnyāsins* nowadays employing their own family members in the affairs of their *āśrams*. They send money to their families of origin. Some call themselves *rāja-saṁnyāsins* which is contrary to tradition. Such transgressions are becoming common nowadays. Family members however may form part of the gathering of devotees but they will enjoy no special privileges." As the head of this institution he gives *pravacana*s morning and evening to the āśramites and on occasions has to address large gatherings.

Saṁśrayanam

Saṁśrayanam is the branding of the bodies of the Vaiṣṇavas of the Vaḍakaḷai sect. It is done by the *ācārya, guru* or religious head. The symbols of the sect like the *śaṅkha, cakra, gadā* and *padma* are heated and placed on the arms of the aspirant to make permanent indelible marks as instructed in the books. As fire is involved only a *gr̥hastha* can perform the ceremony. "Religious heads, if they are *saṁnyāsin*s, are not allowed to touch or use fire in any religious activity. But in practice, a custom has developed, possibly due to compulsions of the aspirations of the devotees. To circumvent the rule of not using fire, a *gr̥hastha* lights the fire but the stamping is done by the *maṭha* head." In the case of his own *āśram,* Swamiji himself performs this stamping on devotees. Rāmānuja himself has laid down the five *saṁskāra*s, viz. *saṁśrayanam, puṇḍram, nāma, mantra* and *pūjā*. Rāmānuja also went through these and it forms the important part of the ordination of all Vaiṣṇavas without fail.

Initiation into Saṁnyāsa

Yatidharmasamuccaya is followed by Vaiṣṇava *saṁnyāsins* especially in the initiation ceremonies and rules of conduct, etc. It is true *saṁnyāsins* of the present day are not able to abide by the conduct rules laid down in the scriptures. Swamiji had to strictly adhere to the stipulated steps of initiation like *virajā homa*, fasts, etc. These are the final acts of a householder aspirant to give up fire ritual for good, before taking up *saṁnyāsa*. Āṇḍavan Swami was chosen by his predecessor to head this *maṭha*. At present, he is the only *saṁnyāsin* in this establishment. "The rule of this *āśram* is that the head has to be a *saṁnyāsin*. If a *gr̥hastha* is chosen then he will have to take *saṁnyāsa* before becoming the head. I give *mantra* initiation according to Pāñcarātra Āgamas. I expect the initiates to devote themselves to the laid down practices throughout their lives."

Activities of the Āśram

"Even though running of colleges, hospitals and religious institutions are theoretically not part of *saṁnyāsa-dharma*, changing conditions make us also participate in service to the community. As heads of institutions with many followers these activities are now accepted as incumbent on them to further the temporal needs of the devotees. No government assistance is received for our activities."

Swamiji would like all orthodox people to adhere to the *saṁskāra*s laid out by the Gr̥hyasūtrakāras, viz., Bodhāyana and Āpastamba. Bodhāyana is the original creator of and arbiter in matters of religious rituals as laid down in the Vedic Saṁhitās especially Kr̥ṣṇa Yajurveda in performance of *yajñas*, *iṣṭi*s, and other *saṁskāra*s. These Gr̥hyasūtras are common to all, whether they are Advaitins, Viśiṣṭādvaitins or Dvaitins. He went on to say that while the Viśiṣṭādvaitins are supposed to continue with rituals (*karma*) throughout their lives unlike the Advaitins, it so happens that the Advaitins in Tanjore area are better versed in performing *yajña*s, etc. But, in general, there was a decline in the knowledge of the Śāstras and performance of stipulated rituals in all the communities which is highly regrettable. In Swamiji's opinion, the Western scholars had done and are doing much more research work and bringing about more valuable literature on our religious and philosophical fields than our own scholars.

Saṁnyāsa Practices

There are no basic differences in the theory and practice of *saṁnyāsa* by all sects even though *ācāra-bheda*s (customary changes) have crept in over time. Removing hair, *upavīta* (sacred thread), carrying the staff (*tridaṇḍī*s, *ekadaṇḍī*, etc.,) and differences in form are followed by *saṁnyāsin*s. "In the Viśiṣṭādvaita schools, we keep a tuft of hair and the *upavīta* as stipulated in the scriptures. *Gautama-Dharma-Sūtra* however lays down that the hair should be removed. In the Rāmāyaṇa it is said that Rāvaṇa came disguised as a *tridaṇḍī saṁnyāsin* to abduct Sītā who took him to be a real *sādhu*. Both systems are in vogue." Swamiji is a *tridaṇḍī* and so will be anyone occupying this position. *Ekadaṇḍī*s are also there. Bhāskarācārya was a *tridaṇḍī*. "Those who follow the Pāñcarātra Āgamas and Smr̥tis, as we do among the Vaiṣṇavas have *tridaṇḍa*, *śikhā* (hair) and *yajñopavīta* (sacred thread). Whereas in the Advaita and Dvaita systems there is no *śikhā* and *yajñopavīta* and they are *ekadaṇḍī*s."

Saṁnyāsa Defined

"The *saṁnyāsin* should give up the three *eṣaṇās*. *Saṁnyāsa-dharma* is intended only for the brāhmaṇas. After taking *saṁnyāsa* he should leave his home and should never enter a house again. He cannot even go into a city or village but can stay only on the outskirts. *Saṁnyāsa* is not for women. Nowadays all the rules of *saṁnyāsa* are distorted to give *saṁnyāsa* to women.

The main job of a *saṁnyāsin* is teaching of Vedānta and he should bring up disciples in the traditional way. Most of the time he is in *bhagavat-dhyāna*. He is an *āhitāgni* before *saṁnyāsa* but after *saṁnyāsa* he has nothing to do with rituals or anything with *agni* — fire. In the Advaita *paramparā* they take *saṁnyāsa* from the *brahmacārin* stage like Śaṅkara who became a *saṁnyāsin* from the stage of a *naiṣṭhika brahmacārin*.

The rules for *saṁnyāsa* in Vaiṣṇavism is laid down in the Yatidharmasamuccaya written by Yādava Prakāśa who was the *guru* of Rāmānuja but who later became Rāmānuja's disciple. *Yati/saṁnyāsin* is intent on his own salvation. He is not meant for politics or social work. He should be completely detached from any outside involvement in society whatsoever. He should have no desire for wealth. But nowadays *saṁnyāsin*s are after all these forbidden things. In this *āśram* we do not travel outside the country."

SWAMI VISHWESWARA TIRTHA

It was a very short interview with Swami Vishweswara Tirtha at a temple in New Delhi where he had come to visit for a short while. There was a large crowd to pay their respects. There was also Uma Bharati an important minister in the Union Cabinet at the time. Swamiji took *saṁnyāsa* at the age of eight. He is now the head of the Pejawar Math in Udupi in Karnataka, which is one of the eight *maṭha*s founded by Madhvācārya, the founder of the Dvaita Vedānta school.

Saṁnyāsa and Mokṣa

According to him *saṁnyāsa* is of two types, one is a *naiṣṭhika brahmacārin* and the other is a *vairāgya saṁnyāsin*. In their system created by Madhvācārya *saṁnyāsa* is the fourth *āśrama*. The *ācārya* did not think *saṁnyāsa* to be the only means to the attainment of *mokṣa*. Only Śaṅkarācārya thought that *saṁnyāsa* is essential for *mokṣa*, he said.

17. Swami Vishvesvara Tirtha, Pejawar Math

According to Madhvācārya a *saṁnyāsin* or a *gṛhastha* is eligible to attain *mokṣa* based on their *sādhanā*. *Niṣkāma-karma* leads to liberation while *kāmya-karma* entangles one in bondage and attachment. A *saṁnyāsin* is entitled to do *pūjā*, *pravacana* and even *homa*, the fire sacrifice; in fact he can do all *karma*s.

Women and Saṁnyāsa

Swamiji said that different opinions exist with regard to enlisting women as *saṁnyāsin*s. He was asked about Śaṅkara's view on the four *varṇa*s and his relegating the position of women to that of śūdras. Swamiji's reply: "Madhvācārya also believed in the four *varṇa*s as Śaṅkara did. But Madhva had said that women also are entitled to do *tapasyā*." The Madhva initiation ceremony for a *saṁnyāsin* is not different from that in other schools. "By this *paddhati* I gave *dīkṣā* to Uma Bharati. She wanted to do *sevā*. She has a project for this purpose in Madhya Pradesh."

General Information

His institutions get donations from the public to run them. There is also revenue from agricultural land that has been left over after the government took away most of it belonging to the *maṭha*. The organization runs centres for women, orphans, schools for children and hospitals.

Philosophy

He gave a short discourse on the various aspects of his philosophy. "According to Śaṅkara, *jīva* is not different from Brahman. When jīva's *cetanā* succeeds in removing ignorance, he becomes Brahman. But in this philosophy, only with the grace of *Bhagavān*, *jīva* is able to lift his ignorance but does not become Brahman. But he becomes *ānanda-rūpī-caitanya*. *Jīva* and *Bhagavān* are different. Both Rāmānuja and Madhva believe that *jīva* is separate from Brahman."

Politics

When asked about his opinion about *saṁnyāsin*s getting into politics he said: "If the *saṁnyāsin*s desire to do so, they may do so as *lokasaṁgraha*. While doing *sevā* in politics, they will do their *tapasyā*. One can be a *saṁnyāsin* while doing *deśa-sevā*."

Note: After interviewing Swamiji I spoke to Mr Rao a follower of Swamiji. I asked him specifically about Uma Bharati and Swamiji giving her *saṁnyāsa*. He said that she (Ms. Uma Bharati) became a *saṁnyāsinī* by about the year 1992. Initially Swamiji was reluctant to give her *saṁnyāsa*. But, he said, because she kept on insisting and he found her capable with the requisite qualities he relented. As a child she used to give *kathā-prasaṅga* and she was also very spiritually oriented. So Swamiji eventually decided to make her a *saṁnyāsinī.* He added she spends almost four hours every day in *pūjā*, she is equally devoted to her political career as much as to her spiritual efforts. Swamiji has felt that as long as one does any work in a detached manner, it is conducive to final enlightenment. As such, there is no contradiction between *saṁnyāsa* and working as a politician or for that matter in any sphere of life. She works for the upliftment of the hill people, the *ādivāsis*."

I then asked Uma Bharati, who was present there, for an interview. But she was very reluctant and said, "Whatever Guruji has said is enough."

SWAMI SUGUNENDRA TIRTHA

Background

Belonging to the Madhva Dvaita Sampradāya, Swami Sugunendra Tirtha is the head of the Puthige Mutt, one of the eight *maṭha*s established by Śrī Madhvācārya in Udupi, Karnataka. He gave the interview in his *āśram* in Udupi. He said he was chosen by his *guru* when he was 12, after his guru who was searching for a successor collected nearly 300 horoscopes and sent them to Kerala to be scrutinized by an expert astrologer. His parents did not know how the *guru* got hold of his horoscope but when the astrologer selected his horoscope saying he is the one qualified, as he had *saṁnyāsa-yoga*, the *guru* went to his parents and said that he wanted Sugunendra to be his successor. The father hesitated and the mother did not accept. The *guru* called Sugunendra and asked him. He had ambitions of becoming a scientist or an astronomer. The *guru* explained to him: "This philosophy is above all that. You will get all these in philosophy also." Soon after, his father agreed and his mother also accepted and he started living in the guru's *āśram* as his *śiṣya* (disciple) and his potential successor. But unfortunately the guru passed away within four months of his stay at the *āśram* and he became the head of the Puthuge Mutt at the tender age of 12. The next 12 years were spent in acquiring proficiency in all the traditional texts like the Upaniṣads, Vyākaraṇa, Nyāya, etc.

Who is a Saṁnyāsin

He defined a *saṁnyāsin* as one who does not have worldly desires as stated by Śrī Kṛṣṇa in the Bhagavad-Gītā. According to him the successor to head the *maṭha* is generally chosen, as he himself had been selected, by consulting the horoscope and by observation. There is only one *saṁnyāsin* who is the head of the *āśram*. When the incumbent *saṁnyāsin* becomes old, he will train his successor *saṁnyāsin* to take over after him. Only a *saṁnyāsin* can be the head of his *āśram* and he has to be a *naiṣṭhika brahmacārin*. There are other Madhva Maths where they have *gṛhastha saṁnyāsins*. There are 16 main *maṭha*s in the Madhva Sampradāya, including the main eight Udupi ones. The Udupi *maṭha*s have *bāla-saṁnyāsins* (*naiṣṭhika brahmacārins*) and the others can have both *bāla-saṁnyāsins* and *gṛhastha saṁnyāsins*.

Temple Worship and Saṁnyāsin

The eight Udupi *maṭha*s are attached to the Udupi temple and their main job is to look after the temple/temples. They have been doing this for the past 700 years and more. The famous Kṛṣṇa temple of Udupi has been entrusted to the original eight *maṭha*s and each one gets the opportunity to look after the temple for two years in succession. He himself took charge of the *pūjā* in the temple at the age of 13, within a year of his taking over as the head. He had learnt the *pūjā-vidhi* by then. Only the *saṁnyāsins* of the eight *maṭha*s are allowed to do the *pūjā*s and touch the Kṛṣṇa icon in the temple.

Family Connection

In answer to the question as to whether the *saṁnyāsin* is cut-off from his family totally he said: "The families of the *saṁnyāsins* can come to the temple only as devotees. But an exception is made with regard to the mother. We should always honour our mother. All other family members have to be treated as devotees including the father. We should respect the father but not prostrate to our father. We prostrate only to the mother because we cannot repay *mātṛ-ṛṇa* (debt to the mother). Your first relationship is with your mother. You can cut the relationship with your father, but you cannot cut the relationship with your mother."

It is said that Madhvācārya was given *saṁnyāsa* by an Advaitin. When asked "do you differ a lot from Advaita," Swamiji said: "In view of *saṁnyāsa* there is not much difference. Philosophy is quite different." Society views a *saṁnyāsin* as a *mārgadarśaka* (one who shows the way how to deal with life), whether in Dvaita, Advaita or any other, according to him. As to whether his *āśram* runs schools, hospitals, etc., he said: "Our intention is to propagate religion. Sometimes we are running model schools also for that purpose. People come and we teach them both philosophy and religion. We also bring out a number of publications. We feel a lot of success has been achieved by our efforts."

Saṁnyāsin in Society

He added that when people invite them for religious functions like *homa*s or *yajña*s they go but they do not attend functions like weddings, etc.

Do *saṁnyāsin*s get respect from society? "*Saṁnyāsin*s sacrifice everything and if they are unselfish then they are respected. *Saṁnyāsin*s are of two kinds, traditional *saṁnyāsin*s and modern *saṁnyāsin*s. We are not only *saṁnyāsin*s, we are *maṭhādhipati*s and *pīṭhādhipati*s and we have our own background. We strictly follow the rules. But some modern *saṁnyāsin*s, they do not have any background, they don't have any framework. People certainly honour *pīṭhādhipati*s who belong to a tradition. They also honour other *saṁnyāsin*s who are prominent in other schools."

As Swamiji had travelled widely abroad, he was asked about the perception that Westerners had about Hindu *saṁnyāsin*s. "Yes, in the Eastern countries people are very particular about life after death. But Western countries are more concerned with the present life in the world. But nowadays they are showing a lot of interest in our view of the world and are curious to learn about the *saṁnyāsin* as well. Sometimes they are surprised to learn that I became a *saṁnyāsin* at the age of 12 and that I am not married. They ask: Is it possible? Sometimes if a *gṛhastha* goes they ask: How many times are you married, How many wives do you have? If the *gṛhastha* answers: I am married only once, they say: How come? The common person does not know much about the culture of India. (Otherwise) they highly appreciate our culture, family values, ancient values."

Future of the Āśram

Day by day more devotees are coming to our *maṭha*. More people are

18. Swami Sugunendra Theertha, Puthige Mutt, Udupi

interested in our philosophy. We intend to have more educational institutions, *pāṭhaśālās*, *vidyāpīṭhas* and temples. Year by year we are getting more positive reaction from all over India. Even non-Madhvas are coming to learn. We impart our Dvaita philosophy, Bhagavad-Gītā, devotion, etc., to all those who come to us. In Śaṅkarācārya's time *saṁnyāsins* were required only to spread spirituality while the kings looked after the mundane matters. Now times have changed, the kings have vanished, the government is secular and nobody is bothering about the spiritual lives of the people. We consider it our responsibility to protect the culture of this nation. Apart from educating people about our culture we also act as counsellors to people who are in need and who come seeking our help. In fact, we are narrowing the distance between a *guru* and *bhakta*. I am specially involved in filling up this lacuna.

Swamiji's *āśram* is producing a lot of literature on the Madhva philosophy. Swamiji himself has written a number of books, he gives *pravacanas* (talks on spiritual subjects) regularly and also runs a journal in English and another one in Kannada. He also travels a lot to meet people. The *āśram* also conducts examinations on the Bhagavad-Gītā which are very popular.

Qualification for Saṁnyāsa

Who is qualified to take *saṁnyāsa* — is it only brāhmaṇas or do you think it is of importance any more? Swamiji's answer: "Saṁnyāsa is a status of mind. Whoever has a higher mind can have *saṁnyāsa*. But *pīṭhādhipati* is different from *saṁnyāsa*." The success of the *maṭha* depends on its head, said the Swami quoting the adage *yathā rājā tathā prajā*. He pointed out how the *āśram* has succeeded in non-devotee circles as well by encouraging self-employment through special schemes: "We should fulfil their materialistic necessities including job, education, etc., for devotees and non-devotees alike.The *āśram* helps the poor by training them in skills such as screen printing, flower making, and other small scale businesses which can help them to succeed. Side by side we tell them to go to the temple, and worship God, and preserve the culture."

Saṁnyāsinīs

Swamiji responded to the question of *saṁnyāsinīs* by saying: "No, in our tradition it is not allowed and we stick to it." Will there be any in the future? "No, in our system each one has his or her own duty. Becoming a *saṁnyāsin* is not meant for all. Why should a woman want to become a *saṁnyāsinī* to attain *mokṣa* or to do something spiritual? In spiritual scriptures and epics like the Mahābhārata they say whatever her duty is, if she renders them truthfully she can get *mokṣa*. Then why should she come to do some other duty. She has her duties cut out for her." So you would reject her? He did not answer that directly but said: "Also, *saṁnyāsa* is a status of mind. One can live as a *gr̥hastha* and keep that status of mind."

Administrative and Financial matters

Swamiji is the administrative head of the *āśram*. The government does not interfere with the function of the *maṭha*. But the government takes away the assets with which to run the *āśram*. All religious institutions are weak. Particularly in Karnataka it is very bad. Temple lands are taken away through the Land Reforms Act. If the temples are not doing any farming on the lands owned by them, the government takes them away. "We had plenty of land earlier. Now because of ceiling limit we have only 150 acres. We find it difficult to manage with meagre resources." There is a trust to govern the institution. Financing is done through donations. Swamiji does not believe in creating endowments. "That is my personal view. You should not have funds. Whatever is needed that will come. Funds will create problems."

General Information

To propagate Kr̥ṣṇa *bhakti* Madhvācārya established the temple at Udupi and installed the icon/statue of Śrī Kr̥ṣṇa. He also made the eight *maṭhas* to take over the worship of Udupi Kr̥ṣṇa in succession. Nowadays it is for two years by rotation but earlier it was for two months in succession. The rule was changed because, earlier, when somebody travelled to Badari for instance, it was difficult for that person to return within 14 months. So 250 years later the rule was changed by Swami Wajiraja. Puthuge Swamiji was in charge of the temple and worship of Udupi Kr̥ṣṇa at the time of interview, and his next turn will be after fourteen years according to this system. He had already been in charge when he was thirteen and subsequently also. He was asked about the controversy surrounding the successor to Pejawar Math who got married and was therefore disqualified. Swamiji said: "Yes he was disqualified according to the rules laid down. They have already selected another person. This is a new development and for the past 720 years there was nothing like that." He mentioned two other instances where after becoming *saṁnyāsins* and taking over as *maṭhādhipatis* they renounced soon after. Consequently they now have two kinds of policies — either to bring in young ones or put in charge older persons. Now everybody has agreed to initiate only those *naiṣṭhika brahmacārins* who are 20 or 25 years old. There is no change as far as the *naiṣṭhika brahmacārin* rule is concerned.

Main Guidelines for Saṁnyāsins

He mentioned the two important qualities of a *saṁnyāsin* as a person who has no desires whatsoever and whose goal is *mokṣa*. He added that *mokṣa* means the termination of the cycle of *saṁsāra*. In Advaita, *mokṣa* is to become one with God; in Viśiṣṭādvaita they say you cannot become one with God. You can achieve equality. "But in Dvaita what we say is that even equality is not possible. Even after death we are devotees of God. For *mokṣa* also there are gradations. We categorize *jīvas* as *sāttvika, rājasika* and *tāmasika*. Only *sāttvika-jīvas* have *adhikāra* for *mokṣa*, *rājasikas* are permanently in *saṁsāra* and *tāmasikas* go to hell." I asked him whether he agreed with that and he said, "It is not a question of agreeing or not agreeing; it is a fact."

He added that *svarga* is *karmaphala* and *gṛhasthas* may aspire for it. *Saṁnyāsins* should do only *nitya-karma*. According to him, the *maṭhas* should have their own concrete philosophy and should develop strong traditions to guide *saṁnyāsins* of all ages spiritually. "We have *virajā homa* before initiation. All ceremonies are in accordance with the Yatidharmasamuccaya and it lasts for three days and then *kāṣāya vastra* is given. We celebrate all festivals, Kṛṣṇa Janmāṣṭamī, Rāmanavamī, Navarātrī and Madhva Navamī. The last is the celebration of the day our founder Madhvācārya passed away." He described that as Madhva's sudden disappearance. Their tradition believes that Madhva was teaching his disciples when he saw celestial beings and disappeared, never to appear again. It is celebrated as *Lakṣadīpotsava*. They also have a *Rathotsava* (chariot festival) with Kṛṣṇa's *mūrti* in the chariot in procession. "We also worship Śiva as God. We worship all gods according to our special philosophy. There are those who worship only Viṣṇu in Vaiṣṇavism but when we worship Śiva we think we are worshipping Viṣṇu inside Śiva — i.e. *antaryāmī* Viṣṇusarvottama. There are distinguishing marks on our foreheads — *gopīcandanam* and the black two lines called *aṅgāraka*."

Swamiji was confident that his *āśram* was doing useful work in society. "We are like pillars and for the survival and welfare of the society the *maṭha* is the basic pillar. We are influencing countless number of people and more and more young people are coming."

Notes: Puthuge Swamiji also mentioned that in the *āśram* complex they feed about 5,000 people who come there every day. He also mentioned that though the tradition says that women should not be given *saṁnyāsa*, Uma Bharati had been given *saṁnyāsa*. He said that it is a controversial point and he left it at that. Swamiji who has been very active since his inauguration has built a Bhagavad-Gītā Bhavan where on the walls the entire Bhagavad-Gītā is chiselled into marble slabs. The inscriptions have been profusely illustrated with the scenes from the Bhāgavata Purāṇa and the epics. He also took us to his pet elephant named Subhadrā. We took part, along with Swamiji, in feeding her with bananas which she ate with gusto and it was a great sight to watch.

SHANMUKHA DESIKA SWAMIGAL

The full designation of Swamiji, who was the head of the Dharmapuram Ādheenam at the time of interview, is Sri-la-Sri Shanmukha Desika Gnanasambandha Paramacharya Swamigal, as given in their publication. Ādheenam means a *maṭha* in Tamil and the Dharmapuram Ādheenam is one of the two very important centres of Śaiva-Siddhānta, the other being at Tiruvāvaduthuṛai. Before meeting the head of the Dharmapuram Ādheenam in Tanjavur district of Tamil Nadu, two professors, belonging to the college run by the Ādheenam, gave an introductory talk on *saṁnyāsa* according to the Śaiva-Siddhānta philosophy followed here. Ādheenam, an ancient institution which has a great number of devotees comprising a sizeable part of the Tamil-speaking population, has been propagating the Śaiva-Siddhānta tradition for many centuries.

Information Gathered from the Professors

Thirukkuṛaḷ as Authority

The professors related first the sources which form the authority for *saṁnyāsāśrama* followed by the Ādheenam. *Thirukkuṛaḷ* the famous Tamil classic work written by Saint Thiruvaḷḷuvar has dealt with *saṁnyāsa*

19. Shanmuka Desika Swamigal,
Dharmapuram Adheenam

in its chapter called "Neetthār Perumai — The Glory of the Renunciates" ("neetthār" is the term in Tamil for *saṁnyāsa*). They quoted profusely from the work to enunciate the principles laid down for anyone who takes up *turavu* (*saṁnyāsa*). There are two types of *saṁnyāsa*, the one taken up by householders and the other by bachelors. It stresses the importance of giving up worldly life from bachelorhood. It also brings out the importance of giving up after a man has led a married life in Chapters 25 to 30. Defining *saṁnyāsa* it says that it is the control of the senses and complete dedication to the service of Śiva. Ideological differences exist between the practice of *saṁnyāsa* according to Śaṅkara and that followed in Dharmapuram Ādheenam. The *jīva/paśu* is coeval with the Lord but it is ignorant of its true nature because of *vinai/mala*s while Īśvara/Śiva is all knowledge. *Jīva* is given its various births by Śiva for giving up the *vinai* or *mala*s which can be achieved only with Śiva's grace. The Lord decides the type of birth and life in accordance with the *vinai* of the soul.

Heads of the Ādheenam

Dharmapuram Ādheenam heads are unmarried and do not have any contact with their families. The family members can come to the *maṭha* like any other devotee and the head will have no objection in meeting them. The head is involved in societal welfare through hospitals and schools. This does not affect his own personal *sādhanā*. The present head is very happy with the work of his institution. But there are times when the current situations, politically and socially, etc., are not favourable for the smooth functioning of the set-up. However, he does not enter into any political transactions with anyone or organization but he does offer advice, if asked for, from the political arena. Socially the head is invited to bless at weddings, births, etc. He does not attend weddings, but blesses them when they visit the Ādheenam.

Founder

The Ādheenam was started by Guru Jnana Sambandhar (not the seventh century Jnana Sambandhar but another great Śaiva *guru* of the sixteenth century, named after him) who was a great scholar and poet. He was the author of many works on *saṁnyāsa*, Śiva worship, etc. The *mantra* of the Ādheenam is *śivāya namaḥ* and *namaḥ śivāya*. The present head is the 26th in the line and he has initiated a number of *saṁnyāsins* as well. He is a very learned man and has the title of *vidvān* accorded to him for his learning.

Ritual and other Information

The head of the Ādheenam gets up early and does Śiva-Pūjā and does the worshipping later at the temple. He will not touch even water till everything is completed in his personal devotions. He also worships at the *samādhis* of the earlier saints of the *paramparā* most of which are situated on the grounds of the Ādheenam. The previous head established a college here to train *saṁnyāsins*. Income for running this set-up comes from the endowment of extensive agricultural lands. Very little income comes from donations. This Ādheenam controls many *devasthānams* of many temples. They have serious problems in collecting revenues from lands and there is no help from the government for any of the activities of the *maṭha*. Things can only improve when there is general involvement of people in religious matters.

Successor

The head chooses his own successor and no one else has any say in the matter. The head also gives *saṁnyāsa dīkṣā* to aspirants. The *saṁnyāsa* initiation is rather simple and not very elaborate. As Śiva is considered Agni, fire is lit and *homa* is performed during the ceremony and *mantra* is given to the aspirants. Only Śaivas are given *dīkṣā*. Initially tonsure is performed. But later they can grow hair if they so desire.

Brāhmaṇas in the Organization

There are no brāhmaṇas so far in their Ādheenam even though traditionally brāhmaṇas have also been Śaiva *saṁnyāsins* in the tradition. The seventh-century Jnana Sambandhar himself was a brāhmaṇa but nowadays they do not come into this Ādheenam maybe because they have their own *āśrams* for *saṁnyāsa dīkṣā*. The *saṁnyāsin* here also wears ochre robes like *saṁnyāsins* in other *saṁnyāsa āśrams*. However, *tiruneeṛu* or sacred ashes and the *rudrākṣa-mālā* (garland of sacred beads) are holy and are worn by the head of the Ādheenam.

Festivals and other Information

The Ādheenam celebrates all festivals connected with Śiva. Educational institutions and hospitals are founded and run by the Ādheenam for which money is donated. *Kuṁbhābhiṣekam* or consecration of temples and regular festivals are also celebrated. A number of publications both on religious themes and philosophical literature (*Tirumuṟais*) are printed and distributed as part of the major activities of the Ādheenam. The head does not travel much. He does *pada-yātrā* on special occasions. Women are not given *saṁnyāsa* in this tradition.

Conversation with the Head

This conversation with the two retired professors, who now work voluntarily at the Ādheenam, was followed by a meeting with the head himself. He was an imposing presence with his mass of hair rolled up on top of the head (*jaṭādhārī*) like Śiva, he said and he also had *kuṇḍala*s or earrings which had six circles/coils. Explaining the six coils he said that it is symbolic of having conquered the six *mala*s like *kāma, krodha, lobha, moha, mada* and *mātsarya*. He also had a big *rudrākṣa-mālā* which is the very mark of his Ādheenam, besides a ring on his finger which indicated purity, according to him.

He mentioned that he belonged to South Arcot in Tamil Nadu, and was initiated into *saṁnyāsa* at the age of nineteen and was the head of the Ādheenam for the past 28 years. He was a very good singer of the Tevārams and that was how he became involved in Śaiva-Siddhānta. He came out of his *pūjā* only at 12.30 p.m. which confirmed what the professors had said, i.e. that he does not miss his *pūjā* on any account. This meeting of the Dharmapuram Ādheenam *turavi/saṁnyāsin* was indeed quite an eye opener.

SWAMI SHIVAMURTHY SHIVACHARYA

Background

As far as his own background was concerned, Swamiji narrated incidents from his boyhood which had a bearing on his future. His predecessor had come to his village when he was nine. The young boy impressed him with his singing devotional songs at the start of the programme to honour the visitor. The elders told the old Swamiji his deep interest in music by relating to him how he made a violin out of a coconut shell. When he was given a real violin, he learnt it and played it in front of the senior Swami.

The elder Swami keenly followed his educational career and sent him, after his schooling, to the college where he studied science which explains his deep interest in latest developments in computers and information technology. Watching every step of his progress, the elder Swami finally gave up his post and placed his young protégé as the Mahāswāmī of the Vīraśaiva *gaddī*. Thus, the elder Swami became the first person to voluntarily retire from his powerful position setting an example to many who cling to their headship in spite of old age and incompetence. Also he was the first in the sense that he wanted the successor to be chosen in a democratic way so that the incumbent will be acceptable to all in the community. By contrast, there had been a bad precedent in the community, when the grand *guru* of the present Swamiji was poisoned by his own disciple-*saṁnyāsins* to capture power.

After BA, Swamiji was sent to Banaras to do his MA and PhD. He got his doctoral degree in 1977. He was a student of Prof. Padma Mishra a student of A.L. Basham in London. He continued his post doctoral studies in Vienna when he got a scholarship. He became the head on 11 February, 1979.

Vīraśaiva Organization

Shivamurthy Shivacharya Mahaswamiji belongs to the Vīraśaiva tradition and heads the many *āśrams* and *maṭhas* of his lineage. The interview took place in his Bangalore, Karnataka office, called Tarala Balu Kendra. He is highly educated both in the traditional Śāstras and in the modern educational system. He is a well-known scholar in Sanskrit. He administers to the spiritual and temporal needs of his community all over Karnataka and outside. Vīraśaivism (heroic Śaiva religion) has its followers residing mostly in areas around Mysore. Vīraśaivas are recognized by the *liṅga* which they wear around their necks. Swamiji gave a very detailed account of his organization, its history, the story of his own initiation, the innumerable social programmes he has initiated and his involvement in safeguarding the religious life of the population as a whole from interference by outsiders, etc.

The head of this organization is invariably a *saṁnyāsin* who is a *naiṣṭhika brahmacārin*. There are other *saṁnyāsins* in the set-up who head the other *maṭhas*. The *maṭhādhipatis* are also called *guru*, *jagadguru*, etc. In the Vīraśaiva tradition there are different types of *maṭhas*. He is the head of some fifteen *maṭhas* and they all follow the same philosophy. The original founder of many of the Vīraśaiva *maṭhas*

20. Swami Shivamurty Shivachrya, Vīra-Śaiva

is considered to be Basavanna. In common with all Hindu practices they also have all the classifications of *saṁnyāsins* like *kuṭīcakas*, *bahūdakas*, *ativarṇāśramīs*, *haṁsa* and *paramahaṁsa*.

Who is a Saṁnyāsin

Swamiji had studied and written about the *Sūta Saṁyukta*, a Sanskrit work. There a *saṁnyāsin* is one who cares for his spiritual upliftment, liberation or *mokṣa*. He has nothing to do with worldly life and is totally cut-off from the world. In general he is in deep meditation for realization of the ultimate truth. Whereas, in the case of a *guru* or Swami of the Vīraśaiva *maṭha*, a *saṁnyāsin* is one who has given up his individual family, but at the same time he is not a person who cares for only his individual upliftment or spiritual advancement. Swamiji added: "Of course, that part is there, but that is not the only thing of main concern." In addition to his spiritual effort, he wants to take people with him. He is more concerned with people who have respect for the religious tradition. Here he loses his individual interest, because of his involvement in the community. He identifies himself with the community and he has no individual existence.

Society and Community

The Vīraśaiva *maṭhas* are very much integrated within the society and with the community. The heads do not have their personal family lives, perhaps one can say they have an enlarged family in the worldly sense. They are very much involved in the family life of their disciples.

Swamiji stressed on the vision of Basavanna in formulating the principles underlining the Vīraśaiva tradition where there is a judicious blend of the traditional understanding of who a *saṁnyāsin* is and of his changed role in the modern context, as being close to and solely responsible to his community. "Basavanna, in himself, combined a social and spiritual life and he did not want to dissociate the two; he wanted them to go hand in hand. According to him this world was a creation of God and is therefore a stepping stone to that (Godly) world."

Following the example of his master he also started a number of educational institutions for the Vīraśaiva community. In spite of vigorous opposition from his community he made admission to the schools and colleges, both technical and arts, open to all communities including Muslims and Harijans. Following this tradition Shivamurthy Swamiji has started many institutions under the Tarala Balu Kendra, one engineering college, one polytechnic and one residential school in Davanagiri which has become the best one in Karnataka. He has arranged for establishment of hospitals in rural areas with the help of the government. His organization has become the biggest in the country running educational institutions in rural areas.

Moral Education and Financial Resources

Even though very successful in spreading the message of modern education especially to rural youth, Swamiji is not satisfied with mere worldly education. He wants to inculcate a system of moral education to all students studying in his institutions. His aim is to produce an ethically oriented educated community of youngsters to ensure a bright future for them and for the country as a whole. Furthermore, he has started a financial scheme of small savings and investing the money to small women entrepreneurs so that they can improve their economic lot. This is also intended to save rural families from alcoholism, litigation, domestic violence and inequality between the sexes.

The financial position of the *maṭha* is very sound. The major institution which holds most of the funds is called Tarala Balu Nidhi started wisely by his predecessor. Swamiji has personally established endowments for all the religious and social projects. The money for these comes from collections and donations. The government pays the school teachers and college lecturers. The government has exempted the *maṭha* from taxation subject to yearly audit of its accounts. Swamiji said that the 1-2 rupee collections from its adherents has amounted to over Rs. 80 lakh which he has put into fixed deposits and he spends only the interest earned on cultural activities. A committee of which Swamiji is the president administers these funds. Once a year a general body meeting is held when Swamiji presents the accounts for approval. Anybody can ask questions. His predecessor had already set a fine example in this regard with respect to the proper maintenance of accounts and an absolute open discussion among members and the committee.

Thus he is able to gather the community's resources for their own betterment. Another rural economic effort Swamiji has started is to create grazing land for cattle. As an environmental project, his society is also planting trees and herbs for the benefit of the community. Some rare species of plants-herbs that are available in the district, have been collected in the nurseries to serve as raw material for Ayurvedic medicines. Swamiji has also undertaken many steps for social and even political education. To prevent his followers spending enormous amounts of money on marriages, Swamiji conducts mass marriages every month where more than 40 couples enter wedded life with Swamiji's blessings.

Singing groups for Spreading Vīraśaiva Philosophy

Besides all these undertakings towards social upliftment, as a religious leader, he considers that he has the obligation to spread religious ideas which is his mandate as a Vīraśaiva *saṁnyāsin*. He has therefore organized singing groups all over to appear before religious gatherings inspiring them with devotional songs. "If they have to sing there, they have to prepare at home. And indirectly it has an influence on the children. So, that is a different atmosphere altogether. All the activities are conducted by women only. Here every week we have a prayer wing. From 6-7 they come and sing *bhajana*s. Women have more time and they can spare more time. The devotional songs contain the crux of the philosophy which instructs both the singers and the listeners." One important festival that is conducted is the Tarala Balu Pūrṇimā. Tarala Balu was the founder of this *āśram* in the twelfth century. To commemorate that event, the festival is held on a large scale when millions take part. Swamiji is taken in a ceremonial procession on a palanquin. Basava Jayanti to honour the founder of their branch of the Vīraśaivas is also observed.

Paṭṭābhiṣeka

Paṭṭābhiṣeka ceremony or the function to anoint or crown the successor takes place when a new head is chosen. The outgoing head, if he is there, will bless the new one and administer the holy *mantra*. It is generally understood that the new one should be acceptable to his own congregation and also to the other *saṁnyāsin*s of other religious heads as far as possible. To the ceremony are invited other *saṁnyāsin*s also who will take part approving the anointed one by blessing him in turn. They do not have *homa* or fire ceremonies. Instead, *pañca-kalaśa*s (five pots) representing the five faces of Śiva are kept during the entire duration of the function.

Importance of Śiva-Liṅga

The importance of the *liṅga* in the life of a Vīraśaiva is to be noted. Right from the next day of the birth of a child, the *liṅga* is introduced. The *liṅga* is tied to the wrist of a child as part of the naming ceremony. The officiating priest is called Jaṅgama who is highly respected by the community. Every morning and evening, the *liṅga* which hangs from the neck on to the chest, is taken out and all the items of worship that is normally done in the temple is carried out, including *abhiṣeka*, etc. They have no temples in Vīraśaivism. They go to the *samādhi*s of their saints to worship.

Specific Characteristics of a Saṁnyāsin

The two important characteristics of a *saṁnyāsin* are, according to Swamiji, that he should be morally strong to honour the faith and respect that he gets from his disciples; and he should have great concern for the welfare of the people. Once these two are there the rest of the things will take care of themselves. The following message is given by Swamiji to the householders: love and affection between the family members should be maintained for a peaceful and prosperous life. If there is any slightest scope of misunderstanding among the members, the family life would be very disastrous.

SIVAYA SUBRAMUNIYASWAMI

Background Information

Satguru Sivaya Subramuniyaswamiji was heading the Kauai Ādheenam or Kauai's Hindu Monastery at the time of the interview. The interview took place in Kauai, an island of Hawaii archipelago. He founded this *āśram* 31 years ago. This is the headquarters of his organization which has a branch in Mauritius. In his Nātha Sampradāya or Nandi Nātha Sampradāya he is known as Gurudeva. The interview started with the definition of a *saṁnyāsin*.

Swamiji explained that the Ādheenams, which is another name for monasteries/*āśrams*, were supported by the *mahārājās* in the past. "The heads of the Ādheenams were advisers to the *mahārājā*s in all political and social matters; they also helped him in gaining the throne and looked after his religious needs. In south India wise men generally lived in an Ādheenam and an Ādheenam was also a place for practising yoga. The Ādheenams would also have a number of temples under their

21. Sivaya Subrahmuniyaswami, Hawaii

control. This Ādheenam in Hawaii has helped in the establishment of 37 temples around the world."

Saṁnyāsin in the Ādheenam

In this Ādheenam "ordination of a *saṁnyāsin* is preceded by study of the scriptures after which he becomes a renunciate *saṁnyāsin*. In this we follow the tradition as closely as we can. We take *saṁnyāsa* very seriously and all the *saṁnyāsin*s here have been with me at least 30 to 40 years. The new ones get initiated after studying for eight to twelve years, if not more. They study the Tirumanthiram, Vedas, etc., and also other books published here. But most importantly it is their own self-inquiry and investigation into the truth inside and their *sādhanā*, the *tapas* they do to transform themselves. It is the transformation that makes the *saṁnyāsin*. *Saṁnyāsa* in our tradition is the path of fire, the *kuṇḍalinī* fire śakti. In my own life I was inspired by Yoga Swami of Sri Lanka and the way he lived his life. He got me started in this path."

General Information, Politics and Society

*Saṁnyāsin*s ordained in this Ādheenam do not marry. They could become *saṁnyāsin*s if they are widowers but not if they are married. Women are not allowed to take *saṁnyāsa* here. "A married man, even if he gets permission from his wife cannot take *saṁnyāsa* here in this *sampradāya*. He cannot do that because he has his *puruṣa dharma* which he has to maintain throughout life; otherwise he would be making bad *karma* for himself. In other words we encourage only those who come straight from *brahmacarya* to become a *saṁnyāsin* here. A *saṁnyāsin* ideally should have begun studying the sacred texts before he has reached twenty-five years of age."

"We belong to a south Indian Ādheenam tradition which as mentioned before is supposed to be a guide for the political forces within the country mainly to keep them on the track of *dharma*. So this Ādheenam also plays this part on this island. In this country, Mauritius and elsewhere too we move closely with politicians, the police, lawyers and doctors and psychiatrists, on every social issue and cultural issue, and give advice as and when required. Here on this island we work with the government counsel and we meet regularly with them, at least once a month. So the Ādheenam here is much respected on the island. We are looked at as the Hindu community.

We have on this island Portuguese, Japanese, Hindu and Puerto Rican communities. They don't look at Hindus as a religious group. They look at it as a group of people that are very helpful and a vital part of the community. So our priests are invited to give blessings at graduation and other big functions. We don't get directly involved socially and politically as such but only give advice whenever they come to us. We don't do any of the work done by say the Ramakrishna Mission, etc., but we do have a Hindu Heritage Endowment to help out orphanages, etc. Cheques are sent to these organizations. Nobody goes there to do any work. Money comes from 43 countries for our work and also for the temple being built here. Initiated members give $1/10^{th}$ of their income to the Ādheenam."

Swamiji mentioned that the successor of his will be chosen only by him.

Hinduism Today

The Ādheenam is very successful in achieving the objectives it has set for itself. It has a very healthy outlook towards honest criticism of its work and is prepared to make the necessary improvements in its working. That way they can serve much better. The Ādheenam has apprised the Indian community of child abuse, wife abuse and has had discussions towards eradicating such evils. Through the magazine *Hinduism Today* by the Ādheenam, Swamiji said, "We have united the Hindus of the world. And that was the intent of starting the magazine, i.e. to reach out to all Hindus."

Swamiji was travelling through South Africa and found that they had no contact with India at all. They were cut-off from India for a long time due to political conditions. They had no idea that there were Hindus in London, and London had no idea that there were Hindus in Guyana and so on. "So, we started a network and it slowly built up over a period of time. It (*Hinduism Today*) has accomplished its missions in a very fine way. Christians and Muslims all get copies for their libraries so that they can see the strength of Sanātana Dharma. It is the only religious publication that sells along with *Times* and *Newsweek* in the news stands especially in India. All sects are treated equally and no bad news is printed unless it has become a subject of public interest like court cases, etc."

Attitude towards Hindu Saṁnyāsins in the West

"Hindu *saṁnyāsin*s are respected like the Christian priests or a Protestant minister. The Hindu *saṁnyāsin* has a deeper look at life as they practise yoga. Hindu *saṁnyāsin*s are highly respected in the West right from the time of Swami Vivekananda. The Śwamis who come here are able to raise a good amount of money for their institutions. They do go back to India and build up their *āśram*s which has benefited many. Swamis like Swami Satchidananda have visited Catholic monasteries in America and helped them to understand the Hindu *saṁnyāsin*. I, on my part, have also taught them how Indian *āśram*s are run like its time schedules, yoga, etc. I have brought out a book called *Holy Orders in Saṁnyāsa* as there had been no such publication detailing the essential nature of Hindu *saṁnyāsin* tradition. It contains contributions from Ramakrishna Mission, Swami Chinmayananda, Swami Satchidananda and others. The Ādheenam follows the practices established in the tradition at Sri Lanka like cremating *saṁnyāsin*s after their death, unlike the practice of throwing bodies into the rivers or burying them as is practised elsewhere."

"The practice of giving *saṁnyāsa* became somewhat lax in the early days of independence in India. In Sivananda Ashram, for instance, they gave *saṁnyāsa* freely to anyone who stayed in the *āśram* for just three years. There was no assessment, training, grooming, etc., conducted in a laid-down fashion. Sivananda's intention was good in the sense that, he probably felt, if he initiated 500 people at least 25 will survive."

Mokṣa

Swamiji defined *mokṣa* as freedom from rebirth. The Ādheenam also believed in liberation while a person is still living (*jīvanmukti*). This is the motto of Śaiva-Siddhānta which is being followed in this Ādheenam as well. This tradition does not initiate women into *saṁnyāsa*. It has a training school for ministers, a training school for priests, and a congregation that has no other religious affiliation whatsoever. There are sacraments for the children of couples whose marriages were arranged by the Swami himself 25 years ago. The Ādheenam celebrated its 50th anniversary recently. A huge temple is being built that is expected to last for a thousand years. This is going to be a unique temple in these islands of Hawaii.

Administrative and other Information

There are five monastic groups in the Ādheenam called *kulams* (family). Each *kulam* has a co-ordinator. Temple administration, tending the cows, astrology, fund-raising, cooking, sales, business, land administration, gardens, publications are all looked after by the respective *kulam*. Each of these meets once a week and decides upon a whole week's programme and then they set their daily activities. Swamiji runs all this through able *saṁnyāsins* who have been doing this work for the past thirty years. Decisions are taken after everyone is consulted and the systems are running smoothly. There are four stewards who may be called members of the board of trustees. The stewards including Swamiji run the whole show. He was confident that all the activities of the Ādheenam will be carried on uninterruptedly even when he is not there any more.

Procedure for entering Saṁnyāsa

A new person wanting to join the set-up has to take his vows for six months at a time. And if he does not come up to the standard after six months, he is given another six more months and so on. At the moment of the interview there was one who had taken vows for two years. It is renewed at the end of two years if necessary. Only the Swamis take lifetime vows. They take it after eight, ten, or twelve years. It is one of the most strict monastic organizations in the world.

Apart from appearing to be a *saṁnyāsin* he should have a philosophical background, and should do *sādhanā* and personal religious practices. From such a person "you can feel the vibration." He is a transformed person and on the road to realization. The *āśram* is a big machine influencing the lives of millions of people. Swamiji's *guru* in Sri Lanka had two million followers and now they are spread out throughout the world — in Europe, Australia, New Zealand, America, etc. Besides arranging marriages, Swamiji gives names to babies in person or through the internet. Five to 10 per cent of those connected and following the religion through the Ādheenam are Westerners. The *āśram* is involved in the lives of all its followers all over the world.

Additional Information

A few more points emerged from discussions with Swamiji and his assistant, a *saṁnyāsin*, who was present at the interview. Many Hindu temples in USA have found it necessary to approach the Ādheenam and Swamiji to resolve any serious problems they encounter. Compared to other Hindu organizations this Ādheenam has been very well established and is a great source of inspiration to other Hindu bodies. This is due to their strict adherence to principles laid down by the Swamiji and the intense training his follower Swamis have had during the course of their life here. Swamiji has done pioneering work in laying down exemplary procedures for persons who decide to enter the Hindu fold. There are very many families who have become Hindus over 30 years and they are happy to bring up their children in their new faith guided by Swamiji and his enthusiastic band of *saṁnyāsins*. Swami Chinmayananda himself sought the help of the Ādheenam for legal advice to run his *āśrams*.

Difference between Daśanāmī and Nātha Traditions

A very significant aspect of the overall *saṁnyāsin* tradition in India was the differences between the Daśanāmī and Nātha traditions. They clearly emphasized that Nātha is a non-*daśanāmī* order even though they also follow Advaita philosophy as the other Śaṅkarācārya *maṭhas*. Within the Nātha tradition there is a southern and northern tradition. The northern tradition follows Gorakhnātha and the southern follows Nandinātha. The Nātha tradition accepts the value and the necessity of temple worship, personal worship throughout one's evolution and at the same time believes in the internal realization of the absolute. When you hear a Swami say those two things together, that indicates a Nātha traditional follower. Daśanāmīs will not say that, as they feel that the concept that one can evolve out of worship is not part of their philosophy. Yoga Swami worshipped in the temple everyday of his life until he died. He was a great *siddhar*. All of the *siddhars* have been associated with temples.

Hinduism: A Way of Life

It would be very counter productive to say that Hinduism is a way of life and thus implying that it is not a religion. This statement unfortunately confirms what has been in the minds of others who do not recognize Hinduism as a religion. This may in the long run harm the interests of the Hindus especially in countries outside India. In

Canada, till 1972 Hinduism was not recognized as a religion. Now it is not so. In the United States there is no "official" recognition of religion. Nearly all the temples have received tax exemption from the IRS as non-profit corporations. Swamiji encouraged the temples to seek the further designation as "church" which is available to any religious organization of any religion which meets certain criteria. Christian, Muslim, Buddhist, Jewish and Hindu organizations in the US have been designated as "churches." Śṛṅgerī Peetham in Pennsylvania, Yogaville in Virginia and Barsana Dham in Texas are three Hindu organizations which are designated churches.

SWAMI VEDA BHARATI

Swami Rama's Ashram is situated in an idyllic setting on the banks of the Gaṅgā far removed from the pilgrimage town of Rishikesh. Swami Veda Bharati who is the head *saṁnyāsin* there is a disciple of Swami Rama and is also a Mahāmaṇḍaleśvara of the Nirañjanī Akhāḍā like Swami Maheshanand Giri. Swamiji said, "The Akhāḍā and Śaṅkarācārya's Daśanāmī system work in parallel. There are seven major *akhāḍā*s. The two biggest ones are the Nirañjanī Akhāḍā and the Junā Akhāḍā. These *akhāḍā*s played great political roles in the past. My master belonged to Nirañjanī, so they came and claimed me. I know I am very unfamiliar with all that. As I am going along, I am finding out more about it."

Saṁnyāsa Defined

In his opinion a *saṁnyāsin* is one who has abandoned the three *eṣaṇā*s; someone for whom this entire creation is his personal family. People have asked me, "What has changed in you by taking *saṁnyāsa*? I said I gained freedom to love." Swamiji was married before taking *saṁnyāsa*. "When I was a householder, I had a great problem. I simply could not figure out who is my family member and who is not. Family claims an exclusive membership. Nobody defines as to on what basis you define this one is a family member and this one is not. So for me, taking *saṁnyāsa* was just having freedom to love." Even at an early age he asked his father to let him become a Swami. "Saṁnyāsa whose characteristic is *vairāgya* is not shutting off anyone. It is not losing someone, abandoning someone. It is gaining the whole universe. It is synonymous with full enlightenment. That is *vidvat saṁnyāsa*. But we are *vividiṣā saṁnyāsins*. *Vidvat saṁnyāsa* is that of the Buddha at the moment of enlightenment (the moment of actually realizing the *mahāvākya*). But ours is a *vividiṣā saṁnyāsa* which means that we want to be away from families and relations and so forth only to pursue that one goal (of enlightenment)."

Personal Background

"I have a peculiar background. I have been a person who had never been to school in his life. I was born near here in Dehra Dun. I have a Punjabi parentage. But we spoke Sanskrit at home, all brothers and sisters. I never had a teacher in any subject, except that my father taught me Sanskrit grammar. I had to memorize Pāṇini and by six and a half years I knew all the four thousand *sūtras*. By the age of seven I studied the *Mahābhāṣya* and Yāska's *Nirukta*. I studied till the age of nine years. And that was the end of my education. Around eleven years I started getting invitations to speak, and at thirteen some scholars saw me presiding as a *brahma* (priest) over a *yajña*. They were surprised and so they went out and wrote one or two articles about me. I was challenged by a *puṇḍit* to translate a passage he randomly selected from the Vedas. When I did that, there were no more doubts about my competence and no more questions were asked after that. Then I got invitations from all over and since then I have been travelling. From February 1947 onwards I have led the life of a wanderer. Six years later I left and travelled to other countries and established organizations here and there."

Swamiji became a *gṛhastha* when he got married in Guyana where he was on a mission. His *pūrvāśrama* wife is an Indian settled in Guyana. He had four children by her — one son and three daughters. "They are in their own places. I had an Ārya Samāj background. I had abandoned it. It never occurred to me at that time that there is any other path than the Ārya Samāj one; all that changed when I came into contact with *gurudeva*" (Swami Rama).

Swamiji was instructed by Swami Rama, who initiated him on Diwali day in 1969 at Minneapolis in the USA into the tradition of what is called Himalayan Yoga. He was instructed to teach the interior processes of *dhyāna-yoga* which is part of the Himalayan Yoga tradition. Since then he has successfully initiated thousands of people into *dhyāna-yoga* and is continuing to do so. The secret of *dhyāna-yoga* is in going to the core of the complex mind and teaching a meditation technique suitable for each individual aspirant. "The *guru* grants you the power of transmission. I had to practise it continuously to gain this power."

Swamiji is invited regularly by many organizations including Sikhs to give this teaching of *dhyāna-yoga*. "It is also regularly done in Minneapolis in my *āśram*."

Role of a Saṁnyāsin

"By being a nothing," was his reply when asked about the role of a *saṁnyāsin* in society. "To be a *saṁnyāsin* one must be a nothing inside one's self. No one is mine and I am no one's — absolute egoless experience. By his presence he influences all those who come in contact with him. He does not go out to seek recognition. If it comes and if it will help with a certain mission, then he accepts. It is a matter of constant self-observation." He added that there were two types of *saṁnyāsins*. Those who choose to live the life of seclusion, absolutely alone with one or more disciples at the most, and those that play an active role, changing the society as needed. My master said, "a Swami has no obligation to anyone. At the time of *saṁnyāsa* the *guru* asks — have you got any debts? If you are indebted, *saṁnyāsa* cannot be given, including kārmic debts." "Just a few days before my taking the vows, I went home to do *pūjā* on Diwali day. I asked my wife for forgiveness for any transgressions. That way you have no debts, no obligations and no kārmic debts. That way you are free. Having that freedom you can bring changes in society, because you are not doing it for political reasons, you are not doing it for recognition, and the moment any selfish thing occurs, then you are transgressing the vow of a *saṁnyāsin*."

Lokasaṁgraha and Spiritual Activity

How does one reconcile activity for *lokasaṁgraha* and one's own spiritual enlightenment? Swamiji's answer: "That is probably the difference between the parallel organization of Śaṅkarācāryas and *akhāḍās*. *Akhāḍās* have always been socially active. It is the *akhāḍās* where the martial arts have been preserved. All the *nāgā sādhus*, they all preserve the martial arts. But now the Śaṅkarācāryas are also active; they run colleges, they run Sanskrit schools, they run hospitals, etc. Enlightenment is not from what I understand an act of selfish withdrawal. It is an expansion. When all become as you, *vāsudevaḥ sarvamiti*, then the *pīḍā* (suffering) of everyone becomes your *pīḍā*. So anyone in any kind of *duḥkha* comes to you. Since you have risen above that *duḥkha* yourself, you can help them, you can guide them. *Kāruṇya* (compassion) is part of development towards enlightenment, and then that *kāruṇya* shows itself towards

22. Swami Veda Bharati

others."

In spite of being a diabetic and a heart patient, he devotes, he said, 20 hours a day to cater to the spiritual and other needs of those who come to the *āśram* for redress or enlightenment. A large number of people keep coming to take his advice constantly and he hasn't been able to take even a walk as he needs to do, according to his doctors' orders, as he devotes all the time counselling those who seek his guidance.

Public Perception of a Saṁnyāsin in India and the West

In Swamiji's view a large number of people in India do not know who a *saṁnyāsin* is. Some even think him to be a soothsayer, a palmist, a problem solver and so on; or they jump to the conclusion that he may be one of those under a cloud. It is a fact many *saṁnyāsin*s have not set the highest example. Now it is at a stage where it is hard to differentiate between a beggar and a Swami. "Only a few come to a *saṁnyāsin* for spiritual advice. However, whenever they detect the slightest true selflessness, then immediately there is that devotion and dedication." There is therefore a very confused picture about how a *saṁnyāsin* is viewed.

In the West they easily understand when they hear one is a monk. But they still do not know much about a Hindu monk and of course there is curiosity. Swamiji was given "the greatest respect among Catholic monks." "Once you exchange the thought on what it means to be a monk then they know that somewhere you are a part of the same community. I was so surprised because I knew nothing about Western monastery systems. I learnt from Catholic Benedictine monks that their vows of poverty, chastity and obedience are similar to our vows. I have stayed in Catholic monasteries and was well received. A traditional Hindu monastery will not accommodate monks from other religions. But modern *saṁnyāsin*s like us, nowadays, do entertain monks from other religions without any reservation. For instance I have a Roman Catholic nun who is staying here and who gives me the same respect that she would give to her superiors."

Saṁnyāsinīs

"The *saṁnyāsinī*s in India have not become well known. Many teachers who are not formerly *saṁnyāsinīs* also are teaching in different countries as *yoginīs*. Anandamayi Maa was not officially a *saṁnyāsinī*, but how many *saṁnyāsinīs* can equal her? "So it is not essential that only one who wears ochre robes is a *saṁnyāsin*/*saṁnyāsinī*. So I don't think it really matters. There is no census of *saṁnyāsinīs* in India. The role of a *saṁnyāsinī* is the same as that of a *saṁnyāsin*. As the variety among male *saṁnyāsins*, so also is there variety among female *saṁnyāsinīs* in the level of education, in the service they give, the mother figure they are, etc. Some of them are political leaders as you know like Uma Bharati and Ritambhara Devi. As you pass during the day you will see some boards of big names of *saṁnyāsinīs* who are running big *āśrams* on the way from here. Each one plays her own role. Some may even be Jaina *bhikṣuṇīs*, they are top notch *viduṣīs*, who are given the title of Āryakās, Āryakā Janamati, for instance. She is an absolute master of Sanskrit. You know she has inspired many others to take this path. She is in Hastinapur in Meerut district. We have some of her books here."

"I have given *saṁnyāsa* to two women. Swami Rama gave one woman *saṁnyāsa* but she went back after a few years. I have given *saṁnyāsa* to two women — Gloria who was earlier a Catholic nun and to a former Taiwanese Buddhist *bhikṣuṇī*. I have also given *saṁnyāsa* to two men."

General Information

While no successor has yet been chosen, a committee of three or four members may be formed who will carry on the work. Members may be male or female. The committee members themselves may choose one among them as the leader. This has happened here in Rishikesh in Sivananda's *āśram* and also in the Dvaita Ashrama of Madhvācārya. Swamiji's assessment of his success and that of his *āśram* is as follows: "I consider not the success of the *āśram* but only the success of the teachings. Any success should be counted as that of the lineage. If one person's meditation improves that is success. I pray for 300-400 people worldwide everyday. I have initiated thousands. Swamiji (Swami Rama) has done much more before me (through this *āśram*). As there are no membership system and rules, it would be difficult to quantify the success. There is no record of many who were taught meditation and countless who were made teachers. For instance, I have here a Trinidadian, and I am going to give him *vānaprastha dīkṣā*. I took him as my pupil there in Trinidad. There was no communication from him for twelve years. Now he wrote to me that he wants to come. So to me having taught one person like that, that is success. I am able to influence all those people for whom I conduct prayers, meditative prayers. Those I pray for always end up being here. The success of an *āśram* depends on the spirituality of its guide."

Administrative Matters

The Āśram's policies are decided by a Trust Committee. Swamiji sets the guidelines for the committee. He also decides for 15-20 organizations all over the world — Singapore, Taiwan, Brunei, Korea, USA, and Canada, etc. The funds of this *āśram* are varied. Western students and visitors to the *āśram* pay "depending on whether they can afford." There are no rich disciples. There are no other donations. Swami Rama built the hospital on the way to Dehra Dun through the help of local populations settled outside: "We are not known among Indians in general. Our Swami brothers go to their rich Indian disciples abroad and collect funds. Our work is all with the local populations in every country. It is all Chinese in China and all Koreans in Korea. Indians in those countries don't even know that I come and that I exist. So, the system in most Western countries is that you give a lecture, you get a fee, you bring back and you support the *āśram*. So that's why after a year I have to be on the move, to run the *āśram* and it also brings people here. In China people come because of their respect to the land of the Buddha. Every one comes with their little gold and red envelopes in which they make offerings without asking for it, at the feet of the teacher, and wait for the blessing."

Specific Qualities of a Saṁnyāsin

The two characteristics of a *saṁnyāsin* are absolute unselfish lovingness towards all without any boundaries, race, culture, country and age without any *pratyāśā*, any expectations of a reward in return; and second, is being *antarmukha*. "In all of our activities we often forget that there is this interior life. So many times Swamis also become involved in social revolutions and their internal life suffers. If you are a serious meditator, then it does not happen." 'Speak only when you are in silence, eat only when you are fasting and meditate on the run' has been the title of seminars Swamiji has spoken. Mental inwardness and interior silence is essential even while caring for other people. The two activities are complementary — the internal and the external. The deeper one goes into the meditative life, the more unselfish one becomes. To Swamiji personally this lovingness without boundaries is most important. Characteristics of the *āśram* — "it should be a place where people arriving feel a lovingness and then automatically and naturally they begin to sense a certain degree of silence. The meditation hall here creates such an ambience."

Festivals

The *āśram* members and guests celebrate Holi, Diwali, etc. The Christians here celebrate Christmas. As part of the lovingness policy, Swamiji participates in all festivals. "To me personally it is of no significance. New year, old year it is all the same." The *āśram* is not ritualistic. The only *pūjā* done here is on Gurupūrṇimā and on the day of Swamiji's (Swami Rama's) *mahāsamādhi*. Swamiji, however, teaches *mānasa pūjā*. No special effort is done for publicity except for a brochure detailing *āśram* activities. Morning 8:30 to 9:30 is reserved for Swamiji's meditation and anyone is welcome to come and sit and meditate with him.

Community Service

Community services are done through the hospital established by Swami Rama. The hospital is actually two institutions — one is the hospital itself, and the other is Rural Development Institute. A lady from Karnataka, Mythili, has dedicated her life for running the 250 centres in the mountains. The staff has to travel by bus for an hour or two and then has to walk 20 miles and go where no doctor ever goes. They are the bare foot doctors as in China. An institute for lepers' children in Dehra Dun is run by the *āśram*. It is run by Swamiji's *pūrvāśrama* wife. There are children studying in their school called Seva Bharati. 300 to 400 children are given milk and some food and medicine every day at the school.

SWAMI AGNIVESH

Let me start with a quote from Swami Agnivesh himself as reported in the *Times of India* newspaper, New Delhi, dated 7 April 2001. The heading reads "I want to counter the blind faith in the saffron robe." He went on to add: A true *sādhu* does not need to hang a label around his neck to show that he is progressive. He actually practises liberalism and secularism in his daily life. Swamiji also made an important observation in that same interview regarding the polarization in Indian society between the people who swear by our cultural heritage but do not want to bring about social equality, and on the other hand there are the communists who want socio-economic parity but reject the holy texts. That in a nutshell summarizes what Swami Agnivesh stands for.

A renowned *saṁnyāsin* of the Ārya Samāj order, Swami Agnivesh is engaged wholeheartedly in political, social and religious activities spread over a number of decades. This interview took place in New Delhi. He readily consented to speak about his life before taking up the saffron robe as a *saṁnyāsin*/renouncer-cum-social worker.

Background

In his own case he voluntarily decided to take the plunge at age 27 along with Swami Induvesh who was 30 years old. How did it all begin? "I was born in a very orthodox Brāhmaṇa family of south India, in Srikakulam in Andhra Pradesh. The part to which my parents belonged is in Orissa and the exact place is Dharampur in Kanjao district, which is on the border of Andhra Pradesh. We still have a large Telugu-speaking community there. I lost my father when I was four. So with my mother I migrated to my maternal grandfather's place at Shakti. He was the dewan in the princely state of Madhya Pradesh in an area called Chhattisgarh. In fact, I was born at Shakti as my mother had gone to her maternal place for my delivery. I did my matriculation from Shakti. Then I went on to Calcutta for University education. After completing my MCom and LLB. I joined St. Xavier's college teaching Business Management and Law there for five years. I also practised law at Calcutta High Court briefly. I was junior to one great lawyer who subsequently became India's Chief Justice of the Supreme Court, Justice Sabyasachi Mukerjee."

Additional Background Information

Swamiji added that while at St Xavier's, he had critically examined the role of foreign missionaries in India and the type of activities that were taking place in places like Nagaland, Jharkand and other areas. As a patriot he considered it his duty to see that his country was not partitioned again on religious lines as happened in the case of Pakistan. Ārya Samāj teachers from places like Punjab, Haryana and other places would come and tell how grim the situation was growing. He, therefore, felt emotionally disturbed. Around the same time he came across the writings of Friedrich Max Müller in which he (Max Müller) had said that it was the opportune moment for India to be converted to Christianity. So, he got a little book published titled *Max Müller Exposed* and got it distributed at a function organized by Max Müller Bhavan in Calcutta where top diplomatic corps and Indian intelligentsia were present. He was at the time 23/24 years old, and his name at that time was Vepakshayan Rao. They wanted to know who was behind it. When they found out, they invited him for a discussion. He then asked them what the answer was to those specific quotations which he had read in Max Müller's writings. They had no answer and they just wanted him not to write and spread such things. They could not answer the questions he had raised based on specific quotations from Müller's books.

The more he read the more he got convinced that just as the missionaries had come here leaving the comfort of their homes, going to the tribal areas with a missionary motive to convert, similarly, unless and until educated young men and women of this country went to the forest areas and lived with our tribal people, we really cannot make an impact. "If Christianity was not to spread in our country, then we should also work with the same dedication and zeal as they do." Basically with this idea he left his job in Calcutta and moved over to Haryana.

My companion there was Indradev Vedarthi who was a teacher and was initiated into Ārya Samāj as a *naiṣṭhika brahmacārī*. Together we planned to raise a band of nearly 200 young Swamis who will pan out to all these sensitive areas and go and work for Ārya Samāj with the main idea not to let these Christian missionaries do their conversion work. We went from village to village to spread this message of what was wrong with our social fabric. Haryana, then a newly carved state (1966), had a lot of potential. Ārya Samāj was highly respected in the rural areas, among farmers and land cultivators, and progressive people took pride in calling themselves Ārya Samājis cutting across party lines. So, by our interaction with the masses, people slowly realized that the real work lies in fighting the caste system, poverty, destitution and things like that, because the Christian missionaries strike at the place where we are the weakest.

This goes for Islam as well; 95 per cent of the converts come from our dalits and the tribal people whom the Hindu orthodoxy has abandoned. They have been discriminated against for centuries. Unless and until we give them back their self-respect and get rid of caste abomination, till then we will not succeed in facing this challenge. With this realization we slightly changed our course of action. Instead of just getting initiation into *saṁnyāsa* and trying to stop conversions, we decided that we should create a new movement where we can reach out to the poorest of the poor in our country, give them empowerment, give them social economic justice and spread that message all over India.

Who is a Saṁnyāsin?

A *saṁnyāsin* is one who is very devoted and dedicated in one's life mission for the service of humankind. He is one for whom the whole life is a prayer to God and who can look upon all human beings as members of one family without distinction of caste, creed, colour, race, religion, etc. At the time of initiation as a *saṁnyāsin*, one is given three vows "give up *vittaiṣaṇā, putraiṣaṇā* and *lokaiṣaṇā*, viz. give up desire for wealth, progeny and fame. It is an institution enjoining on one to stand up for truth come what may. A *saṁnyāsin* should be able to pay the highest price for truth. Goaded by this vision our forefathers divided human life into the four *āśrama*s — *brahmacarya, gr̥hastha, vānaprastha* and *saṁnyāsa*. *Saṁnyāsa* must be the ultimate goal of every human being. When initiated at a very young age, it helps promote transcendence of one's ego, personal ambitions and relationships.

Rāga and *dveṣa* are very binding; they create attachments and through the attachments we get involved in the world all the time. How can one rise above these? How can one be equanimous? How do we relate ourselves to the creator? How does one attain *mokṣa*? There is this whole range of ideas with respect to the *saṁnyāsāśrama*. So, rising above desires, rising above *rāga* and *dveṣa*, aversions and cravings, one has to lead a life of a *sādhaka*. The whole life is a *sādhanā* in order to elevate to that life — to relate to the social, political and economic activities of life.

The fourfold *āśrama-vyavasthā* has been formulated for that purpose. Unfortunately, nowadays, we have only the first two *āśrama*s; the last two are not in force. The founder of the Ārya Samāj, Swami Dayananda Saraswati has said "If anyone can judge himself/herself truthfully, and takes the leap to become a *saṁnyāsin*, that person should be accepted as genuine. The most important thing is for the person himself/herself to judge, and then somebody might also help. The *guru* or whoever initiates can also surely give guidance."

Thoughts on Saṁnyāsa and Mokṣa

As to the question of the textual interpretation of the scriptures regarding *mokṣa*, Swamiji related an incident from Swami Dayananda Saraswati's life. It is said that the founder of the Ārya Samāj was once meditating on the banks of the river Gaṅgā, in fact, Alakanandā, up in the Himalayas early in his life as a *saṁnyāsin*. "After completing his study of the Vedas, Swamiji (Dayananda) used to sit anything up to 18 hours at a stretch in one posture in *samādhi*. On that particular occasion, he was disturbed by the sound of a woman crying nearby. He could see that she was carrying a child in her arms. He then saw her put the child, which was lifeless, into the river. As she was doing this, she was removing a piece of cloth from the child and covering the upper part of her body with it. It was obvious that since she had no spare cloth she had torn half of her own saree to cover the dead body of her child. After talking to her and knowing the truth of her tragic life, Swami Dayananda decided at once that he would not only work for his *mokṣa*, but he will in greater measure fight inequality in society. That prompted him to start the Ārya Samāj and also to reinterpret what the life of a *saṁnyāsin* stands for. Therefore a *saṁnyāsin*, according to Dayananda Saraswati, not only needs to practise meditation to achieve one's *mokṣa*, but has to also realize that one's own *mokṣa* is inextricably wound round the *mokṣa* (liberation/betterment) of the society as well." Swamiji agreed to the suggestion that it is more like the Bhagavad-Gītā's *lokasaṁgraha*.

Eligibility for Saṁnyāsa

When is one eligible for *saṁnyāsa*? According to Swamiji a person, after *brahmacarya āśrama* enters *gṛhasthāśrama* and he should stay in married life, say another 25 years; only then is he eligible for *vānaprasthāśrama* and then *saṁnyāsa*. But it is also not that very strict for there is the provision that any time one feels *vairāgya* in whichever stage of life one is in, he can take up *saṁnyāsa* at once. One may be five years old or 85. A *saṁnyāsin* has to stay away from his family. As a worshipper of God, he should help His creation to be better individuals through his propagation of spirituality which consists of attaining godhood for himself and for others; godhood (God) is defined as

23. Swami Agnivesh, Ārya Samāj

satccidānanda, nirākāra, sarvaśaktimān, nyāyakārī, dayālu, ajanmā, ananta, nirvikāra, sarvādhāra, etc. These attributes of God are to be imbibed and lived through compassion and love towards His creation.

"In order to imbibe these qualities I have to be more truthful, more compassionate, just and loving and kind all the time in every aspect of my life. But when I try to be so, I see all around me the forces of untruth, and violence, injustice rising their ugly head. If I withdraw from society and then think, 'this is not my concern as I am truthful, I am not telling lies, I am not killing,' that does not help; because seeing injustice all around there is an urge to take on the forces of violence, injustice, untruth and tyranny spontaneously."

"So *saṁnyāsa* is spiritual activism, it is not spirituality. Automatically *saṁnyāsa* takes up the activist approach. I have to be truthful within but attack the forces of untruth without. I have to be compassionate within, but fight the forces of violence without. Within and without that is the social dimension. That social dimension gets integrated into one's life. In this system, the *āśram* is for both the individual's pursuit of salvation as well as for social upliftment, social change, social transformation. Fighting injustice, to put it very simply, is key to the worship and prayer and meditation. That is *dharma* as we understand it."

"Here the means itself becomes the end. There is no distinction. It is achieved by practising the ideals of a *saṁnyāsin*, that is trying to live as austere as possible, having as few possessions as possible, devoting as much time as possible for meditation, knowing oneself. Self-realization is the key to the whole effort. I have to know the truth about myself — Who am I — the truth is to be pursued to its logical end. *Vipassanā* meditation helps me. This is part of Buddhism which is an offshoot of Vedas. All knowledge emanated from the Vedic scriptures. Unnecessarily we categorize it as Buddhism. I think the roots are in the Vedas. Vedas are the knowledge given by God in the beginning of creation. Meditation helps me to know myself. Everyday, meditation is necessary to get rid of the ego to the extent possible. I am breathing, but it is not me who is breathing. Breathing has been happening to me. My eyes are seeing, my ears are hearing, it is something else, it is not me. Realizing that truth can make that truth the part of my experiential truth, not like spoken truth or written truth, but something that becomes interior to my being. Then I can overcome my anger and ambitions and whatever else. Then I can relate to the whole universe, to the birds, leaves, everything. There I see the image of my creator. Creator in the most beautiful form, most compassionate form. So meditation of one hour in the morning and one hour in the evening is enough. Then larger meditation is the working life of service. Life becomes meditative. That is how objectives are achieved."

Success in Objectives

"I have been greatly successful in my objectives, even though success cannot be measured in worldly terms. I cannot say that I have achieved my goal. It gives me a lot of satisfaction that I am pursuing my life in the right direction. If I don't achieve *mokṣa* in this life, I will try it in my next life, and next and next. But the direction is correct and I am trying to pursue it as sincerely as possible. At present I am working for the poorest of the poor, the bonded child and slavery-like practices in our country. Also I am continuing my fight against gender inequality, alcoholism and the caste system relentlessly."

In answer to the question of hierarchy in the order he said there is no strict hierarchy in the order. There is a head Swami but a non-Swami can also be the head of the body. The head co-ordinates activities all over the world. "But for my mission, for my pursuit of truth I am totally free and I can do anything. As the direction is right, I can say I am successful 100 per cent in my objectives. When I judge myself, whether I have overcome my ego, my anger and lust and other things, I am quite satisfied. I am able to identify with the struggles of the poorest of the poor not only in my organization, but also anywhere and everywhere in the world. I don't feel any discrimination against people who follow other religions, other so-called racial groups, so-called blacks, whites etc."

One Whole Humanity

"I can see the whole humanity as one family. In fact, I see the whole creation as one organic whole. I feel very pained or anguished when I see animals being slaughtered for food. I just cannot stand the sight of animals being butchered. This is the moment I feel very sad. I feel very sad when I see children being used as labour. I am very sure, as long as humanity does not get rid of killing animals for its own consumption, there will be no end to war, no end to exploitation, no end to violence in society. Even when a flower is plucked I feel sad. That is one reason I don't accept garlands which is customary in India."

Bad Times for Saṁnyāsa

Unfortunately the institution of *saṁnyāsa* has fallen into bad times, said Swamiji when asked about the way society views a *saṁnyāsin*. When it was devised and promoted, it had a lot of significance. The *saṁnyāsin* wore not orange or saffron clothes but wore clothes with the real colour of fire. Fire that purifies, that enlightens. The *saṁnyāsin* gave up all his worldly desires and started living for humanity. But nowadays one sees hundreds and thousands of *saṁnyāsins* who just put on this robe and not live the life of a *saṁnyāsin*. "Then I feel sad. I think the institution is being vulgarized and distorted beyond imagination. Today in India we have very many villages but if you take the census of the total number of Swamis we have thousands of Swamis per village! Even if one Swami could uplift one village then the village could be transformed within no time. Unfortulately they are living in big centres and in religious places like Hardwar, Kāśī, Mathura and other places in hordes and not doing anything; on the other hand they are doing everything contrary and counter productive to spiritual upliftment. They are promoting gender inequality in the name of religion. Generally Swamis are party to denigrating women to an inferior status. This is a great disservice to the institution of *saṁnyāsa*."

The West and the Hindu Saṁnyāsin

As to the way the West views a Hindu *saṁnyāsin* he said: "In the West there is very little understanding about the Hindu *saṁnyāsin*. They have difficulty in comprehending deep, universal perceptions. Their ideas are confined to the book, the institutions of Christianity, Judaism, Islam, the prophets, the rituals in the church, the sacredness of the church. For them it is not that easy to understand the institution of *saṁnyāsa* in Hinduism. Only a few of them, who rise above these narrow connotations, are able to view correctly the Hindu *saṁnyāsin*. There are some fine people out there. But by and large the institutionalized hierarchical way they approach religion and God, etc., makes them have a completely different view of the *saṁnyāsin*."

Interaction with Bombay Muslims

He went on to add: "The other day I was invited to address a very large gathering of Muslims in Bombay, about 50,000 delegates. All of them were males. This was because women are not supposed to join them and sit side by side with them according to their precepts. For me it was a sad experience. I could not reconcile to that and said, 'How come I don't see a single woman?' I found out that they had a separate *śāmiānā* ½ km away from that of the men. There women were having a separate conference where a woman speaker had come. No male speaker can address them. I cannot accept that. They have a man's world and a woman's world. I told them informally that, as an Ārya Samāji, I see God in all of creation. Every particle of creation is the replica of the Creator. Therefore for me it is not important to go to a certain place to say *namāẓ* or prayers. Life is a prayer. Wherever and whenever I am serving society, I am serving God; I am living those ideas in my day-to-day life, in my conduct. For me being religious is being dhārmic, and not just saying prayers or going to the temples and doing rituals. Islam stood for banning idolatry but it is sinking deep into newer and newer forms of idolatry. I told them to read their own tenets and principles as they have deviated from them. They listened with rapt attention and they appreciated also. I told them that they worship graves and put cloths over them which is contrary to the injunction against idol worship. The *kalmā* prayer, says 'God is one and nobody can equal God. Prophet alone is the messenger.' As an Ārya Samājī I recite my own *kalmā* (in Arabic): 'God is one. Every particle of the universe is the messenger of my God.' They clapped and they enjoyed it very much."

Ārya Samāj and Saṁnyāsa

Strictly speaking there is no order of *saṁnyāsin*s as such in Ārya Samāj. *Saṁnyāsa āśram*s do exist in some places like Ghaziabad near Delhi, Aligarh and in other places. There *saṁnyāsin*s meet, read and write. The *vānaprastha āśram* is in Hardwar in a place called Jwalapur. Swamiji's mother lives there at age 80 plus. He recalled that when he mooted the idea of his becoming a *sādhu*, his mother cried profusely. The family depended on him for support. This added to the problem. He assured her that he will not become a Swami. Some time later he invited one great Ārya Samāj Swami to his home. His mother was very happy, prostrated before him and looked after him very well. After he left, Swami Agnivesh jokingly remarked to her, "If someone else's son becomes a Swami, you honour him with such respect, knowing fully well that he does not worship idols and propagate this type of Hinduism or Brahmanism that you do. If your own son wants to become a Swami (he did not complete the sentence)." She immediately started crying but gradually got so much involved in the concept herself. Although some of her daughters live in Maryland, USA and they wanted her to come and stay with them, she refused saying that she wanted to live and die on the banks of the Gaṅgā!

Choosing the Head Swami in Ārya Samāj

He talked briefly of how a head Swami is chosen after the passing away of the current head. Swamis are supposed to have already died a civil death. The property rights, relations, everything gets cut-off when one becomes a *saṁnyāsin*. He himself became Agnivesh from Vepaksha. If the head *saṁnyāsin* dies, another *saṁnyāsin* takes over to run the affairs. He is democratically chosen from amongst the people. Swami Omananda was thus chosen. He was elected by full-fledged delegates from all over the world. Initially he was elected by a few important monks and then they, all the monks from all over the world came and participated in the bigger election.

Role in Freedom Struggle

The Samaj did not merely confine itself to religious and social activities. It was at the forefront of the freedom struggle as well. Pattabhi Sitaramayya, a president of the Indian National Congress and the movement's historian, has written that 70 per cent of those who were in jail during the freedom movement came from the ranks of the Ārya Samāj. All top revolutionary leaders like Bhagat Singh, Lala Lajpat Rai and Swami Shraddhanand, etc., were active members of the Ārya Samāj. Bhagat Singh was born in a Sikh family but all the family members were staunch Ārya Samājis. Bhagat Singh's father was Sirdar Kishan Singh and his grandfather took to Ārya Samāj in Swami Dayananda's time. The family gave up meat eating, alcoholism, etc. They initiated Bhagat Singh into the sacred thread ceremony. His brother is still living in Saharanpur. He is familiar with all Samaj activities.

Criteria of Success and the Future

The criterion for judging the success of the *saṁnyāsa* institution according to Swamiji is how the organization has been purposeful in implementing its principles. "The ultimate judgement should come as to how they have conducted themselves or how they have stood up to tyranny. I would like to ask those *saṁnyāsins* whether they were on the side of right, or whether they were standing up to evil; that is the way to judge rather than finding out how many times you pray or do *havans*. The criteria should be both on the degree of self-realization and more so on the social transformation effected by them."

Normally we judge the *āśrams* by their upkeep, etc. When one thinks of the future of the *saṁnyāsa āśrama*, one is depressed: The whole Vedic culture is becoming extinct — extinct in the sense that modern consumeristic culture is creeping in. Humans and values are becoming reduced to commodities. Family values are distintegrating. On the other hand, science and technology are opening up the frontiers of knowledge which is very inspiring. Today for the first time you can really create an ideal human family with a holistic perspective. But there is the danger of the consumeristic society overtaking this ideal. As a result, the future of such institutions of *saṁnyāsa* is not encouraging. One will have to work very hard to keep the traditions going and recreate some of the original fervour and bring in new meaning.

"We cannot at the same time afford to be dogmatic. The new challenges have to be integrated and again they have to be universal in the real sense of the term. The *saṁnyāsin* outlook should permeate the masses and the right kind of people should take it up seriously. They should not be associated only with the *āśrams* that stand separate from the day-to-day lives of the people. They need to become the real representatives of Vedic knowledge and heritage dedicating their lives to *lokasaṁgraha*. It is absolutely essential that *saṁnyāsa* represents the universal cosmic life after the three necessary earlier *āśrams* — *brahmacarya*, *gṛhastha* and *vānaprastha*. It has to be based on *śrama* — labour, action, unstinted effort, not quietude and rest. All activities must be involved — religious, social, political — to raise our voice against ignorance and injustice to make this world a better place."

Saṁnyāsa and Women

In the Ārya Samāj there are not as many *saṁnyāsinīs* as *saṁnyāsins*. In the Samāj women are as much entitled as men to take up the renouncer's life and they are called *yatis*. For example Vidyuttama Yati is with Swamiji's mother in Jwalapur, Hardwar. She publishes many books.

She is a preacher. She raises her voice against inequalities, injustice. The Samāj has such people all over the world. There are more than a dozen *saṁnyāsinīs* active in the Ārya Samāj. There are no women as yet, heading any *āśram* though. Swamiji tells his Samāj friends, "You talk about gender equality; as long as it is not reflected in the organizational structure, in decision-making process, it will only be on paper." He was hopeful that it would be possible soon.

Daily Routine and Other Matters

As for the routine in the *āśram*: "One gets up at four in the morning. Then there is a two-hour long *sandhyā* prayer. Then they perform *havan*. This is repeated in the evening also. Soon after there is a talk and a question/answer session. They then sit together and have breakfast. Then they observe *mauna* or *svādhyāya*, reading Upaniṣads, etc. Whoever is the head answers questions and clarifies doubts. Again *mauna* and later *havan*, singing of *bhajanas* and some preaching. There is no *pūjā*. Donations keep the *āśrams* going. Receipts are given promptly; even if it is from an anonymous donor, it is acknowledged as such. It is called *gupta-dāna*."

Does the government interfere with the working of the *āśram*? The general laws are applicable to the *āśram*, says Swamiji. "The financial records, property records, should be clear and audited, balance sheets and other documents duly published and distributed." Those apply to *āśrams* as much as they apply to any financial commercial business or educational institutions.

Message to Householders

His message to householders: "Human life is the most important life. Try to realize yourself in this life. Once you have got this life it gives you an opportunity to break the cycle of life and death. Life is *karmayoni*, you have to do your action and yet not get attached to it, so transcendence over the fruits of your action, over *rāga*, *dveṣa*, and maintaining equanimity is important. If you are born into this world, one day you are going to die, what goes on after that? No one knows. Who am I? What happens in this world when I am no more? These questions should be constantly raised within and without and the answers should guide us."

The Initiation

A period of two to five years as *naiṣṭhika brahmacarya* is observed before one is initiated into *saṁnyāsa*. This is in the case of a bachelor becoming a renouncer directly. The initiation ritual has a lot of meaning. You invite somebody who has been your ideal. In Swamiji's case the ceremony was conducted by Swami Brahmamuniji of Hardwar, a great Sanskrit scholar. A *gṛhastha* performed *havan* for the ceremony when he was initiated in 1970.

The Samāj runs *gurukula*s and hospitals. Books, weekly magazines, articles for newspapers, radio programmes, TV shows, etc., are done for disseminating the ideals and activities of the Samāj.

The Emergency

Swamiji then related his role during the Emergency imposed by the then prime minister of India, Srimati Indira Gandhi on the nation. "In 1975 when Emergency was declared, I totally opposed it and joined Jayaprakash Narayan's Movement for Total Liberation. I was heading the Haryana chapter of the movement. I was against the government and I was also against the regime of Bansi Lal in Haryana. The police came to arrest us early in the morning at five. So I decided to go underground. I jumped the wall and went into another person's house and disguised myself in *kurtā-pyjāmā*. I went to Delhi in ordinary clothes and nobody could recognize me. For six months I went to the tribal areas of Madhya Pradesh. I was trying to do whatever that was necessary to defeat the Emergency and the rape of democracy which took place at that unfortunate time. There were threats to my life. The mafia tried to kill me twice in the quarries."

It was not only in India that Swamiji fought against injustice. He went to the Philippines to express solidarity with those fighting President Marcos and his dictatorship. Wherever there is injustice, he has tried to associate himself with the oppressed.

SWAMI SHANKARASHRAM

Background

Swami-Sadyojat-Sankarashram belongs to the Śaṅkara Daśanāmī-Sampradāya. This *āśram/maṭha* called the Chitrapur Sarasvat Brahmin Math, was started by Parijnanashram about 300 years ago. The Chitrapur

24. Swami Shankarashram, Chitrapur Sarasvat Brahmin Math

Sarasvat brāhmaṇa community is a very small community of only 25,000 people and is a very well-educated community. Swamiji hails from a very religious family. During his student years, Sankarashram had read extensively religious and spiritual literature and he was also interested in researches into psychic phenomena and treatises on meditation techniques. He was drawn towards Swami Vivekananda's teachings. He became a very serious *sādhaka* at an early age. The religious atmosphere at home also helped him a lot. All this drew him towards *saṁnyāsa* even during his early years. Coming into contact with a highly evolved soul, he took *saṁnyāsa* at age 19, after his mother gave her permission willingly. He is the eleventh *saṁnyāsin* in the lineage of this *maṭha*. This *maṭha* has always had *saṁnyāsins* initiated before they entered the householder *āśrama* (*gṛhasthāśrama*). Thus he is a *naiṣṭhika brahmacarin*.

Saṁnyāsa and Saṁnyāsin

In his view, *saṁnyāsa* means *tyāga* or sacrifice, and one who places trust on the Lord and Self is a *saṁnyāsin*; furthermore, the *saṁnyāsin* should be prepared to undertake any sacrifice. The *maṭha* follows the Śaṅkara tradition in all matters, religious and philosophical. As a *saṁnyāsin*, he meets his family members also like all other members without any special ties attached. This *maṭha* mainly caters to Chitrapur Sārasvat brāhmaṇa community. It is believed that the Sārasvats originally came from Kashmir and settled in Goa. But later during the Portuguese rule when there was persecution of the Hindus, they had to leave and they settled down further in the south in Mangalore.

The role of a *saṁnyāsin* is a very important one. "Instinctively people feel that they should be more disciplined in the presence of a *saṁnyāsin*. So he does to an extent wield some authority which he can use or misuse. Modern education fortunately has not decreased this kind of feeling." He added that whenever he went to Bombay for instance, he finds even highly educated Sārasvats there have a close rapport with him and are very keen devotees. According to him, the important characteristic of a *saṁnyāsin* is his total reliance on God. A *saṁnyāsin* should keep in mind this spiritual ideal and endeavour to spread it; that will be his first and foremost duty. *Saṁnyāsin* is a model personality who is responsible for maintenance of Hindu spirituality. He insists on the regularity of one's spiritual *sādhanā* for everyone at least for a certain length of time daily even if it is for five minutes only. *Mantra japam* is the main part of spiritual *sādhanā* so that if you have ups and downs, you can still have something you can cling on to, then it grows. The householder has to be initiated into the *sādhanā, mantras*, etc., by a competent *guru*."

Activities of the Saṁnyāsin and Maṭha

The *maṭha* can engage in beneficial activities for the community but there is no compulsion to start any social welfare institutions like hospitals, educational institutions, etc. The *maṭha* is able to channel funds from devotees into worthy causes like running a clinic, organizing medical camps, etc. He, however, added that "my only business is spiritual, that is all. Even the material wealth or whatever there is, I have no right over it, as I am not earning. If somebody wants to donate I believe that it will also help him (the donor), spiritually. *Dāna* is a good *dharma* which purifies."

He has been the head of this *āśram* for only three years so far, and he does not rule out the possibility of starting educational institutions in the future. Even though he devotes most of his time to attend to the problems connected with the *maṭha* and its devotees, he makes sure that he gets time for his own *sādhanā*. "I have to make my own time for self-enlightenment. The interaction with the community brings about a maturity, which is also necessary for a *saṁnyāsin* for enlightenment. It certainly brings about a lot of *vairāgya*," he added.

"In this *maṭha, vaidika*s or priests who perform various rituals are also trained. In fact, even in Śṛṅgerī and Kāñcī Śaṅkara Maths, *Śrīcakra-pūjā* is done; thus *pūjā* is not prohibited in *saṁnyāsāśrams* for *saṁnyāsins*; only *havans/homa* with fire is prohibited. As far as possible the traditional *vaidika paramparā* is maintained here. If someone wants to have a certain special *pūjā* done, they approach the *maṭha* and the *maṭha* organizes the whole ritual. Very many *yajña*s are performed as per the demands of the devotees. Today, there was an *upanayana saṁskāra* which was done with all solemnity with the Vedic recitations, *mantra*s, etc., in the proper traditional style. The *vaidika* training has been going on for very many years. All important Hindu festivals are also celebrated with all pomp and pageantry."

Mokṣa/Enlightenment

Mokṣa/enlightenment for him is more in the nature of self-discovery.

"The more one discovers oneself, the more strength one gets, there is an experience of peace and that is the way to *mokṣa;* and these are positive signs. From the time of Vivekananda, it has been felt that individual *mokṣa* is a wrong understanding of the concept. There is nothing like individual *mokṣa.* If a person attains *mukti,* he will benefit society whether he understands it or not. One who is self-centred can never get to *mokṣa.* Even Vivekananda has said that a *saṁnyāsin's* duty is to do *sevā* for its own sake, which will take him to *mokṣa* automatically." For instance, Swamiji serves his devotees in furthering the cause of religion and spirituality. He also counsels them and men and women, old and young, come to him for guidance, even though he is only 35 years old. "It is some sort of catharsis for them. They do not see my age or the difference in it. That they can open up is their greatness. I help them to the extent possible and sometimes I refer them to psychiatrists as well."

General Information

This *maṭha* has close collaboration with Śṛṅgerī and other Śaṅkara *maṭhas.* How a *maṭha* succeeds will invariably depend on the head of the *maṭha* and on others associated with it. Women are not allowed to take *saṁnyāsa* in this *sampradāya.* "There are a lot of *saṁnyāsinīs* in the north, especially in the Bihar School of Yoga. Swami Sivanandaji has initiated a lot of women into *saṁnyāsa.* I have no comments to make on that. But in this particular *maṭha,* I don't see any reason why one ought to. Because it creates a lot of unrest and upheaval in the community, people not knowing what to do. Certainly not the poor lady who has been initiated." He went on to add that *saṁnyāsāśrams* are more informal in the north whereas in south India the atmosphere is more formal.

Swamiji does not initiate *saṁnyāsins,* in general, but will only initiate his successor. There is an administrative body to take care of the day-to-day administration. The daily *upacāras* are regularly done. There is a committee to look after the *maṭha* in general but Swamiji as the head of the *maṭha* is the sole trustee and ultimately he is responsible for running the *maṭha.* As for sources of revenue, he said that some donations are made by devotees. There is also sufficient land which forms the main source of revenue. This being commissioned as a charitable trust it comes under the jurisdiction of the government to keep track of its activities. As it is not a very wealthy *maṭha* there has been no problem with the government so far!

Chitrapur Sarasvats have four *maṭha*s, viz. Gokarna Math, Kothagalli Math in Goa, Kashi Math and the Chitrapur Math. The Kashi and Kothagalli Maths are Vaiṣṇava Maths. The other two are Śaiva Maths. "This one is a Smārta Śaṅkara Math. The Sārasvats may generally eat non-vegetarian food but it is slowly changing. This *maṭha* is purely vegetarian and does not even use onions and garlic in the preparation of food. *Anuṣṭhāna*s include *japa sādhanā*, meditation, etc. Swamiji also gives *mantra-dīkṣā* to those who want to take it and a certain time is set aside everyday for this purpose. He also goes to pay homage to the *samādhi*s of the earlier heads of the *maṭha*."

Politics and Saṁnyāsa

In Swamiji's opinion *saṁnyāsin*s getting into politics is not a good thing: "At the most they should be able to advise or help people in politics when advice is sought. But to plunge into it is not good either for the politics or for the *saṁnyāsin*s. Because politics is politics, you have to sacrifice certain fundamental rules of a *saṁnyāsin*. It will bring the entire *saṁnyāsa-dharma* into disrepute. There is no necessity for *saṁnyāsin*s to enter into politics as there are others to do that."

SWAMI SACCHIDANANDA OF ANANDASHRAM

Background

"Somehow God made situations in such a way as to make me come to Him," said Swamiji recounting his life. "I expressed to Him that I was not very happy with my attitude towards the activities going on in the world. I wanted to spend some time in meditation and get myself prepared for service." He said, "you go to Rishikesh to Swami Ramdas. He will give you *saṁnyāsa*." Ramdas was not giving *saṁnyāsa* to anybody but he was giving the ochre robes and suggesting the name. "So that way he gave me the ochre robes and asked me to adopt the same. No *virajā homa*. He doesn't do it the traditional way because he himself did not take it that way. His feeling is that those who are ready for *saṁnyāsa* can do it on their own."

Definition of a Saṁnyāsin

Swamiji began by defining a *saṁnyāsin*. *Saṁnyāsin*s can be recognized by the external signs of ochre robes. But it does not always mean real

25. Swami Sacchidananada, Anandashrama, Kanhangad, Kerala

saṁnyāsa. It just means external *saṁnyāsa*. Real *saṁnyāsa* means one who has renounced the sense of I and mine. That is purely an internal matter. Nobody can find out from outside. So to recognize a true *saṁnyāsin* is very difficult. He may have renounced his family and friends and his possessions and all that. That does not mean much and may not be true renunciation: "Saṁnyāsa is not a thing that is to be given or taken. One who is ready can discard the clothes and put on ochre robes. Even if they don't discard the clothes, it is perfectly all right. There are many *saṁnyāsins*, real *tyāgīs*, who wear white clothes. They are also real *saṁnyāsins*."

"I do not follow any *sampradāya*. I was only deep-chanting God's name as much as possible and to be in tune with God constantly. That will lead us to the highest realization. That is Swami Ramdas's teaching. His books emphasize the need to remember God constantly. His concept of God is that He is all-pervading. God is the absolute existence, consciousness, bliss. He himself is manifested as the entire universe. And He is seated in everybody's heart. The world is a manifestation of God. He doesn't call it unreal. Because world as world is unreal but world as God is real."

"*Brahmacarya* is necessary for spiritual progress. Married people can also become spiritually oriented. Swami Ramdas was married. He was leading a householder's life till 38. Then only the great change came within him." In his own case he took *saṁnyāsa* at age 29. A true *saṁnyāsin* must lead the ideal life of a renunciate according to Swamiji. They must not mingle with the householders freely. He must also not engage too much in activities of the worldly type but take to service in a spiritual sense. He must spend more time in meditation and communion with God. In essence he must lead an ideal spiritual life.

Society and Saṁnyāsin in different Parts of India

In Kerala *saṁnyāsins* are not very much respected, in the opinion of Swamiji. In the north however they are literally worshipped. *Saṁnyāsins* who live a real life do get all respect. Of course, *saṁnyāsins* do not care whether they are respected or not. *Saṁnyāsins* from the north who come to the *āśram* have complained of the lack of respect and help from the public of Kerala. They however manage to go to temples for worship and shelter.

Choosing a Successor and the Future

A committee of trustees with five members decides on the choice of the head of the *āśram*. Swamiji was selected by this committee at the Samādhi of his *guru* Swami Ramdas who was called "Pāpā". The *āśram* has become very popular with many people visiting it regularly and a very successful institution. Swamiji said that the head *saṁnyāsin* cannot be responsible for everything. It is a team work actually and everyone living in the *āśram* must contribute towards its success. A booklet containing the rules governing the *āśram* has been published for the guidance of its members. When asked about the future of the *āśram* he said it is in the hands of God.

Saṁnyāsinīs

Talking of *saṁnyāsinīs*, Swamiji mentioned Mātāji as a fine example of a *saṁnyāsinī*. Mataji Krishnabai was the wife of Swami Ramdas, but had renounced the world to follow her husband who became a spiritual leader. She was highly respected and after the death of Swami Ramdas she was in-charge of the *āśram* and was very successful in managing it. He also mentioned Upāsinī Bābā's *āśram* near Shirdi. It was called Kanya Kumari Sthan. Godavari Mata was in-charge of the *āśram* for a long time. "She is no more. In Mangalore there is Ramadevi *āśram*. These *saṁnyāsinīs* are respected as much as the *saṁnyāsins* in society."

Finances and additional Information

As for finances Swamiji said that God is the source of the income of the *āśram* and did not elaborate, implying that it is run by donations. Swamiji has given *dīkṣā* to *saṁnyāsins* in the same manner as he got it. Defining the characteristics of the *āśram* he said that it must be governed by love. Not merely to love anyone who comes but looking upon everyone as God himself. They're following the great tradition set by Swami Ramdas. In answer to a questioner as to why there was no picture of Rama, while reciting Rama's name, Swami Ramdas said that they worship all who come there as Rama.

The *āśrama* feeds anyone who comes here and especially travelling *saṁnyāsins*. Swamiji says feeding is the best *dāna* in this country. He then added that the best *dāna*, however, is spiritual instructions. *Anna-*

dāna gives immediate satisfaction whereas spiritual instructions are for ever.

Rituals

They have no rituals in the *āśram*. Even the usual *āratī* is not waved but kept in front of the pictures. There are no shrines or temples. No *mūrti-pūjā* is practised here. There are no big celebrations. The *samādhi* days of Pāpā and Mātājī are observed with fervour, singing *bhajana*s and chanting and as there is a huge crowd it becomes a kind of celebration. The chanting starts at 6 in the morning and ends at 6 in the evening of the next day, i.e. 36 hours of chanting on the birthdays of Pāpā and Mātājī and on the *samādhi* days. The *āśram* publishes a magazine called *The Vision* and also some books. Swamiji does not travel very much. Earlier he used to travel with Swami Ramdas in his world tours.

SWAMI GURUSHARANANANDA

Background

Guru Sharanananda was reluctant to talk about his background but I was able to piece together some information from his talk. He had a successful academic career but was not satisfied with that life. He therefore chose *saṁnyāsa* and went through the usual rituals like *virajā homa*, etc., for the purpose. After becoming a *saṁnyāsin* he pursued his university education because of his guru's advice. Guru Sharanananda had a doctorate degree (PhD) from Banaras Hindu University and had written his thesis on the *Pramā-khāṇḍa* of Śrī Harṣa's *Khaṇḍanakhaṇḍakhādya*. He eventually took *dīkṣā* from a *sant*, a *mahāpuruṣa*, and became the head of the Udasin Math, Mathura. At the time of the interview he was its head for more than 15 years. I was able to interview him when he was at Varanasi in connection with a lecture on the Bhagavad-Gītā which he gave at the Banaras Hindu University. He had some refreshing ideas on the origins of *saṁnyāsa* and the *saṁnyāsāśrama*.

Origin of the Saṁnyāśarama

In olden times the brāhmaṇa was the link between the *saṁnyāsin* and the *gṛhastha*. The *saṁnyāsin* went begging for alms after everyone had eaten and smoke had subsided in the homes as the Yatidharmasamuccaya says which Guruji interpreted as meaning that they did not encroach on anybody's share but were only given what was left over after everyone was fed in the house. He himself had begged for alms, and lived in a forest and wandered, living the life prescribed for a *saṁnyāsin*. Talking about the *āśram* he said that it is probably modelled after the Buddhist Sangha.

With the coming of Buddhism, the *sangha* or institution of *āśram* came into being for the propagation of Buddha *dharma*. Once there is an institution a number of other things also come into being for the sake of the survival of the institution. Power and money sometimes destroy both the *saṁnyāsin* and the institution as well. Since the link of the brāhmaṇa with *saṁnyāsin*s declined, Śaṅkarācārya also had to create the *āśram*s to protect Vedic Dharma. But in truth propagation of *dharma* is not a *saṁnyāsin*'s job. The *āśram* also attracts people of all sorts. Not all in the *āśram*s are true *saṁnyāsin*s. There are the ones with true *vairāgya*, but there are others not so totally detached. The *maṭha*s also become sites of property. There are also financial implications for running an institution like an *āśram*. So all these sometimes take away from the practice of *sādhanā* for spiritual enhancement. And nowadays politics has also entered the realm of *saṁnyāsa*. He added that politics had no place whatsoever in the life of a *saṁnyāsin*.

Saṁnyāsin and Mokṣa Experience

One who is totally free; he is not for anyone but for everyone; a *saṁnyāsin* has love for everyone as he is everyone. He is an example of total sacrifice. He strives for *mokṣa*. He went on to add that it is very difficult to define what *mokṣa* is. It is a matter of experience and some have it while others don't. In short *mokṣa* is that which frees you from anything and everything. He added that a *saṁnyāsin* is also a counsellor to people who come seeking his advice.

As for rituals he said that he himself had no rituals but that he did *japa* and *pūjā* for the guidance of the others, which is one of the responsibilities of a *saṁnyāsin*.

General Information

Discussing the financial aspects of his *āśrama* he said that it is run purely on donations. He had no fixed deposits, there were not very many resources and also his expenditure on looking after people far exceeded

26. Gurusharanananda, Udasin Math, Varanasi

his income. And yet he had never run out of funds whenever he needed them for specific purposes.

There is a trust which takes decisions and there are persons who take care of the *bhojanālaya* (hospitality), *kośālaya* (treasury) and other day-to-day running of the *maṭha*.

In his closing remarks he said, "A lot of things are changing these days and even the *kāṣāya vastra* of *saṁnyāsins* is giving place to many colours like yellow, etc." Guruji also said that running hospitals, schools and so on distances a *saṁnyāsin* from his/her personal *sādhanā* even though he also does it, because one also has to help those in need. There were so many people waiting to see him that we had to stop at this point.

SWAMI PRASHANTANANDA

Fifty-four year old Swami Prashantananda runs the Bharat Sevashram Sangha in Mumbai, which has its headquarters in Kolkata. The Sangha was founded by Srimad Swami Pranavanandaji Maharaj in 1917. Swami Joganandaji Maharaj was the head at the time of the interview. Swamiji said that, there will shortly be another centre in Nasik, 185 km away, besides the Mumbai centre. The Sangha has in all 39 centres all over India and has five other centres outside India as well.

Background

While he was asked to give details of his personal life, Swamiji regretted his inability to do so. However, from his answers I was able to piece together some information about his entry into the spiritual path. Swamiji was born and brought up in Bihar. He served in the Rourkela Steel Plant as an electrical engineer for six years. After that he resigned and joined this organization in Bihar itself. When his parents were alive, the Bharat Sevashrama Sangha monks used to visit his home. Right from childhood he was somewhat attracted to the monks of the Sangha and their work, and their way of life. But there was no intention to become a *sādhu* himself.

Later on "After this education and service, I thought there are so many things which we read and we teach practically in our daily life, but those are not followed in everyday life. So I could not adjust to family life or a worldly life you can say. So then I left the job and I thought of the monks and how they lead their lives. That resulted in my taking initiation from one of the monks of the Sangha called *guru dīkṣā*. That was in 1959 during my student life. I took the *guru-mantra* and I was also repeating that *mantra* but not very seriously. Later I decided to meet my *guru* and stay with *sādhus* because I was curious to know how they lived their lives. I went to Gayā in Bihar which has a big centre and met the head there. Guruji initially tried to dissuade me from taking to the *saṁnyāsa* way of life but when I insisted he relented. I had explained to him that I have given up my job for good and have come there to live with the *sādhus*. I told him I'll stay, take meals with them and in lieu of that I'll do whatever jobs you'll give to me. So from that day I remained in the *āśram*. After some three or four years as a *brahmacārī* I took *saṁnyāsa* in 1991."

Saṁnyāsa and Saṁnyāsin

Can married persons take *saṁnyāsa* in this organization was the next question: "In our organization it is not allowed. But as per our scriptures there are four stages of life, *brahmacarya*, etc., so one can take *saṁnyāsa* initiation after *vānaprastha*, after marriage and family life. But in our system, one has to be a bachelor. *Saṁnyāsa* is straight from *brahmacarya*. I feel in Kaliyuga whenever one starts leading a family life, he or she gets attached to it, and it is very difficult to come out of that life. It then becomes difficult to become a *saṁnyāsin* after passing through a householder's life. As a family man, he naturally will think of his family members first whereas for us *saṁnyāsins* the whole world is a family."

Role of Saṁnyāsin

How do you perceive the role of a *saṁnyāsin*? "For the self it is enlightenment. We follow the order of our *guru*, to lead one's personal life for enlightenment and side by side to work for the welfare of the society. If one follows these instructions faithfully, automatically it will result in self-realization. Of course, I meditate and continue my *sādhanā* regularly, that goes without saying."

As for working for the welfare of the society: "First we encourage everyone to serve others. In whatever stage you are, attach yourself with an organization and do selfless service; your work may be big or small. When you do good to others, there is an experience of some peace and happiness. Then one starts thinking of the larger purpose of one's role in the world and gradually one is led to a spiritual path. If one just says: you meditate for three hours, study the Vedas, Upaniṣads, Bhagavad-Gītā and other sacred books, that is not practicable. So we encourage people to work voluntarily and selflessly for others which leads to peace, enjoyment, and happiness, doing good. So this is our first duty. After that when the person is ready we teach him/her the higher stage of spiritual enlightenment. We start slowly and then proceed gradually."

Mokṣa and Service

Mokṣa is something to be realized and is difficult to be defined. We are doing it here by serving humanity.

Swamiji then mentioned the relief work that the Samāj engages in. Whenever any natural calamity occurs, we undertake relief work. He then talked about the Samāj's work when Maharashtra was struck by a severe earthquake. "Here also on the receipt of the news of the earthquake in Latur, Maharashtra, we reached there within eight hours and immediately started helping the victims. We had taken materials for the purpose and by God's grace stuff from other sources also started flowing in miraculously. Two districts were badly affected, Latur and Usmanabad. People want to give, but are always worried whether what they donate reaches those it is meant for. Our organization has a reputation of honest work and therefore we were able to collect and distribute material to those needy people."

The Sangha is involved in many other normal activities such as starting and running homoeopathic and allopathic charitable dispensaries in every centre, they also run educational institutions. "In Surat, Gujarat, we have Gujarati medium school. We also run many primary, secondary and higher secondary schools in many places with local and English mediums. We also have one informal school. The children of the vicinity come for *yogāsana*s in the mornings from 8 to 10. They are also taught meditation. There is a women's college in Nagaland. We undertake medical relief work wherever needed through our mobile medical vans."

Swamiji personally goes into the community for service whenever required. He gave blood to one devotee for his heart transplant in Hinduja Hospital very recently. They visit hospitals regularly to help doctors and answer calls for assistance from patients and staff. Swamiji was confident about having achieved full success in all their country-wide activities to help the population, especially those in distress. He attributes the success of his organization mainly to the rules and regulations laid down by the founder Yogacharya Swami Pranavanandaji Maharaj. Anyone who follows these rules will be an ideal *saṁnyāsin*, says Swamiji. He and his *āśram*/Sangha command a great deal of respect as we witnessed from our talks with those around. Swamiji has been to Canada, USA, Guyana, Trinidad, London, etc., where there are centres. He found that Hindu *saṁnyāsin*s are highly respected in these parts.

Future Programme

Swamiji detailed some of the programmes on hand that will occupy the centre for the next five years. The branch here was started in 1992 and is comparatively new. It is a new area coming up and still under development. They stayed in a rented flat in Vasi sector in Mumbai earlier, till they occupied the present *āśram*. They are constructing a big home for cancer patients attending the Tata Memorial Cancer Hospital. There is a guest-house attached to this which at present accommodates six persons. They are expanding to accommodate 45 patients along with their attendants. All those patients and their relatives who attend the Tata Memorial Cancer Hospital are accommodated in these buildings. *Vānaprastha āśram*s are being started in places like Nasik in Maharashtra. There will be a school, a hospital and a *vānaprastha āśram* where senior citizens will be housed. Swamiji said that Nasik was chosen as it is one of the holiest pilgrimage centres and hosts the Kumbha Mela every twelve years when thousands of people come to bathe in the Godāvarī River and worship it. It is also the origin of the river Godāvarī and is revered as much as Gaṅgotrī, the origin of the Gaṅgā.

General Information

The organization has a governing body at their headquarters in Kolkata who decide the successor to head the branches. They look into the qualifications a *saṁnyāsin* has such as his educational achievements, public relations expertise, ability to control his senses, etc. Both the head of the organization and the centres must have achieved a high degree of ethical and moral qualities that is required of a *saṁnyāsin*

27. Swami Prashantananda, Bharat Sevashram Sangha, Bombay

which is valued more than his other qualifications like education, etc. Funds for the *āśram* are through public charity.

Swamiji was first apprehensive about getting funds for the work of his organization. The founder had said that if you are true to the ideals of *saṁnyāsa-dharma* one need not worry about finances as it will come. It sure came as he had said and Swamiji is also wonderstruck by the way in which many people came forward to give generously towards whatever project they had on hand. Running the organization was made easy by the co-operation of the devotees. He added that the success of the Sangha depends both on the head as well as on the collective effort of members in their respective centres, which ensures that the set goal is reached.

Women

Insofar as the induction of women is concerned, the founder totally disagreed with the suggestion that women should be given *saṁnyāsa* and said he did not want to follow the Buddha model. He therefore discouraged it from the start. So their organization does not have *saṁnyāsinī*s. However, there is an independent women's organization, inspired by their ideals started by ladies who have their own system of working unconnected with the Sangha. Its origin is interesting. Some women devotees took *guru-mantra dīkṣā* and some of those who wanted to lead a saṁnyāsin's life, requested the *guru* for initiation. But the *guru* could not give them *saṁnyāsa dīkṣā* because of the rules of the *āśram*. So the *guru* asked those who wanted *saṁnyāsa dīkṣā* to bring saffron coloured clothes (*kāṣāya vastra*) and handed them over to the women. Thus the women's organization started. They have centres in Ahmedabad called Mahila Milan Mandir; there is another one in West Bengal and one in Uttarkashi as well as in Orissa.

Daily Routine

Swamiji then gave details of his routine. "In the early morning at 4:30 we have *āratī*. After that we meditate for some time. We chant the Bhagavad-Gītā followed by *yogāsana*s. At noon there is *āratī* before lunch. Then there is official and outdoor work. Some members go for collection from the public. The evening *āratī* is followed by *prasāda* distribution. We do meditation in the evening also and continue with the office work. The day ends about 10 p.m. We worship all gods and goddesses. We also do *āratī* to our founder along with that for the *Śivaliṅgam*."

Specific Charecteristics of Saṁnyāsa

In conclusion Swamiji pointed out the main characteristics of a *saṁnyāsin* as follow: "A *saṁnyāsin* should speak the truth and take his stand on truth, he should be steadfast in *brahmacarya*, should not have strong likes and dislikes and should not steal. Stealing means not only material things but non-material things also. If a *saṁnyāsin* uses hypnotism to influence others, it amounts to stealing that person! In the *āśram* the code of conduct laid down should be followed strictly. The āśramites should follow the instructions of the head as part of their discipline."

His message to householders was that, they should lead an ideal family life. He compared it to ancient times when so many realized persons were householders. "Nowadays our family life is mechanized and modernized and as a result there is no respect for human values; the human touch is also lacking and there is a lot of tension in inter-family relationships between father, mother, son, daughter, husband and wife. One must strive for a tensionless environment; this can come about not only when material needs are satisfied, but also when there is attention paid to the spiritual needs of the family." He was of the view that the *āśram* can help in this direction.

Festivals

The *āśram* celebrates all the popular Hindu festivals by reciting the Vedic *mantra*s, *āratī*, worship, etc. The organization publishes books and has periodicals both in India and abroad for publicity purposes. At that time there were four *saṁnyāsin*s and two *brahmacārin*s in the *āśram*. Swamiji goes for interfaith meetings both in India and outside. Swamiji is reputed to be a very good speaker and addresses varied audiences both in India and abroad. The *āśram* follows a very strict vegetarian sāttvic diet. There is also no tea, coffee, garlic, onion, etc., in the *āśram*. The *saṁnyāsin*s of this order belong to the Daśanāmī Nirañjanī Akhāḍā and Giri Sampradāya.

SWAMI MAHESHANANDA (OF KAIVALYA DHAM)

Kaivalya Dham is the well-known *āśram* situated in Lonavla near Pune, Maharashtra. It was founded by Swami Kuvalayananda in 1924 to teach yoga. It had trained countless number of yoga teachers all over India and abroad. It has branches in Delhi, Bhopal, Rajkot and Mumbai. Fifty-year-old Swami Maheshananda was the head of the *āśram* at the time of the interview, which he gave in Hindi and that took place in his cottage.

Background

Swamiji became the pupil of Swami Digambarji, the head at that time of the Kaivalya Dham, when he was about 20 years old. He was studying at the time in a college. But once he came to this place he continued to stay on as he liked it very much. He added that he owes everything he has attained to his *guruji*. He is primarily involved in teaching and the entire administrative responsibility is that of the Trust Board consisting of 10-11 members. For instance, Swamiji says, to the question whether a married man or a woman can take over as head, that it is entirely up to the board. He teaches both theory and practice of yoga including *aṣṭāṅga-yoga, haṭha-yoga* and various related practices. The *āśram* also conducts regular daily *pūjā, havan, pravacana*, etc. There is no *guru-śiṣya paramparā* as such in the *āśram*, no one is bound to anyone else, there is no tradition of *dīkṣā*, etc., and "all are free."

Samādhi Experience

He did not respond to the question about his own achievements in the field of yoga. Has he experienced *samādhi*? "That I don't know. I know that we can call *samādhi* as a state of *citta*. This state can be achieved by even ordinary people if they make it their goal. Making the effort depends on the person himself. There are always obstacles arising in the mind. I cannot disclose anything about my own experiences in this regard. If one person does it, it doesn't mean that the other person would do it too. If one person ate 10 *roṭīs*, it does not mean that ten other people would be able to do it. Faith comes from within. When the coconut breaks, then the coconut water flows out, same way faith comes from one's inside. The divine flame from within the heart cannot be shown by open heart surgery. Otherwise surgeons doing surgery would have seen it a long time ago. To see that, we need that special vision."

Saṁnyāsa in Society

When one sees somebody like a *saṁnyāsin* there is a feeling that there is something different, something spiritual, something ādhyātmic about that person. Swamiji was asked to speak about that and he said: "In every country there is place for *dharma*. There is the *guru* to teach *dharma*, philosophy, etc. There are books. While everything is available, what is the present state of affairs? One single Sun cannot keep daytime on both sides of the earth simultaneously. One side is day and the other side is night; it never happens to be the same on both sides. This duality would always stay, this duality would always be there. If in duality there is more or less, there would be imbalance. The teachers can only do it with the help of the others and they can also do it with our help. First they have to help us with their readiness in their mental state. Without somebody's help you cannot help them. The one who is drowning and is not willing to come out of the water can also drown the one who is trying to rescue him." I understood him to mean that society consists of two kinds of people, one in which the spiritual is dominant and the other in which the material satisfaction is important. However, these two are essential parts of society and the one cannot do without the other to realize its own potentialities.

He was sure that those who visit the *āśram* are definitely benefited, by and large. "I have never put conscious effort towards whether people give respect to me or not. Probably people who come here hold me in high regard; but I've never tried to find out about that. That is their wish." As to the success of the *āśram* he said: "*Prakr̥ti* has always been winning and, being only seer or *sākṣi*, *puruṣa* had to stay and sit. So always the *prakr̥ti* wins and therefore, that *puruṣa* has been called *avivekī*, because of his apparent involvement with 24 elements." On being told that there were some foreigners in the *āśram* he said that he had never invited anybody. "They come, it is not mine, this thing is of this organization that is the reason they come; they come in contact and probably they like and that is the reason for their coming again."

General Information

About the *āśram* and *saṁnyāsa* he said that there is another *saṁnyāsī* who has come to stay and learn and practise. Whoever wants to come and learn, he is welcome. So far as the rules governing this body are concerned he pointed to the office which has them. According to him *saṁnyāsins* in India are an unpaid lot while in the West we have paid social workers. "One should take decisions always keeping in mind the most important factors such as person, place, time, etc., and also the direction and ultimate goal. As changes are always taking place, one should change direction as required and the goal too."

28. Swami Mahesananda, Kaivalya Dham, Lonavla

Politics

How about politics? "It is their wish. If they think they would be able to serve from there, that is also another path to serve. It means they are capable of doing social service that way. The object is service to society. They are wrong only in others' eyes but in their own self they are right."

Vedānta and Yoga

He would not elaborate on the differences between Vedānta and Yoga philosophies except to say this: "Śaṅkara has taken the path which he considers right, may be different from the tenets of *aṣṭāṅga-yoga*. This is his choice. Everybody has this liberty to expand more on some aspect, to stress a little less on the other subject. Yoga is old and Śaṅkarācārya's *paramparā* is old too."

Impact on People's Lives

There is no doubt, he said, that people's lives become transformed after they have gone through the courses here. "Their family members are benefited in turn. A person is not only an important member of the family, he is also a member of society; so the society also improves. A person is the building block of all the three. You cannot take out the person and still build a nation, a society or a family. So yoga takes the person as the foundation. Once the individual is transformed, then these three will inevitably be transformed. The *āśram*'s success depends on the work of all the members of the institution not by my efforts alone."

Views on Yoga Research

"I direct research undertaken here and also help others if they want to. If somebody wants to come and discuss it here or if he is self-inspired, he can do the research here. The object is to correct misconceptions and eradicate the wrong beliefs and to know the reality. What is its effect on mind, body? What is written in the books? Sometimes there are exaggerations. The aims of Yoga research should be to sieve the facts, to clean the kernel, to sustain health, sustain life."

There is a hospital run by the *āśram* mainly to utilize the results of the research conducted at the institute. The college here is run on the lines indicated in the yogic principles enunciated by Sage Patañjali in his Yoga-Sūtras. It aims at a cultural synthesis. During the course of nine months all aspects of yoga are covered. The graduates of this college get employment in central schools, in universities or they open their own schools. They also go abroad as Yoga teachers. Women also take these courses. There are women teachers as well.

Swamiji was reluctant to give details of his *sādhanā*. He gets up in the morning and there is *havan* both in the morning and in the evening. They study the ten Upaniṣads, the Bhagavad-Gītā, etc., in the afternoon and late in the evening after meals. All those who want to attend can come and there are no restrictions. Festivals are celebrated here with ceremonial *havans* etc.

TAMAL KRISHNA GOSWAMI

Goswamiji belonged to the International Society for Krishna Consciousness (ISKCON) and gave this interview in Cambridge, England where he was doing his postgraduate studies in religion. He was admitted into the doctoral programme straight after his undergraduate work at the Southern Methodist University, Dallas. He was one of the earliest disciples of Swami Prabhupada who was the founder of ISKCON.

Background

He was born into a Jewish family and described himself of "ethnic Jewish background." When asked to explain the "ethnic" part he smilingly said he was never a practising Jew and had not entered a synagogue till the age of 17 or 18. The family was intellectually oriented and used to discuss freely with him all matters, religious and spiritual. Even while being a non-practising Jew, Goswami said he had an intense belief in God from the age of three or four. His approach to God was non-denominational and he prayed for "protection of all those dear to me in a hierarchical order beginning with my grandparents." Even when one of his grandparents died he continued to pray for the deceased's welfare, such was his faith in God. He grew up and as a teenager, he evinced keen interest in reading books on religion especially Buddhism and Hinduism.

Goswami's parents were divorced and his father and mother remarried. His father at the time of the interview was in Vrindavan as he was a Kṛṣṇa devotee. "All my family members are Kṛṣṇa devotees" he said adding that his mother would be joining the Dallas Ashram of ISKCON. He was the only son of his mother whose second husband had deceased. His half-brother who is professor at IOWA University was also in the ISKCON and spends his vacation in Vrindavan.

Goswami went to Queens College in New York city and would have graduated, majoring in philosophy and music. Midway he felt dissatisfied as he developed doubts about the purpose of the education he was getting. There was no real enlightenment coming from his studies. That was when he started taking interest in Kṛṣṇa Consciousness (KC). That was in 1966. He was into the third year of college and wanted to go to India in search of a *guru*. As it happened in 1967, he went to San Francisco and met Bhakti Vedanta Prabhupada and his disciples whom he had known back in NY. For the first time he went to the Kṛṣṇa temple in 1968. There were only three centres of ISKCON at the time: New York, San Francisco and Montreal. It was really the beginning of the movement. He joined the centre in San Francisco and was one of the 50 members there. Impressed by his leadership qualities Prabhupada initiated him into the organization in April 1968.

Goswami as One of the Leaders

Goswami's innate leadership qualities started to impact on the way the ISKCON movement shaped itself in the West. Almost immediately after his initiation, he took a job to finance the temple's needs. As that was not sufficient, he wrote to Prabhupada who asked him, then, to chant the Hare Kṛṣṇa (HK) *mantra* in public. So he was the first one to organize singing in public, along with his other brother devotees, going out into the streets of San Francisco, Los Angeles and Seattle in a regular procession chanting HK *mantra*. The chanting in the streets soon spread to centres in Germany (Hamburg), France (Paris) and England (London) and the famous chanting became the hallmark of the movement worldwide.

He laughed and said, "We became known from then on as the HK people. Our musical processions were not only to collect funds but they became a major propagating device and also helped distribute HK literature." To imagine these young Americans going out into the streets of San Francisco chanting the HK *mantra*, dressed in an outlandish garb, tells us something about the character and dedication of people like Goswamiji who gave their all to the cause they chose to work for. The HK chant became so popular that the musical "Hair" chanted it in its production and the Beatles made an album on it "which rose to number eleven and then to number 3 in the sales in the 1970s."

Goswami was appointed as one of the twelve worldwide commissioners of ISKCON in 1970 and at the time of the interview he said that he was the only one of the original twelve who was still with the movement. In reply to the question as to how this happened, he confessed that there were times when it was very difficult to hold on to this responsibility. But what kept him going was his "word" to his *guru*, Prabhupada, who had shown him the meaning of life. At about this time he started, in consultation with Prabhupada, the publication of a magazine explaining the movement and enabling the centres to keep in touch with each other. In 1974, distribution and sale of literature was taken up and Goswamiji personally organized a large group of booksellers to travel the length and breadth of the USA in six Grey Hound buses. Over 40 trucks were commissioned to tour the entire USA carrying the ISKCON literature. Regular printing of literature was also undertaken side by side. The effect of all this created a deep impact on the world stage. He also brought in a number of new ideas but always with the approval of Prabhupada.

Who is a Saṁnyāsin

One who is detached from the senses and sense gratification, he is a celibate who is completely dependent on the Supreme Godhead Śrī Kṛṣṇa. The saṁnyāsin's aim is to work for the good of all the other *āśrama*s like *brahmacarya*, etc. He is also to work for the benefit of the world by giving spiritual enlightenment and succour where needed. The greater part of his life should be for personal purification aimed towards *mokṣa*. A saṁnyāsin's entire life is meant for the service of Kṛṣṇa. In the context of the world, it means the service of society, which is a creation of Kṛṣṇa. "We see Kṛṣṇa through Kṛṣṇa's creation. This means a *saṁnyāsin* should serve humanity in any way possible. Best way is to find solutions to the problems of life (*saṁsāra*) which is fourfold: birth, old age, disease and death. To give enlightenment and to help someone to get out of the cycle of *saṁsāra* is the primary duty of a *saṁnyāsin*. A major aspect of the activities of the movement like running a hospital in Bhopal and establishing schools to educate children is to bring spiritual education and enlightenment to all."

Distribution of food to the needy was always emphasized by

29. Tamal Krishna Goswami

Prabhupada. In furtherance of that the organization has set-up Hare Krishna (HK) Food For Life. Millions of meals are served throughout the world. HK devotees have travelled to places like Chechnya in the midst of danger and set-up food distribution centres. "During the Bangladesh war we set-up a huge centre for refugees near Māyāpuri close to the border. I was not allowed to go inside because I declared myself a Hindu. If I had said I was an American, perhaps I would have been allowed to go." Prabhupada had said "no one within 120 miles radius of Māyāpurī should go hungry." So ISKCON gives *prasāda* to the needy everyday. During the Orissa cyclone they went to the houses and recited the entire Bhagavad-Gītā and the profits from this service were sent to the cyclone affected areas through many aid centres set-up by ISKCON.

Daily Routine and Other Information

"Prabhupada has laid down the daily schedule which starts in the morning with *maṅgala āratī* at 4:30 a.m., chanting 16 *mālā*s which takes two hours, chanting, *guru-pūjā, tulasī-pūjā,* Śrīmad Bhāgavatam class everyday for one hour for everyone. All this covers four hours of *sādhanā*." This was done as inoculation against *māyā*, according to Prabhupāda.

Asked whether he felt he had achieved his objective he said, "I cannot say I have succeeded. I do not love Kṛṣṇa enough. I am devoted alright. Symptoms of liberated life are lacking — there is a long way to go. I am a *sādhaka* and not a *siddha*. One should never be satisfied with what one has accomplished. There is always room for improvement." As to how a *saṁnyāsin* is viewed in society he said, "There is tremendous respect for *saṁnyāsins* in India. More reverence is shown in rural areas than in the cities. It is, however, decreasing due to the Americanization of Indian society. What the Moguls and the British could not change in their long stay in India the Americans are doing with the media explosion and the MTV culture. The coming of the MTV generation makes one pessimistic. In 1970 when I went to India for the first time, they were so pious, so very pious; I was touched to the core. I was 25 at the time. I learnt so much then. Indian culture is great and it will be a travesty if it is lost."

Future of the Movement

Goswamiji had a great vision for the future of ISKCON. He wanted to build bridges between academics and his organization. "I would freely allow academics and scholars access to institutions of KC. I will teach others through my work and dedication and through my writings. Our intellectuals should be participating in conferences and spreading the message through personal relationships. I hope to create a real bridge between scholars and our society. Misconceptions about us must be removed. My effort will be not only to approach scholars but also other religious traditions and the general public and educate them about our society's philosophy, our books and our spiritual welfare work. I hope to establish a divinity school in Māyāpurī to teach Vaiṣṇavism for all. We should maintain our temples and continue to look after disciples all over the world."

Women and ISKCON

He was concerned about the negative image regarding women in the organization and said, "I am personally in favour of *saṁnyāsinī*s even though it is not the policy of ISKCON as yet. Even in India there are many *saṁnyāsinī*s in other orders. And in the West women are more social and have economic viability; as such they can easily take to *saṁnyāsa*. Morally women are capable of maintaining celibacy as much as men, perhaps even more, because the consequences are much worse for them than men. Two women in our tradition had been heading in the past the Gauḍīya Sampradāya. Nityananda's wife was the first; the other is Gaṅgā Mātā Goswami. Though there has been no single woman *guru* in ISKCON so far, I hope that it will change."

Administrative Matters

He explained the administrative set-up of the Dallas centre which is generally the pattern for all the centres of ISKCON.

"Temples are governed by the President, Vice-President, and Governing Council. In Dallas there are five members to the council who meet once a week. Departmental heads are members. *Pūjārī*s are trained by previous *pūjārī*s. Prabhupada trained everyone initially. Everyone is trained to do *pūjā*. I do it even now. Ladies also do *pūjā* along with men here; though in India, in general, ladies are not allowed to do *pūjā* in temples. Cooking is shared by ladies. They do not participate in any activity during their monthlies."

"The success of the HK set-up depends on a capable spiritual head who must also have administrative acumen," he said. Goswamiji is justly proud of the innovations he has introduced in the Dallas centre which is one of the most successful centres of the organization. He had instituted various organizational changes after his training in India. "I encouraged devotees to remain as *gṛhastha*s as they are the mainstay of the community. I gradually persuaded the *gṛhastha*s to also leave the temple and live outside the temple. I closed the *gurukula* in the temple and made the children stay in their homes and come to the *gurukul* for study."

"The Dallas centre is self-sufficient financially through public donations, congregational contributions and funds generated from properties they own. There are also membership fees, sponsorship for feeding, income from the Govinda restaurant and sale of books. All these made them self-sufficient. Māyāpurī in India was also earning enough from local support and there was a large funding for Vrindavan as well, the two main centres in India. To ensure financial continuity endowments have also been created," he said.

Message to Householders

"They should hold marriage as a sacred, dhārmic institution in which both husband and wife sustain each other and the children; they should also bestow as much care to others outside the family as well. They should lead a dedicated life mutually and socially, considering always that marriage is not meant for enjoyment but service to humanity. They should rise above the Western concepts of enjoyment of worldly life and treat marriage as a vehicle for *sevā*."

Mokṣa

My last question was whether he had any *mokṣa* experience. He said "Yes, I have had *mokṣa* experience through constant *bhakti*. It is possible to forget oneself in *bhakti*. The different stages in this discipline are: *śraddhā, niṣṭhā, āsakti, ruci, bhāva, prema* and *mahābhāva*. The last was experienced by Radha and Caitanya. I have not experienced that kind of *sāyujya bhakti* as yet. I am still groping."

SWAMI RADHA GOVINDA DAS GOSWAMI (ISKCON)

The birthplace of Śrī Kṛṣṇa, Vrindavan, houses one of the important centres for ISKCON. A beautiful temple in marble with round the clock *pūjā* and celebrations, it is a beehive of activity with innumerable devotees milling around. There is a big guest-house in which this interview with Rādhā Govindaji took place. Born in a village in Bihar, Swamiji studied in Banaras Hindu University completing his philosophy courses.

Background

He read about Prabhupada in a newspaper and attended his lecture in Banaras. He immediately, as he says, surrendered to the great founder of the Hare Kṛṣṇa Movement who had come there with his Western devotees. A year after graduation he joined the Vrindavan set-up and has been there ever since. In ISKCON there are two initiations — first initiation and second. He received the first from His Holiness Gopalakrishna and the second from Prabhupada. He wears ochre robes and has *tridaṇḍa* — three holy sticks indicating his *saṁnyāsa* status. He was a *brahmacārin* at the time of his initiation and had never married. Thus it is a lifelong dedication and devotion of service to his chosen cause. His main preaching is "Kṛṣṇa Kathā" from Śrīmad Bhāgavatam. Everywhere he goes he starts lecturing on this great text on *bhakti*.

Saṁnyāsa

Goswamiji said *saṁnyāsa* is an *āśrama*. The *saṁnyāsāśrama* is meant for persons who are mature in spiritual realization, those who do not have any material desires. They are mad for God, they are hankering for self-realization, to understand God and love him; *saṁnyāsa* is meant for them. "In this society, this *saṁnyāsāśrama* is given to those persons who are experts in preaching and are experienced. It is different in some ways from the Vedic tradition of *saṁnyāsa* where you do not have any money, you do not talk to women, there are no social earnings, nothing. But, in this ISKCON movement, following Shrila Prabhupada we are engaged 24 hours in preaching. We stay in society, we talk to women if necessary to preach, we earn money, but we use this money in the service of God. We have all modern equipment — tape recorder, computer, camera — everything is used in the service of Kṛṣṇa. This is the difference between regular *saṁnyāsa* and ours."

30. Swami Radha Govinda Das Goswami, ISKCON, Vrindavan

He compared Śaṅkara and Shrila Prabhupada thus: "Śaṅkarācārya was very busy in teaching, writing commentaries on Upaniṣads, Bhagavad-Gītā, etc. He wrote so much and he reduced the influence of Buddhism in India and re-established the Hindu *dharma*. He is an ideal *saṁnyāsin*. I think Shrila Prabhupada was the same; after becoming a *saṁnyāsin* he went to the USA, he wrote many books, and he established this great movement. He managed so many wonderful things. When I saw Prabhupada, I was convinced by his lecture, and then I read his books. His books convinced me that his path is the right one. Then I realized that this great soul understood the scripture and he is trying to make other people understand spiritual values. Then I joined this movement, at the age of 21."

"Married persons can take *saṁnyāsa* in this system. *Brahmacārin*s can also be initiated into *saṁnyāsa*. There is no restriction. Once they take up *saṁnyāsa* they give up their married life and, of course, they cannot marry again. This is the Vedic tradition which is being followed. It is forbidden to see the members of the erstwhile family. But in Śaṅkara's case he did see his mother during her last days. He prayed to Lord Kṛṣṇa for his mother. Similarly "to see my parents is not disallowed," said Goswamiji. Even Caitanya Mahaprabhu who took *saṁnyāsa*, always remembered his mother and sent some *prasāda* to her. One who takes *saṁnyāsa* cannot meet or talk to his wife."

Prabhupāda alone is the Ācārya

A *saṁnyāsin* practises chanting, attends *maṅgala āratī*, attends *guru-pūjā*, takes classes, etc. A *gṛhastha* also does all this when he is with the organization. Both *gṛhastha* and the *saṁnyāsin* chant 16 rounds of the *mantra*s everyday. Only Prabhupāda is considered an *ācārya* in ISKCON and no one else. There are many *gurus*; everyone considers himself as a servant of the *ācārya*, i.e. Prabhupāda. Gurus in the system are authorized to give initiation. The saṁnyāsin's main role is to preach in institutions like colleges, schools, in social organizations, and also write books, publish magazines, etc.

"Our ideas are not different from those of Hindu philosophy. To understand God, love him and propagate his glories is also our aim, which is Hindu *dharma* as practised in practical lives. We consider Kṛṣṇa as the only God. But we respect all the *devatā*s of *sanātana-dharma*. Our *sādhanā* begins at 4.30 a.m. Everyone has to attend *maṅgala āratī*. Then we have enough time to meditate and chant. We also have to read the Bhāgavatam everyday. That is also a *sādhanā*. Preaching is also a very important part of our work. We offer our food to Kṛṣṇa and eat it as his *prasādam*. So eating and sleeping in ISKCON is also a *sādhanā*, not to speak about preaching."

Success in Objectives

"I perceive myself successful in the objectives set for us, purely by the blessing of Shrila Prabhupada. He has ordered me to preach and I am following his orders. I see that I am personally succeeding in my efforts and so are all my God-brothers. I also see my grand disciples have succeeded in printing books for the movement in many languages and distributing them all over the country. We have established a TV station and have constructed temples. We keep the temples very clean. The fact that we have attracted highly educated classes to our movement shows how successful we are. Our bookstalls, temples, *kīrtana* singing of Kṛṣṇa devotionals show that we have carried our message to people of all classes. There are so many people who appreciate our work and are very happy attending our programmes. We have been very successful in achieving our objectives all over the world."

Goswamiji added that when he travelled outside India, he saw that people appreciate the movement and Hindu culture. In India, of course, Hindu *saṁnyāsins* are highly regarded. "I cannot foresee the future but my desire is to surrender more and more to my *guru-maharāja*, to work for this society devotedly and wholeheartedly. I see this society as the only hope for the world."

Mode of Initiation

As Vaiṣṇava *saṁnyāsins* they do not discard *yajñopavīta* and *śikhā*. There are not very many rituals as elsewhere in Hindu tradition. ISKCON conducts examinations prior to giving *saṁnyāsa*. There is a Bhakti Shastri course which one has to pass. Bhāgavatam, *Caitanya Caritāmṛta*, Bhakti Rasāmṛtasindhu are some of the texts to be mastered in a six-month period. Tests are given to assess the quality of preaching of a future *saṁnyāsin*. There is a fire sacrifice and exchanging cloth are some of the rituals for a *saṁnyāsin*. The *guru* gives *daṇḍa* finally. According to the Śāstras women are not allowed to take *saṁnyāsa*. *Brahmacāriṇīs* and *vānaprasthinīs* are ladies who have taken the orders and there are no *saṁnyāsinīs* in the order of ISKCON. All these women are called *dāsīs*. They can stay with their husbands, but there is no physical contact. When the husband leaves the hut, she remains celibate and chants and serves Kṛṣṇa. A woman cannot be the head of any *āśram* in this set-up.

Other Information

ISKCON is basically a charitable organization. A number of charitable activities are undertaken such as distributing books, *prasādams*, preaching, etc. Here in the temple there is a president, vice-president, general manager, general secretary and temple commander to look after running of the temple. The rules of governance have already been laid down by Prabhupada. Cooking is done according to the guidelines, what should be cooked, how it should be cooked, and so on. Also rules for singing, *pūjā, āratī*, etc. Donations, life membership, sale of books, etc., are the financial back-up for the organization. Right now there are no financial contributions from outside. Everything is managed within the country. The society is able to tackle all problems including indiscipline, etc. There has been a fairly smooth functioning of the organization everywhere in India. There may be some disgruntled individuals who may criticize the activities of the society but that has not affected the running of temples, etc.

Specific Qualities of Saṁnyāsin

A *saṁnyāsin* is one who has no desire for worldly things and who has conquered lust. This is the first qualification to become a *saṁnyāsin*. Rules are set in the Śāstras and application of them in real life has not become a big problem here, especially with Goswamiji. A *saṁnyāsin* is expected to be absorbed in God all the time. Prabhupāda had laid down that all who join should give up meat-eating, gambling, drug taking, and any kind of intoxication and so on. The positive virtues are taking bath early morning, attending *pūjā* and *āratī*, chanting God's name, dance and *kīrtana* and reading the sacred books. Everyone is considered a Brāhmaṇa when he adheres to HK movement.

4

Endings

THE second and third chapters have brought to light how there are a number of differences in the way scholars as well as *saṁnyāsins*/*saṁnyāsinī*s view the lives they lead and understand some of the common concepts associated with *saṁnyāsa*. We shall first examine what the scholars' understanding is and then look at the views of the *saṁnyāsins*/*saṁnyāsinī*s themselves.

Amongst the scholars chosen for interviews in Chapter 2, some depend on textual information combined with what they have observed closely in their surroundings. Some others are not only textually well informed but combine that with their own experience of living the tradition. One notices that the scholars within a tradition, who also observe the practices within their respective traditions, may approach the topic from a different angle from the others outside the traditon. However, whether one is just a scholar or whether one is both a scholar and a practitioner within a tradition, their understanding still is not the same as that of the *saṁnyāsin*s who live that life and bring in a richness of personal experience into the discussion. The second and third chapters have already demonstrated that. Even though some points covered in this chapter may have been already mentioned in chapters two and three, the focus of this chapter is to compare the views of scholars and *saṁnyāsin*s in a more broad-based manner.

While the earlier chapters cover what the scholars and *saṁnyāsin*s say faithfully, this chapter is about how I, as the author, consider some facts important enough to be reiterated and highlighted in order to understand how both scholars and *saṁnyāsin*s view the concept and the institution of *saṁnyāsa* as well. I also point out the differences between the various *saṁnyāsa sampradāya*s regarding specific issues here. The reader would benefit if the views of the scholars and *saṁnyāsins/saṁnyāsinīs* discussed here are compared with his/her statements in chapters two and three respectively.

Some general observations before we enter this chapter proper are in order here. Amongst the *saṁnyāsins* interviewed a large number proclaim their allegiance to Advaita philosophy, even though they combine other practices as well. Most of the independent *āśrams* started later, like the Ramakrishna Mission also declare that they follow Advaita Vedānta. One ponders on the reasons for this phenomenon.

Some of the probable reasons could be

(1) because the origins of the Hindu *saṁnyāsāśrama* itself is associated with Ādi Śaṅkara of Advaita Vedānta fame who must have been a charismatic figure, having the reputation of bringing back the glory of Vedic Dharma;

(2) Śaṅkara himself advocated that a saṁnyāsin's life is the best for the realization of *mokṣa;*

(3) it is easier to live the life of an advaitin rather than that of a Vaiṣṇava or Śaiva *saṁnyāsin* as Advaita is more inclusive, at least theoretically, in its attitude towards all humans; there are also none of the restrictions of following rituals and also being associated with temples, which would generally follow if one were to declare allegiance to any of the *bhakti sampradāyas;*

(4) what follows from the previous observation is that the *saṁnyāsins* belonging to *bhakti* schools like Vaiṣṇava, Śaiva or Śākta traditions are more sectarian and therefore more restricted as they have to also owe allegiance to one particular Supreme deity unlike Advaita which, in theory, has no preference in the matter and allows a purely knowledge-oriented *sādhanā;* and

(5) thus the appeal of Advaita which has no sectarian bias could be one of the main reasons for those having *vairāgya* towards *saṁsāra* to adopt Advaita.

In general, one does not see independent *āśrams* associated with Viśiṣṭādvaita or Dvaita Sampradāyas. However an exception to that is the Gauḍīya Math started in 1918 by Śrīla Bhaktisiddhanta Saraswati Thakura as its overriding philosophy is based on *bhakti*. This Gauḍīya Math slowly expanded to 64 *maṭhas* "with Caitanya Gauḍīya Math as Śrīla Bhaktisiddhanta Saraswati Prabhupāda's flagship Math" (source for this is Wikipedia). When Bhaktisiddhanta died in 1937 the organization dismantled and many of his disciples founded their own *maṭha*s and became the head *ācārya*s of them as well. The founder of the Hare Krishna Movement called ISKCON in the West, Śrīla Bhaktivedanta Prabhupāda, was himself a disciple of Bhaktisiddhanta Saraswati. Amongst the Swamis interviewed for this project there are two who belong to this ISKCON group.

With that brief preamble let us turn to the interviews themselves. Since there are differences between how the scholars presented their understanding of *saṁnyāsin*s and the institution and how the *saṁnyāsin*s themselves viewed their individual lives and their lives in the *āśrams*, this chapter has been divided into two Parts. Part I concentrates on the scholars' views whereas Part II devotes itself to the views of the *saṁnyāsin*s themselves.

PART I: SHARED VIEWS BY SCHOLARS

There are some ideas which all the scholars share in common. I point them out first and then go on to examine each of the scholar's views individually in the order in which they are presented in chapter 2, starting with G.C. Pandey. As scholars true to their profession, we will see that they also address some questions critically. The views of the *saṁnyāsin*s/*saṁnyāsinī*s themselves follow after that.

All the scholars (Pandey et al., except Srivatsa Goswami) gave full credit to the *saṁnyāsins* for the preservation and progress of Hindu spirituality. They also admitted that the presence of fake *saṁnyāsin*s in no way ruled out the existence of genuine *saṁnyāsins*. Thus R.K. Sharma tellingly said "fake *saṁnyāsins* prove the existence of real *saṁnyāsin*s behind the imitations, just as imitation gold sold in the market." A majority of the scholars spoke about the main difference of the *lokasaṁgraha* or social activities done by *saṁnyāsin*s from the social work done by members living in society as well as by the politicians. While the social worker and politician will mainly concentrate on the material welfare of the people like eradication of poverty, diseases, etc., a *saṁnyāsin*, even while not ignoring the material side, "will also create awareness about the spiritual aspect of one's life" (Sharma and Gautam Patel). They also help in keeping the "*saṁskāra* and *dharma* alive" (Patel). I would go further and add that a politician may possibly have only his own benefit in the next election in mind over and above the amelioration of the material conditions of the people.

Christopher Chapple linked social service with *lokasaṁgraha* or service for the welfare of society and mentioned that it is embedded in Indian culture from "time immemorial" and it is only a further extension of that same function with an attitude of renunciation which the *saṁnyāsins* are following. Pandey felt that *lokasaṁgraha* was not a modern phenomenon; it was part of the textual tradition and was also not just a cultural expression. Since the word *lokasaṁgraha* itself occurs for the first time only in the Mahābhārata and the Bhagavad-Gītā (to the best of my knowledge) one needs to understand that Pandey must have meant these texts. While there were these common threads, each of them also had opinions/views about other dimensions of a saṁnyāsin's life like *mokṣa*, celibacy, women's eligibility for *saṁnyāsa*, etc., to which I now turn.

G.C. Pandey

Using Sāṁkhya as an example Pandey felt that the concept of *mokṣa* has not been presented critically. He was right to point out that *puruṣa* without activity in the stage of *kaivalya* makes it difficult to explain how a *kevalin* (one who has attained *kaivalya*) can serve the role of an *āpta* (a reliable source of knowledge) to instruct about *kaivalya*. Thus if there is no one (an *āpta*) to instruct about *kaivalya* the third *pramāṇa* cited by the Sāṁkhya School cannot be authenticated and is a mere speculation. In fact, the Sāṁkhya tradition maintains that Kapila instructed Āsuri in this knowledge and Āsuri in turn passed it on to Pañcaśikhā. He further added that *saṁnyāsa* is not necessary for *mokṣa*; however, as an ideal such *saṁnyāsins* serve the purpose for training individuals in the spiritual path. One can also add that *saṁnyāsins* by their very presence serve the purpose of indicating that the material world is not the be all and end all of existence and in a visible way remind people to lead better lives.

Pandey spoke with a lot of admiration for the Roman Catholic system as, according to him, "for two thousand years they have meticulously maintained the *brahmacarya* aspect of their priests through a number of their seminaries." While one can agree with these general sentiments, Pandey does not seem to have been aware of the many scandals that have affected some of these priests and their churches, in recent years, about child molestation and other abuses.

While Pandey's observations on *saṁnyāsa* and the *saṁnyāsin* cover some general points of interest, when we examine what Laksmithathachar has to say regarding the Vaiṣṇava *saṁnyāsin* we realize how a general perception very often misses out on the nuances and particular differences that one who is part of a tradition is able to point out.

Lakshmithathachar

Lakshmithathachar who comes in the lineage of Anantācārya, a direct disciple of Rāmānuja, has lived the life of a true Tenkaḷai Vaiṣṇava, so much so, that even today the eldest son in the family is called an Āḻvār after the well-known earliest 12 Vaiṣṇava devoṭees in the Tamil land, who were called Āḻvārs. His erudition in Vaiṣṇava philosophy and theology in no way obstructed his objective analysis of Vaiṣṇavism and he mentioned details of a Vaiṣṇava saṁnyāsin's life that would normally escape a general study.

One generally associates the adoption of *saṁnyāsa* for the purpose of the attainment of *mokṣa* but we learn from Lakshmithathachar that the Vaiṣṇava *saṁnyāsin* is only interested in the preservation of *dharma* in a total sense. Even Rāmānuja's adoption of *saṁnyāsa* was a protest against his wife's being unable to live up to his notion of the maintenance of *dharma*. The Vaiṣṇava *saṁnyāsin* is thus like a *gr̥hastha* but unlike the *gr̥hastha* who has *dharma* as the guiding principle of his activities, the *saṁnyāsin* is totally immersed in the preservation of *dharma* and *dharma* alone. His belief is that "*mokṣa* comes automatically when one follows *dharma*." One can then understand that it is because of this belief that the temple is the site of service of a Vaiṣṇava *saṁnyāsin*. But we also learn from Lakshmithathachar that one of the main distinctions between a Tenkaḷai *jeeyar/saṁnyāsin* from a Vaḍakaḷai *saṁnyāsin* is that, while the former serves in a temple the latter does not.

It is also worth noticing that one is initiated as a Vaiṣṇava *saṁnyāsin* in the Viśiṣṭādvaita Sampradāya, only after he has gone through a married life. What was more surprising to know was that some *gr̥hastha* members like the Āṇḍavan Pillais to which group Lakshmithathachar himself belongs, were given the authority to initiate individuals into the *saṁnyāsāśrama* though they are *gr̥hastha*s themselves. No other *āśram* has this provision as we learnt from the interviews with the *saṁnyāsin*s themselves. What came as even more of a surprise was when he mentioned that an "important function of the Vaiṣṇava *saṁnyāsin* is also to take part in *śrāddha* ceremonies and partake the consecrated food kept specifically for the deities." There was also a *pīṭha* called Dattātreya Pītha in Melkote as Dattātreya is associated with Mahāviṣṇu.

K.T. Pandurangi

We now turn to what the scholar practitioner K.T. Pandurangi of the Madhva Sampradāya had to say about the Madhva *saṁnyāsin*. Both Viśiṣṭādvaita and Dvaita Sampradāyas are Vaiṣṇava schools but they have different views regarding who can or cannot be a *saṁnyāsin*. The *āśram*s are generally called *maṭha*s in Dvaita and one learnt that there were 23 Madhva Maths in all, not just the eight in Udupi established by Madhva himself, as is the common perception. There are also both kinds of *saṁnyāsin*s in the Madhva Sampradāya, the ones who were initiated before marriage and are *naiṣṭhika brahmacārin*s as is seen in the Udupi *maṭha*s, and then there are other *maṭha*s like the Raghavendra, Uttaradi, Rasarāja, etc., where even *gṛhastha*s can be given *saṁnyāsa*. Pandurangi divided the custom as that which prevails on the west side of the Sahyādri Ghāṭs (Udupi) and the eastern side of the Sahyādri Ghāṭs (Karnataka, Andhra, Maharashtra). He also pointed out the stress on austerities such as *ekādaśī-vrata, viṣṇu-pañcaka-vrata* and *kṛcchra-cāndrāyaṇa-vrata* which the Madhvaite in general and a *saṁnyāsin* in particular has to observe, which are more rigorous than the other *sampradāya*s.

Something unique to the Madhva *saṁnyāsin* mentioned was the very special practice of the Madhva *saṁnyāsin* visiting the homes of his *śiṣya*s voluntarily during the *caturmāsya*. He goes and does *pūjā* there and also receives *pāda-pūjā* from the *śiṣya*s in their own homes. Normally one hears of visits by *saṁnyāsin*s only when they are specially invited but this was an exception when the *saṁnyāsin* goes of his own accord to the śiṣya's house to do *pūjā* and receive *pāda-pūjā* at the śiṣya's home itself.

It was interesting to note that Pandurangi was of the view that even during Śaṅkarācārya's time the *āśram*s had not taken root seriously. In other words Śaṅkarācārya did not establish *āśram*s to propagate his Advaita Sampradāya but only started some *pīṭha*s to bring back Sanātana

Dharma. Pandurangi added that the system came to be called Advaita only after Viśiṣṭādvaita came on the scene. Initially it was just protection of Sanātana Dharma from other non-Sanātana Dharma practices. Pandurangi's view could very well be true if one recalls what Śaṅkarācārya himself mentions in the introduction to his Bhagavad-Gītā-Bhāṣya that the express purpose of his writing the *bhāṣya* is twofold: (1) promoting *abhyudaya* (prosperity) for those following the *pravṛtti-mārga*: and (2) providing guidance for those following the *nivṛtti-mārga* (*niḥśreyasa*; liberation).

One is familiar with the aggressive writings of some of the Dvaita followers and Pandurangi said that there was sanction in the Madhva Sampradāya for *saṁnyāsin*s to take an aggressive stand in order to glorify Viṣṇu's supremacy over that of the other *sampradāya*s. His logic for such a sanction was interesting. He felt that this could be in response to earlier aggressive *sampradāya*s that existed before Dvaita came on the scene like those of the Śāktas "who were prone to spread their faiths by forceful means." He developed the aggressive idea further when he said that in Karnataka, Basaveśvara united the six to eight Śaiva sects into one group. Śaṅkara, according to him, "took the lead to save the Vaidikas" and so "Rāmānuja and Madhva had to come to save the Vaiṣṇavas." This seems to be a widely popular view in south Indian circles.

The importance of the presence of a *mūrti* in a Madhva *Maṭha* was highlighted by him saying that whenever any dispute arose regarding "rival claims" to an *āśram* in a court of law, the court will rule primarily in favour of the one who possesses the *mūrti*. The paramount importance accorded to *mūrti* and *mūrti* worship by the Vaiṣṇava *saṁnyāsin* comes out clearly in this observation. Both in the interview with Lakshmithathachar and K.T. Pandurangi the importance accorded to ritual in Vaiṣṇava *sampradāya*s stands out in opposition to what the Advaita *sampradāya*s proclaim. We will see later from the interviews with the Advaita *saṁnyāsin*s themselves that, even while playing down the importance of ritual and *mūrti-pūjā*, the Advaita *āśram*s also have temples and *mūrti*s within them for all practical purposes and *pūjā* to the *mūrti*s either directly by the *saṁnyāsin* or by a priest in the presence of the *saṁnyāsin* is also seen. There is a general ambivalence with respect to principles and practice of ritual, including worship to images/icons in the life of *saṁnyāsin*s and in the *saṁnyāsāśram*s as well.

One of the criticisms of these well established *āśrams* like the Advaita, Viśiṣṭādvaita and Dvaita as well as newer *āśrams*, is that there is a lot of ostentation which is opposed to the very premise of their renouncing the world which is *vairāgya* (dispassion). Pandurangi justified the practice as keeping "up the dignity of the institution" but to my mind that was again a worldly value which should not form part of the saṁnyāsin's concern. Pandurangi also said that the pompous style of being "dressed in finery or sitting on a silver *pīṭha*" does in no way affect the internal state of the mind, "his inwardly *vairāgya*." He went on to say that as long as the *pīṭhādhipati* did not utilise the resources of the *pīṭha* to benefit himself or his relatives it should not matter. One can of course dispute this but that is, by and large, the general attitude towards it.

The Madhva devotees impressing the seal of Viṣṇu like the *śaṅkha, cakra, gadā* and *padma* heated by fire called *tapta-mudrā*s was given a scientific twist by Pandurangi when he said that "It is a kind of medical treatment, this burning with copper on the parts of the body." Of course, no evidence scientific or otherwise was provided for this observation but one can see how, by invoking the scientific aspect, it can lend credibility to any practice, particularly in this modern age. We will also see, later, a similar practice of impressing the seal of Viṣṇu called *saṁśrayanam* mentioned by the Vaiṣṇava *saṁnyāsin* Āṇḍavan.

Saṁnyāsins entering political activity was a question which elicited different answers from different people. Pandurangi was of the view that while politics is outside the purview of a saṁnyāsin's life there can be situations when "if Indian culture is in danger it is the responsibility of these *pīṭhādhipati*s to save Indian culture." And for that purpose, joining a political party in order to advise the average citizen "the rights and wrongs committed in society, they will be fulfilling their responsibility." We will see later the different responses to this question from the *saṁnyāsins* themselves.

While it is well known that women are not entitled to *saṁnyāsa* in the Madhva Sampradāya the Pejawar Swami broke that tradition by giving *saṁnyāsa* to Uma Bharati who was also a politician. Pandurangi did not condemn the Swami for that act but covered it up by saying "This was entirely the Swami's discretion."

Pandurangi's observation that an *āśram* can be started by anyone whereas a *maṭha/pīṭha* is sanctioned only by tradition is worthy of note.

What he meant by *āśram* was not the traditional ones like the Śaṅkarācārya *āśrams* or *pīṭhas, maṭhas* and *ādheenams* which have a long history and are governed by strict rules and regulations. He was referring to the new *āśrams* which have come into being, started by well trained and well intentioned individual Swamis like Chinmayananda or Sivananda which, in turn, have given rise to other *āśrams* started by followers of the above Swamis themselves. Thus, for instance, Swami Dayananda Saraswati was initially a follower of Swami Chinmayananda who in turn was a follower earlier of Swami Sivananda. By the same token we also find individual saintly persons like Advaitananda in our study, starting their own *āśrams* after getting initiated by other saintly persons. It is important to bear this in mind in order to appreciate why the new *āśrams* started by spiritual personalities have been able to bring in innovations into their *āśrams* like changes in the initiation rules, or redefine many a concept like *mokṣa* for instance.

R.K. Sharma

Some of the points covered by R.K. Sharma was mentioned earlier under the common perceptions. When he talked about Swami Brahmananda who had started the Ananda Ashram in New York all that Pandurangi had mentioned about individuals starting new *āśrams* struck a cord. This Swami made it a point to teach Patañjali's Yoga-Sūtras to the inmates as his avowed mission, said Sharma. Comparing the *āśram* in India and the Hindu *āśram* in the USA, Sharma was of the view that "there is a secular atmosphere pervading the ones started overseas." He felt that doing *āratī* to Jesus, Mohammad, Moses and others along with the Hindu deities, proclaim their secular spirit. I was wondering whether this was a concession to the kind of world they lived in. One needs to keep in mind that institutions like *āśrams* also grow when there is a demand for them. The settling of large Hindu populations around the globe has also given an impetus to this growth as the *saṁnyāsins* and the *āśrams* in foreign lands fulfil a much needed and nostalgic connection with the spiritual roots of the diaspora population. An added benefit is that these *āśrams* as well as the *saṁnyāsins* are able to generate funds for welfare activities in India.

Srivatsa Goswami

The scholar-priest Srivatsa Goswami was unequivocal in his declaration that today's *saṁnyāsins* do not fit into the śāstric definition of a *saṁnyāsin*. Of course, he also conceded that it was not possible to follow the strict rules for a *saṁnyāsin* mentioned in the Śāstras. He was particularly against the all round misuse of trust visible in *saṁnyāsin* circles even in Vrindavan with which he was familiar. He did not use the word corruption but that was what was implied when he said that *saṁnyāsins* have amassed "huge assets to the tune of two crore rupees and many of them are personal accounts, deposited by individual *saṁnyāsins*." He quoted the Bhāgavata Purāṇa where it is mentioned that "those who are not well versed in *dharma* will be propagators of *dharma* in the *Kaliyuga*" to emphasize his point about the *saṁnyāsins* (*Bhā.P.* XI.23.36-38).

While Pandey and Sharma gave credit to the *saṁnyāsins* for the maintenance of Hindu *dharma* Goswami was of the view that the tradition was maintained not by the *saṁnyāsins* but by the *ācārya-gurus* and they were all *gr̥hasthas*. He gave the examples of all the *r̥ṣis* in the Vedas and the Upaniṣads being *gr̥hasthas*. It looks to me that there is truth in both these views. While the *saṁnyāsins* were few and far between in the earlier times and the *r̥ṣis*, who were by and large *gr̥hasthas*, did play a significant role in the preservation of *dharma*, once the *saṁnyāsins* grew in numbers and the *āśrams* were also established, they also took on the responsibility of preservation of the *dharma*. Like Pandurangi, Srivatsa did not believe that Śaṅkarācārya started the *āśrams*. He believed that they were started by the disciples of Śaṅkara.

Gautam Patel

The truth about starting an *āśram* mentioned by Pandurangi was exemplified in the Shankar Mandir that Gautam Patel preferred to talk about. The freedom to change the *saṁnyāsāśrama* rules to suit the context, even while staying "within the perceived boundaries of the tradition" was brought into focus by this Mandir. The very word Mandir chosen to stand for an *āśram* emphasized this sanction to change. There are not very many *āśrams* started by *avadhūtas* but this Mandir was started by an *avadhūta*, known as Sant Ramji and the one I interviewed was called Sant Narayandas. Some believe that the Sant *paramparā* is an offshoot from Kabir and it is a coincidence that this Sant was given the "Kabir Award" for establishing "religious harmony between various communities especially Hindus and Muslims." Patel confirmed this by saying that this city where the Mandir is situated has maintained harmony between the two communities "as both Hindus and Muslims venerate him as a man of high spiritual attainment."

Unlike traditional *āśrams* the ones started by independent individuals display a more tolerant attitude towards people of all castes as well as towards women. For instance the "[Shankar Mandir] had given *saṁnyāsa* to a Harijan and took him honourably into their fold." Even though no woman was mentioned who had headed this Mandir as yet in its 168 years of existence (in 2000), there does not seem to be any prohibition against this happening in the future.

This Mandir has also turned the dress code upside down. While in traditional *āśrams* the *brahmacārin* wears white and after initiation as a *saṁnyāsin* dons the ochre robes, in this Mandir, the ones admitted into the Mandir initially don the ochre robes and are called *dīkṣit*s and not *brahmacārins*. Once anyone is chosen as the head of the Mandir he changes over to white robes and is given special *dīkṣā* in the temple. There does not seem to be the usual observance of rituals like *virajā homa*, etc., for initiation as the head. There is also no *mūrti* in the Mandir except a *jyoti* or lamp. When Sant Ramji attained "*mahāsamādhi* a lamp was lighted and it is going on till today" according to Gautam Patel.

The Sant also had a simple definition for *mokṣa* as "*jñāna* or *anusandhāna* is *mokṣa*." As for politics, the Sant echoed Pandurangi's view about *saṁnyāsin*'s entering politics. In answer to that question he said "when the politics of a nation deteriorates to a considerable extent then good people should enter it and improve. Otherwise the politicians will go their own corrupt ways leading the country to ruin." Patel also mentioned that Gandhi had visited this place but there was no independent way to verify that. Gandhi's autobiography or his works do not mention anything about this event. But that need not necessarily rule it out. Given the tolerant history of the place and also its location in Gujarat it is quite possible that Gandhi had visited it.

Patel himself addressed the question of disunity amongst the different factions of *saṁnyāsins* in the past and how there was a new awareness of the need for unity amongst them in order to preserve Hindu Dharma. He also felt that while the Rama Janmabhoomi episode had its downsides, one good thing it accomplished was the bringing together of the various *saṁnyāsin* organizations.

Patel was of the view that the *saṁnyāsin*s had learnt a few lessons from the Christian missionaries and had adopted their methods of building "schools, hospitals and other charitable organizations" under the concept of *lokasaṁgraha*. He, like Sharma, pointed out the difference between the charitable activities done by *saṁnyāsins* and the social work done by others as "schools started by *saṁnyāsin*s begin with a Vedic chant or other prayers. Religion is also taught here as part of the curriculum." This struck me as a significant point as within the secular republic that India has become after Independence, the teaching of religion in schools was not possible. So Patel had a point when he said that through these schools "the *saṁskāra* and *dharma* is kept alive." He brought in the work that Pandurang Sastri Athavale had done amongst the fishermen in Gujarat and how it had changed their lives. He equated Sastri to a *saṁnyāsin* though he was not one in the strict sense of the term. This reminded me of my own article in the *Brahma-Vidya* where I also compared him in that article to a modern-day *saṁnyāsin* (*Brahma-Vidya*, 2000).

Christopher Chapple

Our last scholar participant Christopher Chapple concentrated mainly on the American perception of a Hindu *saṁnyāsin*. He mentioned the Rajneesh episode which brought a bad reputation to the image of a Hindu *saṁnyāsin* in the States mainly because his followers were "spouting some phrases coming from their teacher," and "behaved contrary to what he had seen of [genuine] *saṁnyāsin*s in India." He also talked about the Jain *muni*s and *sādhvī*s and their total dedication to their vows. He expressed the view that "sacrifice for the sake of others was a part and parcel of the ethos of Indian culture" which is what *lokasaṁgraha* stands for. He called this in theological terms as a "deconstruction of the self" where one comes to be aware "of the suffering of others" which then leads one to work for their welfare.

Chapple spent some time talking about the future of *saṁnyāsin*s and the *saṁnyāsāśrama*. He felt that with the emphasis that modern Indian parents place on profitable professions like engineering, etc., as well as the importance given to a secular mind set in modern India and amongst Indians in general, the value of renunciation has been somewhat watered down. Though Chapple's observation could also be coloured by the large presence of Indian engineers, computer scientists and medical professionals in the United States, there is no statistics available on this phenomenon as yet.

In my own experience I have seen highly educated individuals taking to *saṁnyāsa* even in recent years. One of my own colleagues (a lady) and another of my young students (he was about 20 or 21 years old) opted to renounce the world and become renunciates. One of my daughter's medical professional colleagues (a lady) also became a *saṁnyāsinī* because all of them wanted to do so. The two women were very well placed professionally and my student had everything going for him; but they felt they had to renounce all that for a higher purpose in life. So it is very difficult to come to any definite conclusions regarding this phenomenon. Chapple's views as well as my own experience may be at variance, but they both contain some grain of valid truth.

America is probably the country most open to new ideas from anywhere and Chapple gave a couple of reasons why he thought that the *saṁnyāsin*s have succeeded in the USA. He pointed to the connection of America with India through the transcendentalists like Emerson and Thoreau and "in particular with Walt Whitman who himself was like an American *saṁnyāsin*." When Swami Vivekananda visited the Parliament of Religions in 1893 this was given an added boost and many Americans had "this romanticization of the idea of *saṁnyāsa*" he said. The Beatniks and Allen Ginsberg who travelled in India in the 1960s and 1970s introduced the idea of "dropping out" which appealed to the independent minded American mindset and has stayed with them. He also added that not all of it is so romantic as it was counterbalanced by enough people being disillusioned for one reason or another with such people.

This is a fair assessment of the appeal of the *saṁnyāsin* concept in the minds of the American and specially the American youth. His observation that the increased presence of the *saṁnyāsin*s in the States today could also be due to the support they get from the large Hindu diaspora population in the land who "gather round a Swami more as a social thing" rather than a religious expression, since the Swami in his/her personality reminds them of the culture they have left behind, is certainly relevant. He found the *āśram*s also adjusting to the demographic changes in the States by switching over to the Spanish language in Los Angeles for instance. There are ups and downs and it is difficult to predict how these *āśrams* would fare in the future according to him.

Chapple, much like Sharma, talked about an independent *āśram* founded in New York, in this case, by a *saṁnyāsinī*. It is called Yogananda Ashram and still exists in Amityville, New York. Like the Ananda Ashram which Sharma talked about, here also the Yoga-Sūtras of Patañjali was the main focus. It seems that *saṁnyāsins* are also sensitive to the demands of their clientele and the appeal of the Yoga-Sūtras to the American audience, both diaspora and local, could very well help in attracting them to these *āśrams*, since the Yoga-Sūtras definitely is more suited for lessons in self-discovery. Chapple personally remembered fondly the first lessons in vegetarianism which this *āśram* introduced to the American public. He was of the view that this *āśram* was "offering a different kind of education and lifestyle to the public that would go to the improvement of society."

Chapple reflected over the requirement of celibacy for *saṁnyāsins*/*saṁnyāsinīs* as well as for the monastic orders in Christianity in a general way. He referred to some Buddhist texts which nuanced it and suggested that amongst consenting adults "that is OK and that mainly the vow was to avoid marriage." He did not develop this further.

He ended by comparing the Hindu *saṁnyāsins* with the Christian priesthood. He felt that there was "emphasis on community living" amongst the Christian monks whilst there was "a far greater emphasis on individuality" in the case of the Hindu *saṁnyāsin*. This is a common perception amongst most Westerners, as I think they look upon the emphasis of attainment of individual *mokṣa* as of paramount importance to a *saṁnyāsin*. But just as the vows of chastity, poverty and obedience for the Christian monk does not prevent him from interacting with the community, becoming a *saṁnyāsin*/*saṁnyāsinī* in no way prevents one from being in touch with the community. This is amply justified by what we have learnt from the interviews with the *saṁnyāsins* themselves, which we will examine in the subsequent part of this chapter.

PART II: INDIVIDUAL VIEWS OF SAṀNYĀSINS ON COMMON TOPICS

We now come to the views of the *saṁnyāsins* themselves regarding their individual lives as well as their lives in an *āśram*. The saṁnyāsins' views are important even on matters given in the texts for we see that, how they lead their lives as *saṁnyāsins* and how they understand and interpret the rules given in the texts, can depend on many different factors. Again what comes out clearly and has been mentioned many times in the course of the different chapters is that there is no strict correlation between textual information and praxis. One also notices that even *saṁnyāsins* within the same *sampradāya* have different approaches to the same issues. I have concentrated only on some five or six selective issues on which *saṁnyāsins* have different views, as it was not possible to bring in all the differences within this chapter. For those interested in more details the interviews with the *saṁnyāsins* themselves can reveal the differences in detail on a variety of issues. A couple of preliminary observations are relevant here before I examine the individual views of the *saṁnyāsins* themselves.

Since the coming into being of the Hindu *saṁnyāsa āśrams* during Śaṅkarācārya's times (*c*. eighth century CE) not many noticeable changes were introduced in the individual lives of *saṁnyāsins* and the institution as well, till the coming into being of new *āśrams* in the eighteenth century. The exception to this is the Vīraśaiva monastic order which traces its origin to the twelfth century. This order is more or less a sectarian one, catering mainly to its own community members. However, as a reformist monastic order it can be brought under the modern *āśrams*.

A number of changes started to creep in when independent *āśrams* were founded and that is a phenomenon which gained prominence after the Ramakrishna Mission and Math were started by Swami Vivekananda in 1897. He introduced the concept of service to society along with aspiration for individual *mokṣa* as the twin goals of a saṁnyāsin's life which was a major departure from the traditional understanding of what the *saṁnyāsin* stands for. The different names given to the two wings by Vivekananda is also significant as the Mission stands for the *lokasaṁgraha* activities of the *āśram* whereas the *maṭha* denotes the traditional learning and spiritual lives of the *saṁnyāsins* themselves.

Even though Dayananda Saraswati of Ārya Samāj fame had brought in some changes within the Vedic fold itself when he established his Ārya Samāj organization in 1875, the varied approaches and allowances for different interpretations on many issues, was given an impetus, due to the example of the twin branches of the Ramakrishna order. It was during the early twentieth century after the coming into being of the Ramakrishna order, that a proliferation of independent *āśrams* founded by Swamis like Sivananda burst on the scene. In fact, a number of these later Swamis mentioned during their interviews that, they were, in fact, inspired by the writings of Vivekananda to abandon a worldly life and devote themselves to spiritual pursuits, which then ended by some of them starting *āśrams* of their own. What did not happen for nearly 1200 years after Ādi Śaṅkarācārya came on the scene, was made possible by Swami Vivekananda, possibly because of his imbibing some independent views both from the Buddhist concept of the *bodhisattva* and from his travels abroad.

What is interesting to notice is that some of the modern Advaita *āśrams* maintain their association with the older *maṭhas* through their Daśanāmī names. Thus, Sivananda and Chinmayananda (who was earlier a disciple of Sivananda) proclaim their affiliation to the Daśanāmīs by affixing Saraswati to their names and Ramakrishna Mission has retained the affix Purī for their *saṁnyāsins*. In the interviews with the *saṁnyāsins*, some of them made it a point to bring it up. Thus Swami Gokulananda said "We belong to the Daśanāmī *saṁnyāsa sampradāya* started by Śaṅkarācārya. We belong to the Purī lineage of Tota Purī."

General Information

There were some common ideas which the *saṁnyāsins* belonging to different *sampradāyas* shared regarding their lives, as well as the institutions they live in, such as the definition of who a *saṁnyāsin* is and what his/her ultimate goal in life is. However, one did notice individual biases that crept into even the common views. Practically all of them mentioned that their aim was *mokṣa* even though there were subtle differences in the way they defined *mokṣa*. All of them agreed that family ties were completely broken after taking *saṁnyāsa* but how one defines a family was a matter of tradition. Everyone of the *āśrams* is now engaged in *lokasaṁgraha* activities either in a strong sense as is the case with modern *āśrams* like the Ramakrishna Mission, the Bharat Seva Sangha and others, and in a weak sense by the traditional *āśrams* like the Śaṅkarācārya *maṭhas*. There are exceptions to this as well, which will be pointed out below.

All the *saṁnyāsins* were against *saṁnyāsins* entering politics actively, even though they nuanced it by allowing advice to anyone who sought it, including politicians. There were one or two exceptions to this view which will be highlighted in the proper context. No *saṁnyāsin* was opposed to being present when rituals were being performed; Hindu festivals and rituals were very much part of the *saṁnyāsa* set up. The only issue was whether the *saṁnyāsins* themselves performed them or not. In some *āśrams* they did it openly, in some they were spectators without actually being the performers, while one or two *āśrams* stuck to the prohibition of rituals for *saṁnyāsins* in any form whatsoever. All of them stressed the role of *saṁnyāsins* as counsellors for troubled members in society as also the *saṁnyāsins* being visible representatives in pursuit of the cultural value of *mokṣa* and being role models for "the quality of sacrifice."

All the *āśrams* had some initiation rites and rules of succession of their heads, but one noticed major differences in the mode of selection of successors as well as in the intitiation rites. Again the independent *āśrams* had their own innovative ways of initiation into *saṁnyāsa* whereas the traditional ones followed the pattern set into practice over the centuries. The Daśanāmī Maṇḍaleśvara Saṁnyāsins, belonging to *akhāḍās* present a refreshing combination of the tradition of the *āśrams* as well as the activist *saṁnyāsins* and gave the impression of being more democratic in the selection of successors.

Mahamandaleshvar Veda Bharati pointed out that one of the distinguishing characteristics of the Daśanāmī Akhāḍās from the *āśrams* as "*akhāḍās* have always been socially active. It is in the *akhāḍās* that martial arts have been preserved." He was making a distinction between the pursuit of *mokṣa* which was the overriding philosophy of the Śaṅkara traditional *maṭhas* and that of the Daśanāmī Akhāḍās.

The interviews with the Mahāmaṇḍaleśvaras — Maheshananda, Veda Bharati and Advaitananda — bring out these subtle differences and add to our knowledge of how they function differently from the traditional *āśrams* both in the initiation rites, the mode of selection of the successors and in other ways.

One notable point is that those *āśrams* which still maintain that the *saṁnyāsins* have to be *naiṣṭhika brahmacārins* recruit their heads, generally, at a very young age and educate them in their own *āśrams*, into their own tradition rigorously. The traditional *āśrams* that allow householders to take on the headship like the Vaiṣṇava ones, on the other hand, seem to have persons who, generally, have had a secular education and also to have held some other jobs before taking on the headship of the *āśrams*. Also the heads of modern *āśrams* were invariably very well educated, some even holding doctorate degrees (like the Vīraśaiva Shivamurthy Shivacharya and Gurusharanananda of Udasin Math). The level of education of the *saṁnyāsins* sometimes was reflected in the way they answered the same questions.

One factor that has gained prominence in at least some of the modern *āśrams* was the great importance given to the *guru* himself. Ramakrishna Mission worships its own *guru* Ramakrishna Paramahamsa, Swami Vivekananda and Sarada Maa in its daily *āratī*. Similarly, Bhoomananda's Tapovanam Ashram in Kerala pays a lot of attention to *guru-pūjā*. In his own words Swamiji said: "There is no *devatā*-worship; the focus is on the *ācārya* [here]." In fact, the only festival celebrated in that *āśram* was the *guru-pūrṇimā* traditionally dedicated to the Guru. And part of the daily routine at the *āśram* was to offer *puṣpārcaṇa* (worship with flowers) to Swamiji himself at the start of the day. The ISKCON movement also exalts its founder *guru* to such an extent that, in some of the modern *āśrams*, the *gurus* have assumed a status equal to God.

VIEWS OF SAṀNYĀSINS ON DIFFERENT ISSUES

Methodology

A word about the methodology of presenting the views of the *saṁnyāsins*. I try to point out how *saṁnyāsins* both within the same *sampradāya* like, for instance, Advaita, as well as other *saṁnyāsins* of other *maṭhas*/*āśrams*, differ amongst themselves regarding common issues. I also try to point out, wherever possible, how they differ from other *sampradāyas* on the same issues. While the views of individual *saṁnyāsins* have not all been given on all topics, I have tried, as far as possible, to have representations of both traditional and modern *saṁnyāsins* answering the same question. In no way have all differences been addressed and readers who want to know more about the *saṁnyāsins* can always get that from the interviews themselves.

Since some of the modern *āśrams* have branches in foreign lands like that of the Ramakrishna Mission, for instance, the way the Indian Swamis living in foreign lands explain the same concepts has also been attempted. These Swamis can be called as diaspora Swamis as, they, working in foreign climes, have made adjustments to their clientele and topography. It also throws light on how they enable the diaspora community in those parts to maintain their contact with their own indigenous culture. There are also *āśrams* headed by foreign *saṁnyāsins* who sometimes bring in their own understanding to the concepts. I have paid special attention to the views of two modern foreign Swamis living in South Africa (at the time), one belonging to the Ramakrishna Sampradāya and the other to the Sivananda school, as they had to function under the brutal social conditions of political repression called apartheid, which ended only in the last decade of the twentieth century. Similarly the views of Sivaya Subramuniya Swami at Hawaii, who was heading the Kauai Nandi Natha Sampradāya at the time of the interview, have been given some close attention.

Amongst the modern *āśrams* we come across some which cater primarily to their own communities even though they say that all are welcome. The Vīraśaiva Ashram headed by Shivamurthy Shivacharya of Tarabalu Kendra and the Śaṅkara Ashram called the Chitrapur Sārasvat Brahmin Math are two such *maṭhas*, the former catering mainly to the Vīraśaiva community, as pointed out above, and the latter to the Sārasvat Brāhmaṇa community.

I look at the Śaiva-Siddhānta Sampradāyas starting with the ancient Dharmapuram Ādheenam established in the sixteenth century CE, as well as the Kauai Ādheenam, a unique *āśram* established in Hawaii in the USA. Swami Agnivesh stands alone as a representative of the Ārya Samāj *saṁnyāsin*. Then we have Swami Prashantananda (Bharat Seva Sangha), Swami Maheshananda (Kaivalya Dham), Swami Sacchidananda (Ananda Ashram), Swami Veda Bharati (Sadhana Mandir, Swami Rama Sampradāya), and Swami Gurusharanananda (Udasin Math), representing their *āśrams*. I am aware of the fact that there are many more *saṁnyāsins* and *sampradāyas* which this work does not cover. My only hope is that based on my interviews with about 55 *saṁnyāsins*/*saṁnyāsinīs*, 31 of whom are given here, and seeing that, by and large, they have similar ideas with minor differences on basic ideas, even covering other *sampradāyas* may not substiantially change the conclusions arrived at in this last chapter. However, I am sure some other person may be able to come up with more information on that score.

Views of the Saṁnyāsins on Different Topics

Under the Advaitins we have, apart from the traditional four or five *maṭhas*, the Daśanāmīs, and many of the modern-day *āśrams* like Ramakrishna Mission, Chinmaya Mission, Sivananda Ashram and a host of other *saṁnyāsins* who have started their *āśrams* either as affiliated to these modern-day *maṭhas* or as independent *āśrams* like Swami Bhoomananda, Swami Advaitananda and others.

Four of the heads of traditional Śaṅkara *maṭhas* were interviewed; Svarupananda (at the time combining the two headships of Dwaraka Peeth and Jyotir-Math), Bharati-Teertha (Śṛṅgerī Math) and Jayendra Saraswati (Kanchi Kamakotipeetham). The interview with Śṛṅgerī Bharati Teertha was not exhaustive and maybe he would have covered some areas which were not covered in the short interview. While they all covered common ground on the definition of *saṁnyāsa* and similar topics, it was only Jayendra Saraswati who ventured to talk about the Daśanāmī Sampradāya started by Śaṅkarācārya and also associated the *sādhu* "type" (of *saṁnyāsin*) as falling under the Daśanāmī category. He however, seemed to suggest that the Daśanāmī order started by Śaṅkara had now fallen into bad days, as it is the Mahāmaṇḍaleśvaras who now set the rules for it.

One point which both Svarupananda and Jayendra Saraswati mentioned was that most of the *saṁnyāsins* we see, including themselves, were only *vividiṣā saṁnyāsins*, i.e., those engaged in an inward search. This was also mentioned by Swami Veda Bharati when he said, "But we are *vividiṣā saṁnyāsins*." They are not the *vidvat saṁnyāsins* who are, in truth, the realized selves; who are also called *paramahaṁsas*. Swami Advaitananda, who is also a Mahāmaṇḍaleśvara, belonging to the Nirañjanī Akhāḍā added one more distinction by saying that "We fall under the category of *bahūdaka* and *kuṭīcaka saṁnyāsins*. We build *āśrams* and do rituals, give inspiration to people by either scriptural reading or by going out on pilgrimage. So we try to make people follow the path of spirituality."

The Nirañjanī Akhāḍā Mahamandaleshvar Maheshananda Giri also gave a different explanation for the origin of the Daśanāmī organization. First of all one needs to recognize that the *akhāḍā* has establishments also called *āśrams*. The *āśrams* seem to be headed by *ācārya* Mahāmaṇḍaleśvaras whereas the *akhāḍās* were more loosely places of residence and training in physical exercises. There are so many versions of the origin of the Daśanāmī Sampradāya started by Śaṅkara and what Swamiji mentioned was perhaps what the *saṁnyāsins* within the *akhāḍās* themselves believe and hence it is important.

According to Swamiji Daśanāmī (ten names) constituted the four *āśrams* devoted to the propagation of Sanātana Dharma and the six *pīṭhas* engaged in worship of the five devas and Kārttikeya, thus totalling ten (Daśanāmī). The heads of the *pīṭhas* are known as *ramata pañca* (wandering five, not six) and they are required to move around and preach philosophy and religion. He did not give any account of the origin of the institution of Mahāmaṇḍaleśvara or Maṇḍaleśvara amongst the Daśanāmīs.

One important information which Maheshanandaji mentioned was about the loss of contact between the north Indian and south Indian *maṭhas* that happened during the "Mohammaden times," as the three north Indian *maṭhas* were "practically destroyed." Later "as late as 1942-43, the north Indian *maṭhas* were again re-established, but the close relationship with the southern *maṭhas* that should have been there, is not there."

He also mentioned that a married man can also head the Nirañjanī Akhāḍā. Of course, after being given *saṁnyāsa*, he ceases to have any contact with his family.

Choice of Successor

All the three traditional Advaita *maṭhas* mentioned that they would choose their own successors: the Śṛṅgerī chief added that only his successor, chosen by him, will be initiated into *saṁnyāsa* by him, while others who want to become *saṁnyāsins*, will be initiated into *saṁnyāsa* by *saṁnyāsins* already there in the *āśram*.

The Daśanāmī Maṇḍaleśvaras also choose their own successors but the choice had to be approved by other Maṇḍaleśvaras as well. Thus it was more a consensus than just an individual choice. One other special feature of the Daśanāmī Sampradāyas is that the *saṁnyāsins* are ordained at the time of Kumbha-Melās.

In the case of the Ārya Samāj, as understood from Swami Agnivesh's answers, it appeared that there were no individual *āśrams* headed by individual *saṁnyāsins*. The organization as such has a head and individual *saṁnyāsins* are more or less independent to choose their line of action within their organization's guidelines.

The foreign *āśrams* affiliated to their respective headquarters, like the Ramakrishna Mission, would have their heads appointed by the headquarters. Others not affiliated choose their own heads, according to their own rules.

Some of the heads of *āśrams*, particularly the modern ones like Bhoomananda Tirtha, Swami Sahajananda, Swami Veda Bharati, etc., have trustee committees with the head playing an important role in decision making like choosing a successor, for instance. Though Swami Veda Bharati started off as an Ārya Samāji, later he took over as the head of the modern Sadhana Mandir (at the time of interview) affiliated to Swami Rama's Himalayan Yoga, which he joined as a *saṁnyāsin* in 1969. Sivaya Subramuniyaswami mentioned that he himself as head, will name his own successor. Swami Saradananda of South Africa said that there was a "managing committee consisting of all member trustees belonging to the monastic order. The trustee monks will choose the head by consensus or by election from amongst themselves." The Ananda Ashram of Ramdas also had a committee of five trustees who would decide on the choice of head of the *āśram* (Swami Sacchidananda).

It was interesting to note that in the traditional Madhva Sampradāya, Sugunendra Tirtha was chosen after his horoscope was consulted and it indicated his having *saṁnyāsa* qualities. This was the only instance where I came across horoscope consultation as part of a selection process for a *saṁnyāsin*.

Family Ties

Traditional *āśrams*, by and large, have no connection with family members after they take up *saṁnyāsa* and the family members are also treated like any other member of society. Swami Sugunendra of the Udupi Madhva Math came up with a very interesting tradition in his *āśram* which allows even the head Swami to prostrate before his mother. He said "An exception is made with regard to the mother. We prostrate only to the mother because we cannot repay *mātṛ-ṛṇa* [debt to the mother]. You can cut relationship to your father, but cannot cut the relationship with your mother." No other Swami had anything similar to say regarding family members.

In actual practice, however, the principle of cutting ties absolutely with the family is very often not followed and it is also widely known amongst the public. Āṇḍavan Swami himself said "One finds *saṁnyāsins* nowadays employing their own family members in the affairs of their *āśrams*."

Amongst *āśrams* in foreign lands, following either the Ramakrishna or other orders, some are affiliated to the headquarters in India and tend to follow the rules set by them, and others are independent and set their own rules. For instance, the Vedānta Yoga Centres founded by Vishnudevananda to which Mahadevananda belongs, does not have this affiliation and so does not follow strictly the rules set by Sivananda, even though in most cases they do. Thus, Swami Mahadevananda in Montreal nuanced contact with family by saying, "There is no question of staying with the family. There should be a lapse of at least 12 years after taking *saṁnyāsa* and visiting one's birthplace as such."

The Ramakrishna Centre in South Africa which, for a long time till 2007, was not affiliated to the Calcutta headquarters, as well as Sahajananda's Sivananda Yoga Centre believe that a *saṁnyāsin* has nothing to do with family members after *saṁnyāsa* much like the *āśrams* in India. Sivaya Subramuniyaswami of the Kuaui Ashram also held the same view. Swami Radha Govinda of ISKCON, Vrindavan, cited the example of Śaṅkarācārya going to see his mother during her last days and added "Similarly it is not disallowed to see my parents. Even Caitanya Mahaprabhu always remembered his mother and sent some *prasāda* to his mother." He added that a *saṁnyāsin* cannot meet or talk to his wife.

Travel Abroad and Attire

When it came to travel across the seas the traditional *saṁnyāsins* were non-committal. In fact, the three interviewed had not travelled outside India and amongst them Jayendra Saraswati had gone to Nepal if that can be considered a foreign land. In any case Nepal does not involve crossing the seas. The Śṛṅgerī chief was the one least interested in travelling even within the country. It did not appear that the Swamis were vehemently opposed to it as there was a history of the Purī (Govardhana Peeth) Śaṅkarācārya travelling overseas in the past.

During the responses, Swami Svarupananda came out as more liberal when he said that he had no objection to travel abroad but "one should only go to countries where Vedic knowledge is respected." One interesting way in which Mahamandaleshvar Maheshananda answered the question of travel abroad was "Unless India is completely cured of its ills it becomes a farce or hypocrisy to go outside and talk about these things." Thus it appears the Daśanāmīs have no objection to travel outside *per se*. He seemed to be concerned about the hypocrisy of preaching about our culture when things at home were not all that it preaches.

The Viśiṣṭādvaita Āṇḍavan Swamigal bluntly said "In this *āśram* we do not travel outside the country."

The Madhva Sampradāya does not allow travel across the oceans. However, Swami Sugunendra did travel overseas in 2005 in spite of the prohibition to do so, and had to face certain consequences before taking on the headship of worship at Udupi temple by rotation called *paryāyam*, in 2008. As widely reported, Sri Vishweswara Tirtha, the head of Pejawar Math and the senior monk of the Udupi Aṣṭamaṭhas (eight *maṭha*s) led the protest and it was declared that, since Sugunendra Tirtha had crossed the ocean against scriptural authority, he could not perform the Mahāpūjā of Udupi Kṛṣṇa by touching the Deity. He was allowed to occupy the Sarvañja Peeth at the *paryāyam* rituals, but not touch the Deity.

Regarding the ochre robes that identify a *saṁnyāsin* both in India and abroad, some of the Swamis working in foreign lands, both Indian and of foreign origin, had different views for practical reasons. Swami Sahajananda of South Africa had no problem staying in the same ochre robes whenever and wherever he travelled but Swami Saradananda, again from South Africa, was willing to wear other clothes "if the place and context so demands." Swami Subramuniyaswami only wore his ochre robes wherever he went. He also wore his hair coiled on top of his head like the Śaiva Swami Dharmapuram Swamigal and would stand out in any crowd. Swami Dayatmananda, an Indian Ramakrishna Swami working in the *āśram* in London also had no problem changing into other clothes when travelling outside the *āśram*. Swamiji said "While external things like robes, etc., are also necessary to mark a *saṁnyāsin*, when I go out in public I put on pants, as I don't want to be stared at. I want to be at peace and this way nobody notices who I am."

Lokasaṁgraha

Āṇḍavan Swamigal was forthright in his statement that the *saṁnyāsin* "is not meant for social work." He, however, added "though running of hospitals and religious institutions are theoretically not part of *saṁnyāsa-dharma*, changing conditions make us also participate in service to the community." The sensitivity of the *saṁnyāsin* to changing conditions is brought out clearly in that statement. Some of the modern Advaita Āśrams like the Ramakrishna Maṭh, proclaim social service/ *lokasaṁgraha* as of equal importance as seeking individual *mokṣa* and make it part of their mission. The traditional Śaṅkara Maths do not proclaim that as part of their programmes even though all of them engage in some form of working for the welfare of the community in keeping with the changing times. They, along with the *akhāḍā*s, also undertake social service activities but the importance is more to disseminate spiritual education. Thus their prime task is educating people about Vedic Dharma even though all other acitivites are also encouraged in a weak sense.

It is here that we notice the difference of functioning of *āśram*s established in foreign lands even of the very same branches. Thus Ramakrishna Ashrams called Vedānta Centres in places like the UK and the USA are not at all into *lokasaṁgraha* but in disseminating Hindu spiritual values mainly based on Advaita ideals. Lokasaṁgraha is thus dictated by the needs of the clientele they serve. Swami Mahadevananda (Canada) mentioned that "The social work undertaken by the *āśram* is mainly in India in the form of running schools, etc."

When there is a need, as in places like South Africa, the branches of the Ramakrishna and Sivananda Ashrams do *lokasaṁgraha* but in a manner suited to local conditions. Both Swami Saradananda and Sahajananda of South Africa mentioned how they built schools, hospitals, etc., but handed them over to the government after building them. This could do with the troubled atmosphere that still prevails in these lands which makes it difficult for organizations to run them and so handing them over to the governments is a wise move. One also notices that some Swamis like Swami Veda Bharati for instance, who engage in *lokasaṁgraha* in India, also travel to foreign lands and use the funds they collect there for such activities in India.

Unlike India, where secularism has been defined in such a way as to make it difficult for Hindu *āśram*s to function, countries like the UK, USA, and South Africa have a uniform policy of treating all religious organizations equally, and therefore the privileges enjoyed by other religions are also equally available, in general, to the Hindu *āśram*s as well. Thus most of these organizations come under the charitable acts and are free to speak about their lineages and beliefs in an open way.

Personal Rituals and Worship of a Deity

As for participation in the ritual of worship, there is broad agreement amongst all the *saṁnyāsin*s that it was essential, in order to serve as guidance for the general public to follow a dhārmic path. Of course, one need not participate directly and some of them got around the prohibition by allowing regular priests to perform the ritual of worship of the deity, though one can be present at the ceremonies themselves. We witnessed Swami Dayananda, head of the Arsha Vidya Gurukulam, a former Chinmaya follower, present at an *upanayana* ritual ceremony, even though he did not do the actual ceremony himself. Dayatmananda, on the other hand, mentioned that in his *āśram*, the *saṁnyāsin*s themselves do the worship. "We also do Kṛṣṇāṣṭamī, Rāmanavamī, etc., all Hindu festivals. We do it ourselves and not through a priest. That is yoga, not what one does but what it does to us."

Mahamandaleshvar Swami Maheshananda nuanced the practice of rituals by saying that the head/*saṁnyāsin* is the one capable of giving advice to people as to how to perform *pūjā*, as he is well versed in the texts. He however added that the rituals are not performed by the *saṁnyāsin*s themselves. In other words he was capable of giving instruction for performance of ritual to others even though he himself would not do them. This was also confirmed by Swami Veda Bharati.

As for the question of performance of rituals combined with knowledge in the different *sampradāya*s the answers were revealing. Since Śaṅkara himself vehemently opposed their combination, the Advaitins paid lip service to that belief, but as seen in the *āśram*s did not strictly observe that opposition. Thus, Svarupananda was very frank when he said that for Śaṅkara, *karma* and *jñāna* were opposed to each other, but he himself was caught in between. "I am myself caught in a trap and I do my *dharma* (by which he meant *nitya-karma*)." He was convinced that he was not going against his own *siddhānta* for he added, "When *karma* is done as per the rules of that particular situation and is dedicated to God in his *saṁkalpa mantra*, it becomes *akarma*." He probably was taking refuge in the Bhagavad-Gītā message of dedication of all *karma* to God as *karmayoga*.

All this was within the context of one's personal *karma* called *nitya-karma*. Neither Śṛṅgerī nor Kāmakoṭi Swamijis said anything to the contrary. We also witnessed their support for deity worship; we watched Śṛṅgerī Swamiji directly participating in Śāradāmbāḷ worship and we saw the Kāñcī Swamiji, visiting the Rameshwaram Temple and being authorized to perform *abhiṣeka* to the *Śivaliṅgam* there.

Āṇḍavan Swamigal's reply was refreshingly different. He said "while the Viśiṣṭādvaitins were supposed to continue with rituals throughout their lives unlike the Advaitins, it so happens that Advaitins in the Tanjore area are better versed in peforming *yajñas*." The reversal of roles speaks of the way the lived world differs from what is given in texts themselves.

Gurusharanananda of Udasin Math said that he himself had no rituals but he does *japa* and *pūjā* for the guidance of others "which is one of the responsibilities of a *saṁnyāsin*." Advaitananda had a practical angle when he said "When I am within the social context, I have no problem of peforming *pūjā*. Then how can I preach not to do *pūjā*? So, if we do, our neighbours do, and our kids do, which are all for the welfare of the society."

Swami Sacchidananda of Anandashram said that they had no rituals whatsoever and there were no shrines or temples with *mūrtis* in the *āśram*.

The ISKCON *saṁnyāsins* called Goswamis or Dasas freely do worship to Caitanya Mahaprabhu; in fact, the *saṁnyāsin* alone is entitled to do so in their *sampradāya*, and therefore the *saṁnyāsin* is the priest as well.

Saṁnyāsinīs

As for *saṁnyāsinīs*, both Śṛṅgerī and Kāñcī just dismissed them by saying "Śaṅkara Maths do not initiate women as *saṁnyāsinīs*." However, Svarupananda again struck a different note. He struggled to keep to the tradition, even while accommodating the spiritual aspirations of women by building a special place for them on the banks of the Narmadā called "Ubhaya Bharati Mahila Ashram."

One statement of Jayendra Swami was puzzling. He said that while a *saṁnyāsin* should follow the *saṁnyāsa-dharma*, "it is not necessary that one should follow exactly what is written in the texts; it can vary here and there depending on the times." He was therefore, it seems, willing to introduce some changes within the *saṁnyāsa-dharma* but that did not include admitting women as *saṁnyāsinī*s in the near future. Since he did not elaborate, I could not get any further information on that. Swamiji was known for trying to help in solving the Ayodhyā dispute. Did he have that in mind when he made that statement, I was not sure.

There is no dispute whatsoever of admitting women as *saṁnyāsinī*s in the modern Advaita *āśram*s in India. Almost all of them are open to women and even in South Africa, in the midst of apartheid, there was established an *āśram* affiliated to the Ramakrishna order in South Africa meant exclusively for ladies called Sri Sarada Devi Ashram, headed by a *parivrājikā*. This changed attitude towards *saṁnyāsinī*s was due to the efforts of Swami Vivekananda, who set in motion the opening of the gates of *saṁnyāsa* to women as well, even though the Sarada Math itself came into existence only in 1954. No more was there any doubt about the eligibility of women for *saṁnyāsa*. Even some modern movements like Bharat Seva Sangha, whose rules do not permit women as *saṁnyāsinī*s, find ways to get around the restriction. Thus, Swami Prashantananda of the Bharat Seva Sangha, founded in 1971, gave an interesting answer to the question of *saṁnyāsa* for women which his Sangha does not permit. He said that some determined women devotees of the Sangha started their own independent organization by taking *mantra-dīkṣā* from the *guru* and then requested the head for initiation. The *guru* found an ingenious way of getting round the rule. He asked them to bring "saffron coloured clothes and handed them over to the women. Thus the women's organization was [formally] started." Today there are centres in Ahmedabad, West Bengal, Uttarkashi and Orissa. It is called the Mahila Milan Mandir.

What is surprising is that even the traditionally orthodox Madhva Math has inducted a woman (Uma Bharati) into their ranks. She was initiated by Pejawar Swami Vishveshwara Teertha, who is one of the eight Udupi Swamis of the *sampradāya*. When asked about it he said "[Madhva] had said that women also are entitled to do *tapasyā*. By this *paddhati* I gave *dīkṣā* to Uma Bharati." One got the impression that it was her status as a prominent political leader that eventually swayed Pejawar Swami to give her *saṁnyāsa* somewhere in 1992 (according to one of the informants). Neither the scholar Pandurangi nor Puthuge Swami, another one of the eight Udupi Swamis addressed this question directly when asked about it. What surprised me was whereas Pejawar Swami Vishveshwara Teertha was opposed to Sugunendra Swami's travelling overseas against the Madhva tradition, he himself had given *saṁnyāsa* to a woman which is prohibited in the Madhva Sampradāya and seems to have got away with it!

On the other hand, Sivaya Subramuniyaswami of Hawaii, who was pretty progressive otherwise, also was not in favour of giving *saṁnyāsa* to women in his *āśram*. He was upholding the tradition of Yoga Swami of Sri Lanka Saiva Sampradāya whose disciple he was.

A late entrant, the ISKCON, also known as the Hare-Krishnas, totally oppose giving *saṁnyāsa* to women. Unlike all the other modern *āśrams* which are present in the countries outside India, the ISKCON movement started not in India but in the USA. Śrīla Bhaktivedanta Prabhupāda was a disciple of the founder of the Gauḍīya Math and it was he who, when he fell out with the *maṭha*, travelled to the States and started it in America. However, his opposition to women being given *saṁnyāsa* stems from the original Gauḍīya Math rules.

However, what is not given wide publicity is that *saṁnyāsinīs* were not a novelty in the *akhāḍās*. The Junā Akhāḍā within the Daśanāmī Sampradāya "comprises entirely of *saṁnyāsinīs* and there are about eight women Maṇḍaleśvaras in the *akhāḍā*. In the Nirañjanī Akhāḍā and other *akhāḍās* also there are a few *saṁnyāsinīs*. They deal more with women than with men" (Mahamandaleshvar Maheshananda). Swami Maheshananda and Swami Veda Bharati, both affirmed that the Junā Akhāḍā had existed from a long time ago, maybe from the time of Śaṅkara in the Daśanāmī Sampradāya. And the participation of this Junā Akhāḍā in Kumbha-Melās, as long as memory goes, also confirms that.

Varied Approaches to Initiations

The traditional *āśrams* had rituals like *virajā homa*, etc., and some of the modern-day *āśrams* like the Ramakrishna Mission and Chinmaya Mission have retained them. But others have brought in their own innovations and there are many variations in the way they initiate their own *saṁnyāsins*. Independent rules were also in vogue in the South African Ramakrishna order headed by Saradananda at the time of interview. So the rules of succession, initiation and other matters for this *āśram*/ centre were framed by those who started it like Swami Nischalananda and Shivapadananda. This Centre follows the traditional *virajā homa* initiation rites but there is a preliminary period of more than eight years of training for the *brahmacārin* before he can be considered for *saṁnyāsa*.

The Dharmapuram Ādheenam has a simple initiation ceremony of lighting the fire, doing a *homa* and giving the *mantra* to the aspirants. This is also a sectarian *āśram* as only Śaivas are given *dīkṣā* (Dharmapuram Swamigal).

The Vīraśaiva Swami Shivacharya also mentioned that the initiation ceremony in his *sampradāya* was rather simple. "The outgoing head, if present, will bless the new one and administer the holy *mantra*. They did not have *homa* or fire ceremonies. Instead *pañca-kalaśa*s (sacred vessels) representing the five faces of Śiva are kept during the entire duration of the function."

Swami Bhoomananda of Tapovanam *āśram*, had simplified greatly the procedure for initiation. He had "instituted a special *saṁkalpa* in Sanskrit which the prospective candidate recites and becomes a *saṁnyāsin*. There is no other ritual" (Bhoomananda).

Anandasram started by Pāpā Ramdas did not have any rituals, whatsoever, for initiation into *saṁnyāsa*. The head gave the ochre robes to the aspirant and suggested a new name. There was also some ambiguity when Swami Sacchidananda mentioned "Those who are ready for *saṁnyāsa* can do it on their own." This has potential for misuse in the future I felt. There is only continuous recitation of *Rāma-nāma* here and no other ritual or worship.

In Swami Dayananda's *āśram* (Arsha Gurukulam) there were different rules of initiation for men and women. While the traditional *virajā homa* and *aṣṭaśrāddha* (eight death ceremonies) were done for the men, they "are not peformed for the women" according to Swamini Pramananda, who was initiated by Swami Dayananda. "We only take up the *mantra* given by Swamiji at the time for *anuṣṭhānam* (regular practice)." She somehow justified the non-performance of rituals for women by saying that "one sees that *karma*s (rituals) were not being done by women even in the *gṛhasthāśrama*. So there is no sense in talking about *karma-tyāga* for women. *Saṁnyāsa* for women was more in the attitude" according to her.

Swami Radha Govinda Goswami (ISKCON, Vrindavan) said: "In this society *saṁnyāsa āśrama* is given to persons who are experts in preaching and are experienced. We are engaged 24 hours in preaching. We stay in society, we talk to women if necessary, we earn money, but we use this money in the service of God. This is the difference between regular *saṁnyāsa* and ours."

Politics

The general view amongst a large number of Swamis was that politics was an area primarily not meant for them. But almost all of them were not averse to giving politicians advice if it was sought (Mahesananda, Āṇḍavan Swamigal, Dayananda of Gurukulam), some even suggesting that they must use their influence to set things right when they go wrong. "We don't interfere in politics. We must, however, have the power, if people go wrong, to correct it" (Bhoomananda). Swami Ranganathananda, the President of Ramakrishna Math at the time of interview, said: "Any service is good and if politicians can serve truthfully their cause, there is no harm for a politician-*saṁnyāsin* to do so." Swami Maheshananda of Kaivalya Dham was of the same view as Swami Ranganathananda: "It means that we are capable of doing social service that way. The object is service to society."

Then there is the example of Swami Agnivesh of the Ārya Samāj who, in keeping with the history of that organization, had always participated actively in politics. Swamiji himself was a subject of interest during Indira Gandhi's emergency days. He said, referring to that period: "In 1975, when emergency was declared, I totally opposed it and joined Jayaprakash Narayan's Movement for total liberation." There were a couple of *saṁnyāsin*s who felt that politics should be left to others. "Because politics is politics, you have to sacrifice certain fundamental rules of a *saṁnyāsin*. It will bring the entire *saṁnyāsa-dharma* into disrepute. There is no necessity for *saṁnyāsin*s to enter into politics as there are others to do so" (Shankarasram).

Pejawar Swami of the Madhva Sampradāya who gave *saṁnyāsa* to Uma Bharati, nuanced his reply as follows: "If the *saṁnyāsin*s desire to do so, they may do so as *lokasaṁgraha*. While doing *sevā* in politics, they will do their *tapasyā*. One can be a *saṁnyāsin* while doing *deśa-sevā*." When I asked Uma Bharati herself she was reluctant and just said "Whatever *guruji* has said is enough."

No Swami working in the West expressed an opinion on the topic of politics except Sivaya Subramuniyaswami (Hawaii). "We belong to a south Indian Ādheenam tradition which is supposed to be a guide for political forces within the country, mainly to keep them on the track of *dharma*. So this Ādheenam also plays this role on this island." In pursuance of this belief this organization does move closely with politicians wherever they have their *āśrams* like Mauritius, etc., but mainly giving advice on "every social issue." So in essence it did not differ from what the Indain Swamis mentioned as giving advice "when sought for by politicians."

The above gives a sampling of how Swamis look upon politics in connection with their lives. The interviews themselves in the third chapter will give more information on that matter.

Saṁnyāsins as they View Themselves

Almost all the *saṁnyāsins* strongly believe that they act as counsellors in society which was echoed by the scholars as well. They also strongly believed that they have a large part to play in the preservation of Hindu *dharma* over the ages. "Without *saṁnyāsins* I think the society will degenerate. They are the *mārgadarśakas* (Sugunendra Swami). There is no doubt about it" said Dayatmananda. "We maintain a balance in society. If all follow the path of enjoyment, the world will be destroyed" (Gokulananda). They also generally consider that they have respect in society. However, Swami Sacchidananda of Anandashram added that in the south, particularly in Kerala, the *saṁnyāsins* did not enjoy the respect that *saṁnyāsins* enjoy in the north. This notion was also expressed by Swami Gokulananda who said "The *saṁnyāsin* is still respected, particularly in the north. They have a great regard for us." Sankarashram seemed to suggest as much when he said "*Saṁnyāsāśrams* were more informal in the north whereas in south India the atmosphere was more formal." Advaitananda put it succinctly as "I do not think a Hindu will reject a *saṁnyāsin* based on my experience." That echoed Dayananda Saraswati's (Arsha Gurukulam) remark about there being a slot for a *saṁnyāsin* in the psyche of the Hindus and Indians in general. Tamal Krishna Goswami (ISKCON) remarked that "There is tremendous respect for *saṁnyāsins* in India. More reverence is shown in rural areas than in the cities." He also observed that this was decreasing "due to Americanization of Indian society."

There was also a feeling amongst quite a few of the *saṁnyāsins* that too much of *lokasaṁgraha* involvement as well as administration of an *āśram* takes away time from personal *sādhanā* and, in any case, that was not the prime duty of a *saṁnyāsin* (Maheshananda, Āṇḍavan). Āṇḍavan also said that this is primarily for obtaining *khyāti lābha* (fame) and "accumulation of wealth, which are forbidden by Śāstras." One could divide the *saṁnyāsins* as activist *saṁnyāsins* and scholar *saṁnyāsins*. The activist *saṁnyāsin*, whose prime example is Swami Agnivesh, calls it "spiritual activism," for whom *lokasaṁgraha* in many forms did not seem to detract from personal *sādhanā*. For the scholar *saṁnyāsins* (Maheshananda, Dayananda Saraswati, Advaitananda) the primary concern is only with personal enlightenment. Bhoomananda seemed to be comfortable in both roles. The Kaivalya Dham stands out as a sole *āśram*, amongst those interviewed, which combines traditional teaching on yoga and research into the areas of yoga.

Almost all the *saṁnyāsins* interviewed were also concerned with the loss of revenues due to government interference. As Mahamandaleshvar Maheshananda mentioned, "Government does not help except to levy taxes. Neither do they help nor do they stop hindering, especially on the tax issue." The south Indian *maṭhas* like Śṛṅgerī, Dharmapuram Ādheenam and Madhva Maths, were all uniformly of the view that the large lands which helped them to support their establishments were gradually being seized by the government and so their activities, particularly charitable activities, were being jeopardized. As some of these *maṭhas* feed nearly 5000 people and more on special festive occasions (Sugunendra Swami), this can affect the level of their *lokasaṁgraha* activities. It is here that *āśrams* like Vīraśaiva and Śaṅkarāśram, who cater to their own communities, score, as they are supported by generous support from the community members themselves. By and large, all modern-day *āśrams* depended on public donations for their varied activities.

There was a general concern amongst all the *saṁnyāsins* (both Advaitins and others) about the loss of Vedic culture and Hindu values with the proliferation of Western ideas in modern times.

Mokṣa

The purported goal of any *saṁnyāsin* is to achieve *mokṣa* and so it would be good to look at the way the *saṁnyāsins* understand the concept of *mokṣa*. While the traditional *saṁnyāsins* still gave a textual definition of *mokṣa* which was also echoed by *āśrams* like the Ramakrishna and Chinmaya Missions, there were many other ways of defining *mokṣa* as well.

For Bhoomananda the dissolvement of the ego is enlightenment which is another word for *mokṣa*. Sankarasram was of the view that there was "nothing like individual *mokṣa*. One who is self-centred can never get *mokṣa*." He seemed to understand Vivekananda as saying that *sevā* done for its own sake "will take him to *mokṣa*." *Āśrams* like the Vīraśaiva and Bharat Seva Sangha, along with the Ramakrishna Math, do not draw a distinction between "working for one's *mokṣa* and working for social betterment." Swami Ranganathananda paraphrased it as "It is the service of God in human form that is the core of a saṁnyāsin's life." The one will lead to the other is how they nuanced it. On the other hand, the Hawiian Swami believed in the traditional definition of freedom from rebirth as *mokṣa*.

For Swami Agnivesh "one's own *mokṣa* is inextricably wound round the betterment of the society as well." He explained further that "the *āśram* is for both the individual's pursuit of salvation as well as for social upliftment, social transformation. Fighting injustice, to put it very simply, is key to worship, prayer and meditation." I understood that for Swami Agnivesh fighting injustice is equal to *mokṣa* in a certain sense.

For Prashantananda (Bharat Seva Samaj) *mokṣa* is something to be realized and cannot be defined. "We are doing it here by serving society." Maheshananda (Kaivalya Dham) answered the question as to whether he had had *samādhi* experience by saying, "I don't know." For him it was a state of *citta* and "this state can be achieved by even ordinary people if they make that as the goal."

One came across another way of looking at *mokṣa*, akin to the Vaiṣṇava sense, when some of the Swamis equated it with absorption in God. Tamal Krishna Goswami said, "Yes, I have had *mokṣa* experience through constant *bhakti*. It is possible to forget oneself in *bhakti*. I have not experienced *sāyujya bhakti* as yet. I am still groping." Swami Sahajananda did hint at his own experience of *mokṣa* when he said, "I have had spiritual experiences in my path towards *mokṣa*. *Mokṣa* can come after intense *tapasyā*. My master gave me the bliss of God." Sacchidananda also echoed that when he said "I was only deep-chanting God's name and be in tune with God constantly. That will lead us to the highest God-realization." For Dayananda (Arsha Gurukulam) "*mokṣa* is a *puruṣārtha* [a goal] sought by all humans. *Mokṣa* is freedom from *saṁsāra*" and all the limitations of *saṁsāra* like birth, death, etc. He seemed to imply that a state of freedom of the mind is what is called *mokṣa*. Veda Bharati (Sadhana Mandir) understood enlightenment/ *mokṣa* as "an expansion." It is more a matter of experience. "It is not an act of selfish withdrawal. When all become as you, then the *pīḍā* (suffering) of everyone becomes your *pīḍā*. Since you have risen above that *duḥkha* yourself, you can help them, you can guide them." This seemed to have resonances of the bodhisattva ideal.

Gurusharanananda (Udasin Math) said it was difficult to define *mokṣa* and it was a matter of experience. "It frees you from anything and everything."

New Information Gleaned from Saṁnyāsins

Some information, not generally known to the public came out in the interviews with the Swamis of different *sampradāyas*. For instance Āṇḍavan Swamigal pointed out that the title "Āṇḍavan" was used for the Vaiṣṇava sect of Vaḍakaḷai, also known as the monkey school (*markaṭa* school) whereas the other Tenkaḷai Vaiṣṇava sect known as the cat school (*mārjāra*) calls its Swamis "Jeeyar". Andavan Swamigal also clarified that the word *andaṇar* in Thiruvaḷḷuvar's *Thirukkuṛaḷ* (Tamil work) though generally understood as a brāhmaṇa actually stood for a *saṁnyāsin* (*turavi* in Tamil). The Shankarasram (Chitrapur) mentioned that his *maṭha* trains "*vaidika*s or priests who perform various rituals. As far as possible the traditional *vaidika paramparā* is maintained in this *āśram*." So this sectarian *maṭha* doubles up as a religious place as well as a *saṁnyāsāśrama* for its clientele.

It is generally believed that the *paryāyam* or worship by rotation at the Udupi Krishna Temple by the head *saṁnyāsin*s of the eight Madhva Maths takes place for two years which means that a person's chance will come after fourteen years from his first chance. Sugunendra Tirtha (Madhva) revealed how this was a change in the rules brought in by Swami Wajiraja 250 years later, after the first rules were changed, for practical reasons. Initially, it was a rotation for every two months. "The rule was changed because earlier when somebody travelled to Badari, for instance, it became difficult for that person to return within 14 months" when his next headship would be due. That prompted the change but only after 250 years since the rule was laid down by Madhva. He also mentioned that in the entire history of the *sampradāya*, for the first time in 750 years, a person (successor to Pejawar *maṭha*) was disqualified because he got married.

Dharmapuram history was interesting. One normally emphasizes the Sanskrit works that deal with *saṁnyāsa* and the importance given to *saṁnyāsa* (*neetthār* in Tamil) in the Tamil *Thirukkuṛaḷ* is not widely known. There is a whole chapter in that work on "Neetthār Perumai" (third chapter: The glory of Renunciates). "Turavu" is also used for *saṁnyāsa* and a whole chapter is devoted to it (chapter 35). Even though the founder of this Ādheenam, Jñāna Sambandhar (not the original Thiru Jñāna Sambandhar but another *guru* named after him) was a Brāhmaṇa, nowadays Brāhmaṇas do not go for *saṁnyāsa* there.

Chidananda (Chinmaya Mission) was perhaps the only one who alluded to how *saṁnyāsin*s, like him, appeal only to the educated classes. He mentioned openly that "we are not taking care of the poor sections." This is an important observation as there is a large population in India that comes from the poorer sections. The *saṁnyāsa* tradition, as Chidananda seemed to suggest, is becoming increasingly an elite institution. He added that "it is the gods who take care of the poor." I have alluded to this in the first chapter and pointed out how the traditional *saṁnyāsin*s differed from their modern versions in the kind of clientele they cater to. But the distinctions may become more and more blurred as India plunges into the market of economic prosperity measured only in terms of the profit motive.

Having lived in South Africa, as I have done for a period of three years, one cannot but acknowledge the great courage displayed by the two South African *saṁnyāsin*s (Niscalananda and Sahajananda) who instead of giving in to despair at the time of apartheid, started the Ramakrishna Centre and Sivananda Vedanta Centre respectively, and took on the role of serving others and helping them to tide over the difficult apartheid days. They played an immense role in maintaining the Hindu spiritual heritage alive, even when they were practically cut-off from India due to political reasons. To start a separate women's wing called Sri Sarada Devi Ashram was another act of great significance. As women are the most affected in any crisis, one can only imagine how this oasis of spirituality must have worked for the comfort of those women, suffering enormous difficulty of discrimination under apartheid. The organizations started by them continue to build bridges between the native African population and also between different religious communities to this day.

The Hawaiin based Sivaya Subramuniya Swami mentioned that "Initiated members give one tenth of their income to the Ādheenam [organization]." This is normally not done in *āśrams* in India or elsewhere and seems to have been incorporated from the practice in other Western religious orders. Swamiji also had something to say about the difference of the Nātha Sampradāya from the Daśanāmī Sampradāya, both of whom worship Śiva, and are, in a certain sense advaitic. He emphasized that the Nātha Sampradāya is clearly non-Daśanāmī and also had a northern and a southern tradition following Gorakhnātha and Nandinātha respectively. The Nātha traditions believe in the value of temples and personal worship "and at the same time believe in the internal realization of the absolute." The Daśanāmīs do not accept worship as part of their philosophy.

This Hawaiian Swami also has become world renowned for starting the magazine called *Hinduism Today*. With Hindus spread in almost all corners of the world today and most of them not being in active contact with their culture, this magazine in Swamiji's words has "united the Hindus of the world" to learn about each other. "It is the only religious publication that sells along with *Times* and *Newsweek* in the news stands, especially in India."

Retrospect and Prospect

It is relevant now to ponder on the future prospects of the *saṁnyāsa* organizations after having talked to so many of the *saṁnyāsins* themselves. We have looked at the historical evolution of the Hindu *āśrams* and also have an idea of how these *āśrams* are viewed both by scholars and by the *saṁnyāsins* themselves. Is it possible to predict some prospective image of the *saṁnyāsins* and the *āśrams* in the near future? Whether it is possible or not I have decided to take the plunge.

If Śaṅkarācārya was important for the retrospective angle, Vivekananda was the catalyst for the second phase in which a number of innovations came into being. Now with the phenomenon of globalization and increasing use of information technology, a new third phase is already on the move and will continue to play a significant role in the shape of things to come. I have briefly referred to this new phase in the first chapter; but technology is moving even faster than one can keep pace with these days. In the third phase it will be those *saṁnyāsin*s who can channellize the new technologies for their purposes who will make a mark both in India and on the world stage. We have already seen signs of that in Swami Ram Dev's Movement. Chidananda (Chinmaya Mission) expressed the same view forthrightly when he said "*Saṁnyāsāśrama*s also have to change according to the times."

We have also noticed above that *mokṣa* has been defined in many different ways by the *saṁnyāsin*s themselves and social service (*lokasaṁgraha*) has been elevated to a status almost equal to personal *mokṣa*. It seems as if the prospects are that even paying lip service to personal *mokṣa* may become a casuality in the third phase. It also seems that individual charismatic leaders like Lekh Raj of Brahmakumari fame or Sri Sri Ravi Shankar of the "Art of Living" movement will become as common as the *saṁnyāsin*s themselves.

Indians have also become more materialistic and consumer hungry, interested in earning more wealth and success in the world. "Today for the first time you can really create an ideal human family with a holistic perspective. But there is the danger of the consumeristic society overtaking this ideal" (Agnivesh). A large number are imitating the lifestyles of the West and with that will come, as already witnessed, increased tensions and stress as well as lack of mental peace. The future spiritual leaders like Sri Sri Ravi Shankar will cater to such people, as we see in the case of Deepak Chopra in the West.

The initiation into *saṁnyāsa* will probably be confined to the traditional *āśram*s which will have their own clientele. There will be a recognition of the pitfalls of recruiting *naiṣṭhika brahmacārin*s at a tender age in these *āśram*s and the tendency would shift to retaining the *brahmacarya* clause but looking for candidates spiritually oriented but more mature in age. Will all *āśram*s, including the Śaṅkara Math, gradually move to selecting as their heads those who have already gone through the *gṛhasthāśrama*, like the Vaiṣṇava Maths, is something which needs to be watched for. Perhaps the traditional Śaṅkara Ashrams and the Madhva Sampradāya will tend to retain their heads as *naiṣṭhika* *brahmacārins* even while taking care to recruit more mature candidates. Sugunendra Tirtha (Madhva) already hinted at that in his interview.

The stage is increasingly set for new individuals working outside the *saṁnyāsa* robes, like Sri Sri Ravi Shankar. He himself is the disciple of Maharshi Mahesh Yogi who started the trend of a *brahmacārin* wearing white clothes, wearing his hair long, taking on the role of a traditional spiritual leader, preaching not *mokṣa* but bringing about peace both individually and worldwide, through positive thinking. That is the message that Sri Sri Ravi Shankar seems to be spreading as well. So, along with the *saṁnyāsins*, such persons will be equally sought after for spiritual comfort even if they are not *saṁnyāsins* in the strict sense of the term. Unlike what happened with the advent of the Ramakrishna Mission, when new *āśrams* were started, there will perhaps be individuals becoming *gurus* catering to the new breed of successful Indians. Women will also become increasingly more important both as *saṁnyāsinīs* and as independent spiritual leaders like Amritanandamayi Maa, known as the hugging Swamini.

Foreign Hindu *saṁnyāsins* are now a common sight both outside and inside India. While some foreigners head Indian *āśrams* abroad (Sivananda Vedanta Centre, ISKCON, Self-Realization Group), I will not be surprised if foreigners, both men and women, do become heads of *āśrams* in India as well. There is already the precedent of the Mother in Pondicherry, though she was strictly not a *saṁnyāsinī*. There is also some hope that more spiritual personalities, not tied down to *āśrams*, will have time to enter into interfaith dialogues in India similar to what happens in the West. Sri Sri Ravi Shankar has already demonstrated that such dialogues can lead to a more harmonious understanding between different religious groups.

I do not predict that the traditional *āśrams* will go out of circulation. In fact all the Swamis of the traditional *maṭhas* interviewed were positive that their establishments will prosper in the future. They will have continued support from traditional groups within the country and their popularity, it seems, will also grow more within the diaspora Hindu community who have already shown their support by generous donations to these *āśrams*. There may also be members from the diaspora communities entering these traditional *āśrams*, as is happening even now. Also their influence in rural areas, as opposed to the urban centres, will continue as before.

But there will be parallel spiritual organizations which will cater to an economically successful clientele. Individual *guru*s, as already witnessed in the ISKCON and Swami Narayan groups, will compete with the Śaṅkarācāryas, Āṇḍavans and Jeeyars et al., for spiritual leadership. The trend as of now is in favour of non-*saṁnyāsin*s, wearing white robes of a *brahmacārin,* talking about the "Spiritual Aspects of Wealth" and explaining spirituality as "Deepening the mystery of the Self." However, it looks to me that, whatever incarnation the *saṁnyāsa* ideal of renunciation may take, it will always be present in one form or another, for the spiritual hunger in people is an enduring phenomenon. Spreading the message of spirituality will also depend on charismatic individuals, whether in the robes of a *saṁnyāsin* or in non-*saṁnyāsin* robes.

Appendix

Questionnaire

THE Chair in Hindu Studies in the Department of Religion of Concordia University is carrying out a study on "The Saṁnyāsin and the Saṁnyāsarama based on Sanskrit Texts." One part of the research aims at studying the *saṁnyāsin* and the *saṁnyāsāśrama* as they exist today in India and in the countries to which Hinduism has spread through its *swāmīs*. This will be done with a view to compare and contrast the role of the *saṁnyāsin* and the *saṁnyāsāśrama* in the different countries in which they operate.

Some major themes have been addressed in this questionnaire. Please give your answers to the following open-ended questions. Your co-operation is greatly appreciated.

Name of the Swami ....

Age ....

Country of origin ....

Name of Āśram ....

Location ....

Name of the Founder ....

Established in ....

Name of the head of the Āśram ....

Affiliation ....

No affiliation ....

I. PERSONAL DATA

1. In your view who is a *saṁnyāsin*?
2. Could you give a brief account of your background?
3. What made you decide to follow this path and when?
4. Are you allowed to marry before taking up *saṁnyāsa*?
5. After taking up *saṁnyāsa* does he/she stay away from family?

6. How do you perceive the role of a *saṁnyāsin* in society?

7. Describe the role of saṁnyāsin with reference to:

   (a) Self

   (b) Society

8. How would you perceive the role of a *saṁnyāsin vis-à-vis*

   (a) Spiritual education

   (b) Overall welfare of the members (service to community)

9. In your opinion how can the above objectives be achieved?

9a. Do you think you have been successful in achieving these objectives as a *saṁnyāsin*?

   Yes___________ No____________

9b. If yes please quantify your achievements

   (i) 25% (ii) 50% (iii) 75% (iv) 100%

9c. If no, please state your reasons.

10. How does the society you live in view a Hindu *saṁnyāsin*?

11. Could you comment — how Western perception differs from that of the perception of a Hindu *saṁnyāsin* in India?

12. How do you see your role as the head of the *āśram* in the next five years?

13. What is the procedure for choosing the successor of your *āśram*?

II. SAṀNYĀSĀŚRAMA/MONASTIC ORDER

1. What is the function of your *āśram* in society?

1a. How effective do you think your *āśram* has discharged its perceived objectives to the society?

1b. Are the functions of your *āśram* the same as conceived originally for a *saṁnyāsin* in India?

1c. In which areas would you emphasize the success of your *āśram vis-à-vis* the members?

2. On what factors does the success of the *āśram* depend?

   (a) on the head *saṁnyāsin*

   (b) on other factors

3. Is there an understanding of the role of *saṁnyāsin* and the order in circles other than the devotee circle?

3a. Please elaborate.

4. How do you visualize the future of you *āśram* in your situation?

III. SAṀNYĀSINĪS

1. Unlike in India, there are more *saṁnyāsinīs* heading *āśrams* outside India

   Agree__________ Disagree__________

1a. Give your comments.

2. In your opinion is the role of the Hindu *saṁnyāsinī* the same as that of a Hindu *saṁnyāsin vis-à-vis*

   (a) Self (b) Society

2a. Have there been *saṁnyāsinīs* so far in your order?

   Yes__________ No__________

2b. Has your *āśram* had a *saṁnyāsinī* heading it in the past?

   Yes__________ No__________

2c. If yes, could you please tell when, and how long?

2d. If no, please give reasons.

IV. ADMINISTRATIVE AND FINANCIAL ASPECTS OF THE ĀŚRAM

1. Are there any guidelines set by the government for the *āśram*?

1a. If yes, please specify any modification the *āśram* made in order to comply with the guidelines?

2. Please comment on the changes/adjustments made to the functioning of your *āśram* compared to that generally observed in an āśram in India. Please elaborate.

3. Who sets the guidelines for the internal day to day functioning of the *āśram*?

   (a) Head *saṁnyāsin*________ (b) Governing body________

   (c) Collectively

4. What is the source of income to maintain the āśram? Please specify,

   (i) Funds raised locally

   (ii) Outside resources

5. How is its continuity assured?

6. What are the checks and balances put in place to ensure proper functioning of the *āśram*.

6a. How do you eliminate unwanted elements from the *āśram*?

6b. What disciplinary measures are in place in your *āśram*?

7. What are the two important defining characteristics of

   (a) a *saṁnyāsin*

   (b) the *saṁnyāsāśrama*

8. What message would you like to give to the householders?
9. How are new *saṁnyāsins/saṁnyāsinīs* chosen in your order?
10. Who initiates them? Could you describe the initiation ceremony?
11. What made you choose the path of a *saṁnyāsin/saṁnyāsinī*?

TALKING POINTS

1. Clientele — Indians or others — percentage-wise
2. Rituals
3. Festivals
4. Any educational facilities (schools, colleges for religious purposes or is it general? Any Hospitals, helping leprosy patients, sick people, arranging for operations, etc.
5. Do you have publications or any other media effort to educate public?
6. Do you travel around the country and abroad?
7. Any distinguishing marks and robes? Is robe optional?
8. Is there a hierarchy within the *āśram*?
9. Routine of the head swami?
10. Community service — frequency (once a week/month)?

Glossary

abhayam	—	fearlessness.
abheda	—	non-difference.
*ācārabheda*s	—	differences in spiritual practice.
ācārya	—	spiritual teacher.
ādhīnam/ādheenam	—	the Śaiva-Siddhānta *saṁnyāsa* organizatioin in Tamil Nadu.
adhyātmic/ādhyātmic	—	spiritual, pertaining to the self.
adhyayana	—	Vedic learning.
ādi	—	ancient, first.
ādivāsī	—	tribal.
Advaita	—	non-dual Vedānta philosophy.
agni	—	fire.
agnihotra	—	daily fire ritual.
agnisaṁskāra	—	fire ritual.
ahiṁsā	—	non-violence.
ajanmā	—	birthless.
akarma	—	negation of action.
akhāḍā	—	place for training in arms generally associated with the Daśanāmī system; it is also the headquarters of the Nāgā sect which is the military wing of the Daśanāmīs.
ambāḷ	—	goddess.
āmnāya	—	history or lineage maintained in *āśrams*.
anāsakti	—	detachment.
andaṇar	—	Tamil word meaning brāhmaṇa or *saṁnyāsin*.

āṇḍavan — title given to the head *saṁnyāsin* of the Vaḍakaḷai section of Vaiṣṇavism.

antarmukha — turned inward.

aparigraha — without possessions, non-acceptance of gifts.

apartheid — segregated political system in South Africa under white rule.

āratī — ritual waving of lighted wicks.

āryakā — an erudite Jain *saṁnyāsinī*.

āsakti — attachment.

aṣṭaśrāddha — funeral rites done for all worldly relations, including one's personal self; performed when taking initiation.

*āśram*s/*ashram* — abode of *saṁnyāsin*s.

aśrama — the four stages of one's life — *brahmacarya, gr̥hastha, vānaprastha* and *saṁnyāsa*.

ātman — individual spirit/self.

ātmajñānin — knower of self.

ātmano mokṣārtham jagaddhitāya ca — liberation for oneself as well as working for the welfare of the world, motto of the Ramakrishna Mission.

ātmasantuṣṭi — self-satisfaction.

ātmavicāra — discourse/discussion on *ātman*.

avadhūta — one whose ego is destroyed, final stage of *saṁnyāsa* when one attains total transcendence of the body.

avadhūtinī — female *avadhūta*.

avatāra — incarnation of the divine.

Āyurveda — life science, ancient Indian medical system.

bahūdaka — one of the four divisions of *saṁnyāsin*s.

bhagavatdhyāna — meditation on Bhagavān.

bhajana — devotional song.

bhakti — devotion.

bhakti yoga — *bhakti* as yoga.

bhāṣya — commentary.

bhāva — feeling generally used by a devotee to describe his/her devotion towards the *iṣṭadevatā*.

bheda — difference.

bhikṣuṇī/bhikkuṇī — female mendicant, generally used for a Buddhist female mendicant.

bhikṣu — mendicant.

Brahmā — the deity associated with the function of bringing the world into existence.

brahmacārin/brahmacārī— student/bachelor.

brahmacarya — stages of student/celibacy.

brahmamīmāṁsā — also called Vedānta.

Brahman — absolute reality of the Upaniṣads.

brahmatattva — the principle of Brahman.

brahma-vidyā — spiritual knowledge.

buddha — enlightened one.

cakra — wheel, divine weapon of Bhagavān Viṣṇu.

cāturmāsya — the four month (monsoon) period when *saṁnyāsins* are allowed to stay in one place.

dama — self-control.

daṇḍa — staff as insignia of *saṁnyāsa* status.

daṇḍī/daṇḍin — staff holder.

Daśanāmī — ten monastic orders believed to be started by Śaṅkarācārya with names such as vana, tīrtha, etc. These names are also associated with the four *āśrams* started by Śaṅkarācārya.

dīkṣā — initiation.

devatā — divine being, deity.

dhyāna — meditation.

duḥkha — sorrow, suffering, pain.

Dvaita — dualism, dualistic Vedānta philosophy.

eka-daṇḍī — monk with one staff, generally associated with the Advaita monks.

eṣaṇā — desires.

gadā — mace, a divine weapon of Viṣṇu.

gr̥hastha — householder.

Gr̥hyasūtra — ritual text for household rituals.

guru-mantra — *mantra* given at the time of initiation by *guru*.

guru-pūrṇimā — full moon day on which the *guru* is honoured.

haṁsa — swan, one of the four divisions of *saṁnyāsins*.

homa — fire sacrifice.

iṣṭi — a kind of *yajña*.

Īśvara — the ultimate pictured in an anthropomorphic manner like Viṣṇu, Śiva, etc.

īśvarānugraha — divine grace.

jagatguru — world teacher.

janeū — sacred thread, same as *upavīta* or *yajñopavīta*.

jayanti — generally used for birthday of *deva*s and saints like Kr̥ṣṇa-Jayantī, Śaṅkara-Jayanti etc.

jeeyar — title for the head of the Tenkaḷai Vaiṣṇava *maṭha*.

jijñāsā — thirst for spiritual knowledge.

jīvanmukta — one liberated while still living.

jñāna — spiritual knowledge.

jñāna-niṣṭhā — established in the pursuit of spiritual knowledge.

jñāna-yoga — yoga that is knowledge.

jñāna-kāṇḍa — Upaniṣads.

Kaliyuga — the fourth last age in the Hindu calculation of time; the other three in order are Satyayuga, Tretāyuga and Dvāparayuga.

karma	—	Vedic rituals, duty.
karma-kāṇḍa	—	ritual part of the Vedas.
karma mīmāṁsā	—	philosophy based on the ritual part of the Vedas.
karmayoga	—	*yoga* that is action.
kāruṇya	—	compassion.
kāṣāya vastra	—	ochre robes.
kevala jñāna niṣṭhā	—	intense pursuit of knowledge.
khyāti lābha	—	fame.
kīrtana	—	devotional musical composition.
kṣamā	—	forgiveness.
Kumbha-Melā	—	periodic Hindu gatherings held at Prayāga, Hardwar, Nasik, and Ujjain every twelve years.
kuṭīcaka/kuṭīcara	—	*saṁnyāsin* living in a hut, one of the four divisions of *saṁnyāsins*; the other three are *bahūdaka, haṁsa* and *paramahaṁsa*.
lokaiṣaṇā	—	desire for honour, fame, wealth, etc., in the world.
lokasaṁgraha	—	welfare of the world.
mahābhāva	—	last stage in the *bhakti* discipline.
Mahāmaṇḍaleśvara	—	title bestowed in the Daśanamī Sampradāya for a leader and respected monk.
maharāja	—	honorofic title for senior *saṁnyāsin*s.
mahāsamādhi	—	passing away of a saint.
mahāvākya	—	great sayings in the Upaniṣads generally considered to be four; they are *prajñānam brahma, ayam ātma brahma, tat tvam asi, aham brahma asmi.*
mālā jāpa	—	counting the beads as a form of worship.
manana	—	reflection.
mānasa pūjā	—	mental worship.
Maṇḍaleśvara	—	title of a respected monk in the Daśanāmī Sampradāya.

maṅgala āratī	—	early morning worship with lights.
mantra	—	sacred syllable.
maṭh/maṭha/mutt	—	monastery.
mokṣa	—	liberation from the cycle of birth/death/ rebirth.
mukta	—	liberated soul or person.
nāga sādhu	—	term for naked mendicant in the Daśanāmī Sampradāya.
naiṣṭhika brahmacārin/brahmacārī	—	lifelong celibacy.
nāma	—	one of the *saṁskāra*s of Vaiṣṇavas.
nāmam	—	religious mark worn by sectarian groups like the Vaiṣṇavas, Madhvas, etc.
Nandinātha Sampradāya	—	Śaivaite Nātha monastic tradition of south India and Sri Lanka.
Nārāyaṇa-sevā	—	welfare work for the poor and afflicted.
nidhi	—	fund.
nididhyāsana	—	meditation.
nirākāra	—	without form or shape.
nirguṇa	—	without qualities.
niṣṭhā	—	steadfast in discipline.
nitya	—	daily, for ever, permanent.
nirvikāra	—	without form, immutable.
northern Nātha tradition	—	the monastic tradition of the followers of Gorakhnātha.
nyāyakārī/ nyāyakārin	—	giver of justice.
Oṁ	—	a *mantra* normally identified with the ultimate reality whether Brahman or a personal god.
padma	—	lotus.
pāpa	—	vice/demerit.
paramahaṁsa	—	last of the four divisions of *saṁnyāsin*s also called *vidvat saṁnyāsa.*
Paramātmā	—	Supreme Being.

pariṇāma	—	real change as opposed to *vivarta* which is apparent change.
parivrājikā	—	wandering female mendicant.
pāṭhaśālā	—	Vedic school.
pīḍā	—	suffering.
pīṭha/piṭh/peeth/ peeṭham	—	monastery, generally used for the main monastery.
perumāḷ	—	Tamil term for Viṣṇu.
pūjā	—	worship of a devotee.
pūrṇimā	—	full moon.
prāṇa-pratiṣṭhā	—	infusing life into an icon in the temple through rituals.
prasāda, prasādam	—	consecrated food given to devotees at the end of a religious function.
pratyāśā	—	expectation in return.
pravacana	—	discourse.
pravṛtti	—	involvement.
puṇya	—	virtue/merit.
Pūrva-Mīmāṁsā	—	philosophy of rituals/one school of Indian philosophy.
pūrvāśrama	—	earlier stage of life.
puṣpārcana	—	worship with flowers.
putraīṣaṇā	—	desire for progeny.
rājayoga	—	king of yogas; another name for Patañjali's eightfold yoga.
ṛtam	—	physiological and moral order mentioned in the *Ṛgveda* / Vedic literature.
ruci	—	taste, a stage in *bhakti* discipline.
sādhaka	—	practitioner of spiritual path.
sādhanā	—	spiritual practice.
sādhu	—	ascetic also called *yati, swāmin/swāmi/ swami/saṁnyāsin, śramaṇa, bhikṣu,* etc.
Śaiva-Siddhānta	—	Śaivaite philosophy.
samādhi	—	eighth limb of yoga.

saṁśrayanam	—	branding of the symbols of Viṣṇu on the body by the Vaḍakaḷai school of Vaiṣṇavas.
sampradāya	—	tradition.
saṁsāra	—	world.
saṁsārin/saṁsārī	—	worldly man.
saṁskāra	—	ordained ritual, subtle impressions of experience retained in the mind/*citta*.
Sanātana Dharma	—	traditional designation for what is now known as Hinduism.
saṁkalpa	—	determination, declaration of religious intent.
śaṅkha	—	conch-shell.
saṁnyāsa	—	mendicancy.
saṁnyāsī/saṁnyāsin	—	renouncer, same as *sādhu*.
sant	—	saint, sage.
Sāra	—	Tamil term for Brahman as used in Vaiṣṇavism.
sarvabhūtahiterataḥ	—	those involved in welfare of all.
sarvakarma-parityāga	—	giving up all actions.
sarvaśaktimān	—	all powerful.
Śāstras	—	sacred texts.
satccidānanda	—	reality, consciousness, bliss, denotes Brahman.
sāyujya bhakti	—	*bhakti* that results in oneness with the *iṣṭadevatā*.
sevā	—	service.
śāmiānā	—	decorative tent used for celebrating events like wedding, etc.
siddha/siddhar	—	spiritual adept.
siddhānta	—	philosophy, conclusive theory and practice.
siddhi	—	spiritual accomplishment.

śikhā	—	hair, top knot.
śloka	—	verse.
śraddhā	—	faith.
śrāddha	—	ceremony to honour the *pitṛ*s/manes.
śravaṇa	—	listening to sacred texts.
śruti	—	Vedas/Vedic corpus.
śuddha caitanya	—	pure consciousness.
sukha	—	happiness.
sūtrakāra	—	author of *sūtras*.
sūtras	—	condensed texts that convey a lot of meaning.
svāhā	—	mantra during ritual offering.
svayam prakāśa	—	self-shining, self-luminous.
tantra	—	esoteric practices on body and mind.
tapas	—	austerities.
tarpaṇa	—	ritual in memory of one's ancestors also called *śrāddha*.
tat tvam asi	—	Upaniṣadic *mahāvākya* indicating the identity of the *jīvātman* and *paramātman*.
Tenkaḷai	—	a Vaiṣṇava Sampradāya also called the cat/kitten school or *mārjāra mārga*.
tri-daṇḍī	—	monk with three staffs, generally a Vaiṣṇava *saṁnyāsin*.
tyāga	—	sacrifice, renunciation.
upadeśa	—	instruction, advice.
upāsanā	—	personalized form of worship.
Uttara-Mīmāṁsā	—	also called Vedānta philosophy.
Vaḍakaḷai	—	a Vaiṣṇava Sampradāya also called the monkey school or *markaṭa mārga*.
vairāgya	—	detachment, dispassion.
vānaprastha āśrama	—	the third of the four stages of *brahmacarya, gṛhastha, vānaprastha* and *saṁnyāsa*; forest dwelling sage.
vibhūti	—	sacred ash.

vicār/vicāra — contemplation.

vidvat saṁnyāsin — enlightened *saṁnyāsin* also called *paramahaṁsa.*

vidyā — education, spiritual knowledge.

virajā homa — fire rituals performed to initiate one into the *saṁnyāsa-āśrama.*

Viṣṇusahasranāma — thousand names of Lord Viṣṇu.

Viśiṣṭādvaita — the Vedānta philosophy of qualified non-dualism.

vittaiṣaṇā — desire for wealth.

vividiṣā saṁnyāsa — *saṁnyāsa* in pursuit of enlightenment.

vrata — religious observance, vows.

yajña — Vedic sacrifice.

yajñopavīta — sacred thread; also used for the ceremony or *saṁskāra* of initiation when the sacred thread is given along with the *Gāyatrī-mantra,* same as *upavīta* or *janeū.*

yantra — geometric symbol designed for concentration, mainly used in Tantra.

yati/muni — *saṁnyāsin.*

Bibliography

Abhisiktananda, *The Further Shore:Three Essays* (1st edn., 1975, rpt. 1984), Delhi: I.S.P.C.K.

Agehanandabharati, *The Ochre Robe: An Autobiography* (2nd edn.), (1980), Santa Barbara: Ross Erikson.

Aiyer, V.V.S., *Thirukkural* (trans) (1998, 5th rpt.), Trichy: Sri Ramakrishna Tapovanam.

Bose, A.C., *Hymns from the Vedas* (1966), New York: Asia Publishing House.

Cenkner, William, *A Tradition of Teachers: Sankara and the Jagadgurus Today* (1983), Delhi: Motilal Banarsidass.

Chakraborti, Haripada, *Asceticism in ancient India in Brahmanical, Buddhist, Jaina, and Ajivika societies, from the Earliest Times to the Period of Sankaracharya* (1973), Calcutta: Punthi Pustak.

Cushmon Anne and Jerry Jones, *From Here to Nirvanā* (1998), New York: Riverhead Books.

Dalton, Dennis, *Mahatma Gandhi: Nonviolent Power in Action* (1993), New York: Columbia University Press.

Dazey Wade, "Tradition and Modernization in the Organization of the Daśanāmī Saṁnyāsins", *Monastic life in the Christian and Hindu Traditions: Studies in Comparative Religion* (1990), Austin Creel and Vasudha Narayanan (eds.), New York: Edwin Mellen Press, Lewiston.

Ganapathy T.N., *The Philosophy of the Tamil Siddhas* (1993), New Delhi: Indian Council of Philosophical Research.

Ghurye G.S. (with L.N. Chapekar), *Indian Sadhus* (1st edn., 1953 , 2nd edn., 1964), Bombay: Popular Prakashan.

Hiriyanna, M., *Outlines of Indian Philosophy* (1993, first Indian edition), Delhi: Motilal Banarsidass.

Iyer, Raghavan N., *The Moral and Political Thought of Mahatma Gandhi*, 1973, New York: Oxford University Press.

Khandelwal, Meena, *Women in Ochre Robes* (2004), New York: State University of New York Press.

Miller, David and Dorothy C. Wertz, *Hindu Monastic Life: The Monks and Monasteries of Bhuvaneshwar* (1976), Montreal: McGill-Queen's University Press.

Olivelle, Patrick, *The Ashrama System: the History and Hermeneutics of a Religious Institution* (1993), Oxford University Press.

———, *Rules and Regulations of Brahmanical Asceticism and Renunciation* (1992), Oxford University Press.

Pandeya, Rajendra P., "The Vision of the Vedic Seer", Sivaraman. K (ed.), *Hindu Spirituality* (1989) New York: The Crossroad Publishing Company.

Pechilis, Karen (ed.), *The Graceful Guru: Hindu Female Gurus in India and the United States* (2004), New York: Oxford University Press.

Rukmani, T.S., "*Saṁnyāsa* and some Indian Reform Movements in the 18th, 19th, and 20th centuries", *Brahmavidya: The Adyar Library Bulletin* (1998), vol. 62: 23-50.

———, "Saṁnyāsins in a Temple Context", in Himanshu Prabha Ray (ed.), *Archaeology and Text : The Temple in South Asia*, (2010), New Delhi: Oxford University Press.

Sarkar, Sir Jadunath, *A History of Daśanāmī Naga Sannyasis* (1946), Mahanirvani, Allahabad.

Swami Sadananda Giri, *Society and Saṁnyāsin — a History of the Daśanāmī Saṁnyāsins* (1976), Rishikesh: Kriyayoga Ashrama.

The History and Culture of the Indian People: The Classical Age (1988), Bombay: Bharatiya Vidya Bhavan.

Tripathi, Bansi Dhar, *Sadhus of India: the Sociological View* (1978), Bombay: Popular Prakashan.

Yoshitsugu, Sawai, *The Faith of Ascetics and Lay Smartas: A Study of the Sankaran Tradition of Sringeri* (1992), Vienna: Sammlung de Nobili, Institut für Indologie der Universitat, Wien (Institute of Indology, University of Vienna).

Index